UNIVERSITY OF ST. THOMAS LIBRARIES
WITHDRAWN
UST
Libraries
TERRORISM IN NORTHERN IRELAND

TERRORISM IN NORTHERN IRELAND

GENERAL HALL, INC.
23-45 Corporal Kennedy Street
Bayside, New York 11360

Copyright © 1983 by Alfred McClung Lee

All rights reserved. No part of this publication may be reproduced, stored in a retrieval system or transmitted in any form or by any means, except for the inclusion of brief quotations in a review, without the prior permission of the publisher.

Publisher: Ravi Mehra
Editor: Joanne Eckett
Associate Editor: Eileen Ostermann
Composition: *Graphics Division,* General Hall, Inc.

LIBRARY OF CONGRESS CATALOG CARD NUMBER: 83-80158

ISBN: 0-930390-50-4 [paper]
      0-930390-51-2 [cloth]

Manufactured in the United States of America

TERRORISM
IN NORTHERN IRELAND

Alfred McClung Lee
Brooklyn College and Drew University

GENERAL HALL, INC.
Publishers
23–45 Corporal Kennedy Street
Bayside, New York 11360

To Dr. Elizabeth Riley Briant Lee
in gratitude

Contents

	Acknowledgements	vii
	Preface	1
	Introduction: Ways of Looking at Terrorism and Revolt	5
1.	Interethnic Conflict in the British Isles	19
2.	The Stuff of History	43
3.	Human Rights in the Orange Statelet	59
4.	Revolt Renewed	77
5.	Learning to Be Violent	99
6.	Terror in Upper-Class Strategy	125
7.	Terror in Middle- and Lower-Class Strategies	143
8.	Terror as Theater	168
9.	Quests for Peace	200
10.	Is There No End To It All?	234
	Index	241

NORTHERN IRELAND

Source: British Information Services

ACKNOWLEDGEMENTS

This book is not a collection of previously published articles even though parts of it owe much to materials originally brought together for such purposes. It is an effort to present in an integrated form what I have been able to learn about tensions and social conflict in Northern Ireland during ten field trips there since 1955 and from available documentary materials.

The footnotes in this work indicate my indebtedness to a wide range of commentators and investigators, politicians and observers, representing as many aspects of and views on Northern Ireland troubles as I could gather. In addition, a number of individuals have been especially helpful with observations and criticisms and with helping me to obtain useful materials. Those now deceased include Kenneth H. Connell and Harry Midgley. Others helpful have been Denis P. Barritt, Kevin Boyle, Rev. David J. Bowman, S.J., Ronald H. Buchanan, Rev. Maurice Burke, S.M.A., Leo P. Chall, Marybeth Crowley-Farrell, Earl E. Davis, Matt Diskin, Rona M. Fields, Elspeth Flynn, Irving Goldaber, Bruce T. Grindal, Maurice N. Hayes, John A. Jackson, Robert E. Kennedy, Jr., Rev. Charles Kyle, David R. Lowry, Seamus P. Metress, Joseph and Nancy O'Donaghue, Liam G. O'Dowd, Thomas J. Rice, Bill Rolston, P. Joy Rudd, and A.E.C.W. Spencer. Ann Guida has helped with the index.

In the preparation of this book, it has been helpful to discuss parts of it with Ellsworth T. Carrington, Edward and Elizabeth Huberman, Glenn Jacobs, Louis Kriesberg, and Andrew Tierman. Franco Ferrarotti's studies of violence elsewhere have been helpful. Julie and Gerald A. Fitzgerald, James Michael O'Kane, and Howard Elterman read the manuscript and provided many useful suggestions.

Research for this work was supported by a series of grants from The City University of New York PSC-BHE Research Award Program. Since 1975, Drew University has made facilities available to me as a Visiting Scholar in Sociology. The librarians of Drew University, the Graduate Center of The City University, and New York Public Library have been most cooperative many times in many ways.

Some of my previous publications from which I have extracted materials to use in this book are the following:

"Insurgent and 'Peacekeeping' Violence in Northern Ireland," *Social Problems*, vol. 20, no. 4 (Spring 1973), pp. 532–546. "To What Is Northern Ireland's Civil War Relevant?" *Holy Cross Quarterly*, vol. 6 (1974), pp. 94–100. "Efforts to Control Insurgency in Northern Ireland," *International Journal of Group Tensions*, vol. 4 (1974), pp. 346–358. "Northern Irish Socialization in Conflict Patterns," *International Review of Modern Sociology*, vol. 5 (1975), pp. 127–134. "Is Ulster's Conflict Religious?" *Church & State*, vol. 29, no. 5 (May 1976), pp. 9–11. "Interethnic Conflict in the British Isles," *Anthropology and Humanism Quarterly*, vol. 4, nos. 2–3 (June/September 1979), pp. 6–16. "Human Rights in the Northern Ireland Conflict: 1968–1980," *International Journal of Politics*, vol. 10, no. 1 (Spring 1980, pp. 1–146. "Nonviolent Agencies in the Northern Ireland Struggle," *Journal of Sociology and Social Welfare*, vol. 7, no. 4 (July 1980), pp. 601–623. "Mass Media Mythmaking in the United Kingdom's Interethnic Struggles," *Ethnicity*, vol. 8 (1981), pp. 18–30. "The Dynamics of Terrorism in Northern Ireland: 1968–1980," *Social Research*, vol. 48, no. 1 (Spring 1981), pp. 100–134. "Riflessioni sul Terrorismo nell'Irlanda del Nord," *Critica Sociologica*, no. 59 (Autunno 1981), pp. 6–19. "Terrorism's Social-Historical Contexts in Northern Ireland," *Research in Social Movement, Conflicts and Change* (Greenwich, Conn.: JAI Press, Inc.), vol. 5 (1983), pp. 99–131.

The publishers of these journals have given permission to use materials from the above articles in the present book. Since the materials have been considerably rearranged, amplified, updated, and rewritten for the present purpose, it would be difficult to specify derivations from each of the articles. I have also adapted, with permission, a resumé chart from my book, *Multivalent Man* (New York: George Braziller, 1966), in chapter 5. I am indebted to the publishers, as copyright holders, for these permissions.

Ravi Mehra, President of General Hall, Inc., cooperated in the planning of this volume and has now brought it to publication. His interest and diligence are appreciated.

As always, my wife and fellow social scientist, Elizabeth Riley Briant Lee, has provided psychological support and has made many suggestions and criticisms that have greatly improved the whole product. A substantial part of this took the form of sharing in my field experiences in Northern Ireland as well as in our monastic lives at home as individual researchers and writers.

Alfred McClung Lee
Drew University, Madison, New Jersey

Preface

A preface can well be used to bare an author's intentions and biases. I should like, therefore, to indicate what led me to a series of investigative journeys to Ireland during several decades and to the writing of a series of articles and this book.

The evolving patterns of English aristocratic and authoritarian practices and controls have fascinated me ever since my boyhood reading of such racist and class-ridden propaganda as that contained in the then popular English boys' stories, the Jack Harkaway series.[1] Their contrasts with the forthright egalitarianism of Mark Twain's *Tom Sawyer* and *Huckleberry Finn* interested and perplexed me. Public school teachers assured us that all our ideals of fair play, civil liberties, and even democracy had come to us directly from the English. Yet, for reasons then not at all clear to me from our history books, we had fought a revolution of sorts against the English and had gained our independence from them. We had even fought against them a second time in 1812–15. There must have been some point in our fighting to free ourselves, and keep ourselves free, from the control of such fine people!

The problem bothered me for a long time — until I got around to reading the Declaration of Independence and what Tom Paine and Thomas Jefferson had said, as well as some of the more accurate and comprehensive accounts of Anglo-American relations. For a far shorter period than for the Irish, the Americans had been English colonials, but those documents make clear how far-off Westminster arbitrarily made basic policy decisions for them concerning their lives and against their interests.[2]

When I was growing up in an area at one time described as part of "Greater Ulster," western Pennsylvania, I learned that "all of us" were more or less "Scotch-Irish" with perhaps some traces of Welsh, English, and even Huguenot and "Pennsylvania Dutch." "Scotch-Irish" did not mean, it was insisted, that we were actually part Irish. The "Irish" were Roman Catholics, many of them recent immigrants, and not well placed in employment and other community connections. Even though the "Scotch-Irish" did not in general appear to me to look different genetically from the Roman Catholic "Irish," the "Scotch-Irish" were Presbyterians or some other kind of Protestant, native-born, and had better accesses to income and social prestige.

Since some of my closest boyhood friends were "Irish," the artificiality and unfairness of this invidious distinction early became clear and annoying to me. Why were Protestant Swedes and Germans so much more readily absorbed into the town economic and social life than were the families of my Irish Catholic friends? When I was able to listen to discussions among some of my father's black and other nonwhite legal clients, I broadened the question in my mind even further: Why did people have to pass as WASPs in order to participate fully in community life? For that matter, how could the "Celtic" Scotch-Irish be Anglo-Saxon enough to be thought WASPs? And the WASPs did not appear to be any more or less attractive as individuals than did other people. As part of all this, in the backlash of World War I, how could our whole town and district get so caught up in the Ku Klux Klan madness that my father had to pay both an economic and a social price for providing legal representation to blacks and Roman Catholics?

These questions about the nature of "democracy" and about ethnic and racial prejudices eventually led me into many lines of investigation.[3] They also pushed me toward looking at the English and other social-historical roots of and parallels to such beliefs and practices. Because the Irish scene through the centuries has been a significant testing ground for English imperialistic practices,[4] I have concentrated my attention in the present studies not only on that island but also on the conflict since 1968 in one part of it, in the United Kingdom province of Northern Ireland consisting of six of the nine Ulster counties. Within its setting, its historical background, this conflict tells a great deal about the persistence of beliefs, policies, and practices to earlier versions of which we in the United States owe so much of our own ethnocentrism, racism, classism, and faith in authoritarian procedures.

The foregoing has perhaps raised and not answered a question to which a frank answer is due at the outset of this book: Whose side am I on?

At the risk of arousing annoyed disbelief among many concerned with Irish problems and in spite of whatever interpretation may be placed on the foregoing, I contend that this book is an effort to serve equally all the people of the British Isles. In that sense, it is both pro-English and pro-Irish; more broadly, it is pro-human.

Vividly aware as I am of what the Irish have contributed to the peopling, freedoms, and cultures of the New World, as well as of what they have suffered and still accomplished in Ireland, I have a special non-religious-denominational pro-Irish as well as broadly pro-human (a humanist)[5] bias in my views. At the same time, although I may at times give the impression in the following that I am anti-English, such a notion is not accurate. My criticisms are of unrepresentative and exploitative functionaries of the English establishment, not of the English people. Similarly, my criticisms of the ecclesiastical establishments and their politico-economic maneuverings are not to be taken as reflecting upon religious beliefs or on the people who hold them.

Criticisms that I make are not directed against the long-suffering deprived levels in the British Isles but against the habitual myopia and offhand brutality of their controlling Irish, Northern Irish, and English establishments. In that still class-ridden society, those in elite positions take few opportunities to come to know people in the wide ranges of British society as fellow human beings. Like the perceptive journalist Bernard Weinraub, I cannot but censure the "blatant prejudice against the Irish, the anti-Semitism, the smugness, the flabbiness and lack of intellectual tension" that characterize so much of English political, business, and "intellectual" leadership.[6] In my estimation, the repression and exploitation common in England appear more clearly in the colonial atmosphere of the six occupied Ulster counties only because they are more openly carried to an extreme there. They do not differ in kind from similar abuses suffered by the poorer classes in England and especially by the lower-class ethnic and racial minorities in the large urban areas.

These patterns of self-glorification and of rejection or hatred of others not only simplify the exploitation of the subordinate groups principally affected but lead again and again to bitter tensions and violence. The situation thus raises many significant questions: Is social violence learned? By whom? When? Is it characteristic of certain groups, in certain social strata? Under what conditions? What are its personal and social costs? What do people expect to gain from it? What does it actually accomplish? When violence is so counterproductive because of the long-lasting and unhealing sores that it leaves, why do people resort to it rather than to more peaceful alternatives?

The riots, insurrections, and wars of our period repeatedly confront social scientists as well as policy makers with these questions. They are difficult ones to try to answer. Too often, hackneyed formulas rather than fresh and basic analyses provide the accepted but usually futile answers.

The wars of this century, and especially the urban riots in the United States and elsewhere in recent decades, have stimulated a tremendous volume of literature on violence, its causes, techniques, and control. Nevertheless, few social scientists regard the above questions to have been well enough answered by the formal studies now available. Examples of social violence are complicated, difficult to observe and analyze. Repeated studies in many different contexts are needed to form the comparative basis for substantial theory construction with which to help make diagnoses more accurate and prescriptions for change more helpful.

The civil conflict in Northern Ireland since 1968 presents opportunities as a locale in which to probe for more light on the above questions: The area is small. The participants are highly literate and vocal. The historical contexts of the struggle are set forth extensively in contradictory manners by writers representative of the three major partisan segments of the population and by some others, but comparisons of such writings can yield significant convergences.

On the basis of my personal observations and interviews and through digging into available documents, I attempt in this work to clarify the social roles of violence in both its current and historical social contexts. I have been concerned with searching for alternatives to violence, for social resources through which necessary social changes can be achieved without violence's social wounds. It is hoped that the conclusions reached can be helpful not only in prompting a better theoretical understanding of violence and of actual Northern Ireland violence but also in prompting policy making of a more constructive and useful kind.

Notes

1. Bracebridge Hemyng (Samuel Bracebridge, 1841–1901), Jack Harkaway series of children's books (New York: Street & Smith, n.d.), 28 vols.; (Chicago: M. A. Donohue & Co., n.d.), 11 vols.

2. C. A. and Mary R. Beard, *The Rise of American Civilization* (New York: Macmillan, 1927), 2 vols., esp. vol. 1; Conyers Read, ed., *The Constitution Reconsidered* (New York: Columbia University Press, 1938).

3. As examples: A. McC. and E. B. Lee, *The Fine Art of Propaganda* (New York: Harcourt, Brace, 1939, new ed., Octagon Books, 1972, and San Francisco: International Society for General Semantics, 1979); A. McC. Lee and N. D. Humphrey, *Race Riot* (New York: Dryden Press, 1943, new ed., Octagon Books, 1968); A. McC. Lee, *The Daily Newspaper in America* (New York: Macmillan, 1937, Octagon Books, 1973), *How to Understand Propaganda* (New York: Rinehart, 1952), and *Fraternities Without Brotherhood* (Boston: Beacon Press, 1955).

4. See, for example, L. P. Liggio, "English Origins of Early American Racism" (Ms. study presented before Columbia University Seminar on Irish Studies, 1974).

5. A. McC. Lee, *Toward Humanist Sociology* (Englewood Cliffs, N.J.: Prentice-Hall, 1973), and *Sociology for Whom?* (New York: Oxford University Press, 1978), chap. 2.

6. Bernard Weinraub, review of Anthony Sampson's *The New Anatomy of Britain* (New York: Stein & Day, 1972), in *New York Times Book Review,* 18 June 1972, pp. 1, 18, p. 18 quoted.

INTRODUCTION

Ways of Looking at Terrorism and Revolt

Sensational acts that appear to threaten "law and order" seize the attention of government policy makers and administrators. Theft, arson, murder, and terrorism — even nonviolent but substantial representations of dissent — demand immediate attention. Considerations of the contexts of such events and especially of their multiple causes is usually laid aside for some future agenda or merely ignored. As that apologist for the radical right in the United States, William F. Buckley, Jr., states: "...to spend one's time in probing the *cause* of our social maladies ... distracts us from coping with crime."[1] In the present book, consideration is given to contexts and causes overlooked in such a view. If a government is truly representative, it works to deal constructively with such causes before politically explosive tensions become threatening.

The causes of terrorist events are complex. What they might be is often a controversial issue. To try to cope with causes rather than only with the perpetrators of the events makes political and economic leaders attempt to face crime-producing characteristics of their society. It is far less complicating to rely on punitive and "corrective" measures aimed at those considered to be criminals. Such measures may do little or nothing to reduce the frequency of such threats to the status quo. As usually conceived and carried into practice, they are often actually counterproductive — as they can currently be seen to be in the case of Northern Ireland's civil conflict.

Terrorism, like violence and intimidation, can refer to significant kinds of human behavior that many people have at times practiced. But in more common usage, these terms are emotionalized and polarized: Other people use "violence" against our interests, try to "intimidate" us, and even "terrorize" us, but our similar behavior is given other labels. We or our agents employ "influence" or, if need be, "legal force" or "appropriate coercion" as a "security measure," as a way of reestablishing "law and order." Thus such terms have collected connotations in popular usage that make them emotive name-calling symbols to be contrasted with protective generalities for behavior acceptable to us that is the equivalent.

Both journalists and scholars like to write about the depredations of West Germany's Baader-Meinhof gang, Italy's Mafia and Red Brigade, the Palestine Liberation Organization, the Ku Klux Klan, and the Irish Republican Army. In doing so, they often try to portray a kind of viciousness that is entirely dissociated from the sort of behavior with which they and their readers presumably feel at home. They seldom spend the required effort to probe personal and social factors that produce such organizations rather than more peaceful ones. They do not get sufficiently outside of their own social preconceptions to see the many facets of terrorism. It is so much easier and so much less critical of the status quo to treat the acts of the organizations mentioned as pathological deviations from the "normal" than to see how "normal" society produced the organizations and in many senses is involved in them.[2] In contrast, many writers prefer to think of how middle-class groups faced with deprivation and even oppression are likely idealistically to get together and adopt resolutions of protest and perhaps also to attempt programs of peaceful demonstration and lobbying.

A dictionary defines terrorism as coercion through fear, fright, or dread.[3] Another dictionary sees terrorism as a "method of governing or of resisting government,"[4] but political and journalistic apologists would only associate that "method of governing" with "authoritarian regimes," "guerrillas," or "subversive elements" and not at all with the "forces of law and order" and "democracy."

Social scientists try to employ the word terrorism more objectively, more in line with traditional dictionary definitions, but they too often permit themselves to let the term refer only to discretely defined phenomena rather than to things as parts or phases of larger and changing contexts. The word is not often enough perceived as referring to end products or symptoms of much more significant and basic developments. For example, one writer goes to pains to differentiate the work of the intimidator, who, "unlike the terrorist, merely threatens injury or material harm in order to arouse fear of severe punishment for noncompliance with his demands." The "terrorist does not threaten," he says; "death or destruction is part of his program of action." He also contrasts governmental "terror," which he calls "law enforcement," with "terrorism in its proper sense." The latter, he asserts, "implies open defiance of law and is a means whereby an opposition aims to demoralize a governmental authority, to undermine its power and to initiate a revolution or counter-revolution."[5] As we shall see, at least in Northern Ireland, these categories are far from being so discrete; the police also often ignore or defy the law. There are terrorists who wear three-piece suits, ride in Rolls Royces, and sit in the seats of corporate and government power.

Political terrorism, the focal point of the discussion here, thus involves the threat of injury, death, or destruction of property in order to coerce individuals, groups, communities, or governments or to replace them or their control structure. This includes both "enforcement terror used by political authorities and agitational terror used by their opponents"[6] — to the extent that these forms of terror can be differentiated. They often interpenetrate. Thus the "tactics called terrorism are ideologically neutral. They can and have been used by any group on behalf of any cause."[7] As the novelist Joseph Conrad uses a character to summarize his own experience: "The terrorist and the policeman come from the same basket."[8] This observation points toward significant similarities in the life histories of people who terrorize.

Even though terrorism is acceptably defined as a means of coercion that exploits fear or fright, the dread of violence to persons and property, the mass media employ the term selectively. They ordinarily use it only to designate antiestablishment efforts. Terrorism by governmental functionaries is translated into accounts of measures to "restore peace," "maintain law and order," or "restabilize society." That those protective labelings have class and other sectarian biases is habitually ignored. The social contexts of rebel terrorism and reasons for the failure of nonviolent alternatives are rarely set forth in adequate detail in the mass media. Even whether the actions of dissidents are or are not potentially or actually "violent" does not keep establishment-oriented media from indiscriminately calling many of them "terrorist."[9]

Sensational offenses that are considered "political" are, if anything, more confusing to policy makers and administrators than are other kinds of "crime." Democracy presumably assures the right of dissent, but what forms of dissent should be deemed "legal" and what forms "criminal"? As Max Lerner notes, "political offenses have been the despair of jurists because of their relativist character." With such persons as George Washington and Eamon de Valera in mind, he adds that "political attempts cease to be crimes as soon as they have succeeded in overthrowing the regime."[10] The tendency of governmental agents to increase and expand the categories of political events called "criminal" reflects a rigidifying tendency in social structure, a greater unwillingness to face social needs and accept the costs of social change.[11]

Sudden and sweeping surges of social change are called social revolutions. Modern mass literacy and mass communication media have drastically modified how they occur, how they can be stimulated, and how they might be counteracted. They have forced complete rethinkings of strategies. As a leading counterrevolutionary theorist concludes: "Whether or not there is more discontent in the world than was formerly the case, ... the means of fanning it and exploiting it are infinitely greater than they used to be, because of the increase in literacy and the introduction of wireless and television sets in large numbers." Defensively he adds that instruments of mass communication are seldom manipulated as skillfully by "those involved in protecting the existing order" as they are by their opponents.[12] This contention is scarcely supportable by evidence. He is pointing to the manner in which sensational news breaks may force critical or even subversive ideas to be given some passing reference in the establishment media. He is not recognizing the constant, day-by-day impacts of orthodox media with their ritualistic justifications of nothing more than limited variations on status quo ideas.[13]

To suggest the extent of the communication upheaval in revolutionary strategies, look at the American example of the 1770s. American propaganda, printed as well as oral, ideologized and built morale for the struggle fairly well among the colonists. Agitators did this: by distributing reports of events such as the Boston "massacre" of 5 March 1775; by infiltrating the royal postal service and using its distribution facilities; by enlisting public readers of pamphlets, handbills, and newspapers; and by inducing some of the king's own propagandists to serve as double agents. The latter included James Rivington, the king's printer and publisher in New York City,[14] and that ideological zigzagger, Hugh Gaine, editor of papers in New York City and New Jersey.[15]

In spite of their energetic efforts, colonial leaders lacked the facilities effectively to reach the masses in Britain and on the Continent. Rebel propaganda could reach only sympathetic foreign leaders, some of whom, especially on the Continent, proved helpful.[16] But the ease with which the American-born Dr. Edward Bancroft as an English agent frustrated France's plan to stimulate revolt in northern Ireland in 1779 highlights the situation. Sent to agitate an uprising among Ulster Presbyterians, "where grievances similar to those suffered in America were actively nurtured," this spy went there, did nothing, and then advised the French that a revolt was impractical. "An English spy's advice on this occasion decided the policy of the Court of Versailles."[17]

Neither the Ulster Presbyterians nor the Americans could then obtain the foreign publicity for an event that is possible today. As Emerson said, the "embattled farmers" at Concord bridge in 1775 "fired the shot heard round the world,"[18] but it took a great many years for that message to carry so far. Meanwhile, George III is said to have characterized the American revolution as "a Presbyterian war" because of the very heavy involvement of Irish Dissenters in Washington's armies, but the separate Ulster revolt led by Presbyterians was delayed until 1798 and became a futile one.[19]

In contrast with eighteenth-century Americans, current Northern Ireland rebels find effective ways to speak to British and other publics around the world in spite of the pro-British prejudice typical of major media. Bombings, maimings, and killings have provided negative publicity as they are reported and interpreted, but marches and hunger strikes have carried the main burden for dramatizing positively the current rebellion, for enlisting support, and for spreading skepticism concerning British policies, intentions, and practices. In a modern effort at revolt, the propaganda struggle is a crucial factor.[20] Whether the partisans in Northern Ireland have exploited their propaganda opportunities as effectively as they might is developed elsewhere in this work.[21]

In consequence of both the communication revolution and the more general technological and industrial revolution of which it is a part, evidences and consequences of social revolution now appear frequently in headlines and on television. Few of us do not feel, at least at times, that sweeping social changes are personal threats. Alleged fomenters range from Christian agitators to Marxists, from John L. Lewis and F. D. Roosevelt to Richard M. Nixon and Ronald Reagan, from copywriters for the left to those for advertising on Madison Avenue, and from Charles Darwin and Thomas A. Edison to Sigmund Freud and Albert Einstein.

Social revolution is a far-ranging, pervasive, usually radical change in a substantial aspect or in many parts of a society. It can take place more or less quickly and is sometimes accompanied by violence, but this is not necessarily so. Thus, we have revolutions characterized in terms of a salient aspect as sexual, scientific, technological, or educational, but they are broadly societal in their ramifications. They typically "make waves" throughout society.

If a social revolution does not involve violence or the sudden and forcible replacement of a powerful elite in control, it may appear to be "inevitable"; those who might oppose it may find it expedient to make the best of the sweeping modifications in social power structures it brings. A coup d'état may or may not be related to a social revolution; it may merely be a way of perpetuating the status quo.

Violence is a social revolution's most horrifying aspect. Even the threat of a reign of terror is easily exaggerated. It can seem to menace all sense of security and portend the unhinging of all social relationships. Violence can quickly get out of control. It can become confused, irrational. Organized participants in violence often confess to feeling that its manifestations are chaotic. Once armed conflict begins, private grievances and goals and the criminally inclined exacerbate it.[22] At a peak, it is usually focused on replacing a power elite with another in control of one or more aspects of society—political, economic, ecclesiastical, entertainment. The replacement of a principal power elite may also mean a change in the character of the predominant social class and possibly also in the predominant ethnic group.[23]

In discussing the power-restructuring focal point within some revolutions, one need not perceive it as narrowly as does Friedrich Engels. He restricts his definition of revolution to the seizure of power and calls that "the most authoritarian thing there is." He describes it as "the act whereby one part of the population imposes its will upon the other part by means of rifles, bayonets, and cannon." Even after succeeding in such a seizure, "the victorious party ... must maintain this rule by means of the terror which its arms inspire in the reactionaries."[24]

On the contrary, the power-restructuring focal point of a social revolution may well consist of throwing out an entrenched minority that has ruled by rifles and cannon. It may involve installing in its place popularly acceptable representatives with a broad mass base of support, people in far less need of bayonet support than their predecessors.

Few can ponder the implications of violent social revolution disinterestedly, without a sense of dread, insecurity, or revulsion. Like disease, pollution, international war, nuclear disaster, and death, it haunts us. In our present social atmosphere, discussions of social revolution are so infected with special-interest biases that some reasonable degree of objectivity through noninvolvement is nearly impossible. These biases are not only ones of social class and politico-economic ideology but also of vested vocational interests and, especially in the Northern Ireland and Arab-Israeli cases, of ethno-religious identity and ideology.[25]

Think of how Karl Marx's vocational bias led him to be overly optimistic concerning the potentialities of Ireland as a starting point or fulcrum for a social revolution in the British Isles. In 1870 Marx contended that for English proletarians, "the *national emancipation of Ireland* is no question of abstract justice or humanitarian sentiment, but *the first condition of their own social emancipation.*" That was almost half a century before the Russian revolution of 1917. It was at a time when Marx was concluding that England was "the *only* country in which the material conditions for this [the workers'] revolution have developed up to a certain degree of maturity. Therefore to hasten the social revolution in England is the most important object of the International Working Men's Association. The sole means of hastening it is to make Ireland independent."[26]

Marx gave too much weight to the "material conditions" and neglected the powerful nonmaterial controls in both Ireland and England that made and still appear to make remote a social revolution of a drastic sort on either island. The provocation in Ireland to revolt was surely great enough, and this preoccupied Marx. He observed the absentee landlord exploitation of the Irish, the depression of British wages through the "*forced immigration* of poor Irishmen,*"* and the consequent division of British workers into "two hostile camps," to the economic and political disadvantage of both. He compared the relationship to that of blacks and whites in the United States. "This antagonism among the proletarians of England is artificially nourished and supported by the bourgeoisie. It knows that this scission is the true secret of maintaining its power." He even claimed that "Ireland is the only pretext the English Government has for retaining a *big standing army,* which, if need be, as has happened before, can be used against the English workers after having done its military training in Ireland." This allegation is frequently repeated today. Marx hopefully added: "England today is seeing a repetition of what happened on a monstrous scale in Ancient Rome. Any nation that oppresses another forges its own chains."[27]

As late as 1916, V. I. Lenin continued to echo much of this Marxian view concerning the Irish-English situation. He welcomed the aborted "Easter rising" in Dublin that year as one of the revolts by small nations that would prepare the way for the general European social revolution he and his associates in international communism wished to foment. He labeled it the "misfortune of the Irish ... that they have risen prematurely, when the European revolt of the proletariat has *not yet* matured." At the same time, he asserted that "only in *premature,* partial, scattered and therefore unsuccessful, revolutionary movements do the masses gain experience, acquire knowledge, gather strength, get to know their real leaders, the socialist proletarians, and in this way prepare for a general onslaught, in the same way as separate strikes, demonstrations, local and national, outbreaks in the army, outbursts among the peasantry, etc., prepared the way for the general onslaught in 1905 [in Russia]." Probably Lenin's one statement on which all students of actual revolutions could agree is this: "Whoever expects a 'pure' social revolution will *never* live to see it."[28]

Thus, these revolutionaries permitted their vocational involvement in ideologizing for social action to color optimistically their diagnoses of the

British situation and their prescriptions for it. Perhaps, however, no strategies would have worked at that time for their goals any better than those proposed.

For this discussion of ways of looking at revolt, let us follow a few steps further consequences of vocational bias among ideas of other students of crucial power struggles in social revolutions. Let us do this by contrasting the theorizings of selected establishment, revolutionary, and reformist intellectuals.[29] In doing so, we actually come up with a half dozen principal orientations that permeate both strategic planning and the propaganda themes incident to such struggles. There are two each because of significant polarizings of viewpoint within each of the three groups. Their relevance to Irish efforts is noted below.

Not unpredictably, when establishment social scientists anatomize revolutions, they discover that a struggle for control has less of a chance of succeeding against a power elite guided by well-trained, experienced, and adequately equipped social theorists! An intelligentsia motivated to be loyal presumably can direct skillfully the deployment of military might, specify correct politico-economic policies and strategies, and thus reliably cope with revolutionary threats. In other words, these social theorists contend that elites in control of politico-economic power, in order to maintain the status quo, have no choice under current conditions but to depend upon astute social scientific guidance in military morale building, in politico-economic relationships, and in the maintenance of mass loyalties.

These establishment social strategists usually visualize themselves as serving "the majority" (most often through an oligarchically dominant elite), but their faith in the majority's support for that elite and themselves may be as shaky as it is in Northern Ireland and the rest of the United Kingdom. They therefore typically point out: "It is fatally easy to underestimate the ability of a small number of armed men to exact support from exposed sections of the population by threats."[30] In another book, the strategist quoted admits that "no campaign of subversion will make headway unless it is based on a cause with a wide popular appeal." In their rhetoric, too, such persons like to make a kind of pseudo pass at liberalism by saying that any person "convinced that his country is wrong ... should cease to support it and take the consequences." At the same time, the "fact that subversion may be used to fight oppression, or even that it may be the only means open for doing so, does not alter the fact that soldiers should know how to suppress it if necessary."[31]

Conversely, they stress that disaffection by established intellectuals and especially by social scientists from the support of controlling elites is a significant step toward a successful social revolution.[32] An outsider might be so impolite as to interpret this as a species of blackmail or at least self-seeking special pleading: Cherish us or else!

Among establishment social theorists, individuals vary in their views and behavior, in their interpretations of commitment and of the probable course of the current struggle, between at least two poles: They may tend toward being (1) complacent and uncritical jobholders, compliant instruments of what seems to be becoming a more and more efficient police-state structure. On the other hand, they may see themselves as (2) engineers of adaptive change, of social revitalization, who can most effectively work within the status quo. In the present Northern Ireland conflict, such persons have produced many extensive analyses and proposals under military, governmental, and business auspices. These operators often brush aside social scientific "outsiders" as misguiding meddlers, "also rans," or "wild people"; but they may also try to exploit without thanks or credit the ideas of such "outsiders" to the extent that they can!

Such theorists as Marx and Lenin, who are committed to violent revolution as the necessary way to change society, also assign a similarly crucial role to intellectuals—of their own type. They look with contempt upon the wisdom of the social scientists of the establishment. They even assert that the incompetence or venal bias of such "lackeys" simplifies their own work of subversion for insurgents. As would-be midwives of societal reorganization, they place their faith in the "inevitability" of a shift from "decadent" ruling elites to representatives of a larger mass of the people. They contend that a more democratic distribution of power and opportunity is coming. They aver that those who try to maintain the status quo are inevitably to be defeated through their inability to retain mass support and through the inadequacy of their diagnoses and strategies. As the influential Irish revolutionary theorist James Connolly (1868–1916) asserts, "the development of the system of capitalist society leads inevitably to the increasing conservatism of the non-working-class element, and to the revolutionary vigour and power of the working class."[33]

Revolutionary social theorists thus devote themselves to analyzing past experiences and present potentials and then to adapting policy and strategy recommendations to the constantly changing opportunities they think they confront. That is how they say they can speed the arrival of the inevitable. Without the guidance of suitably dedicated and informed social theorists, they contend that a revolutionary effort is doomed to defeat.[34] Once again, an impolite outsider detects a threat or at least special pleading in their message: Cherish us or else!

Here, as before, within the role of revolutionary ideologist, individuals exhibit interpretations of commitment and behavior that vary between at least two poles: The polar types may be called "revolutionaries for the hell of it"[35] and "revolutionaries for a program." The latter are the more common. In other words, the first group of intellectuals contends that any social upheaval may shake out at least some social gains; after "victory," the "people" can decide what to do with what they have won. This notion has often pervaded the pronouncements of the Provisional Irish Republican Army during the current Northern Ireland struggle, even though it does also have something of a program.[36] Others insist on plotting and fighting for a more precisely defined reorganization of an institution or of society. They agree with T. E. Lawrence on the danger of "the old men" who come out again after the revolutionary enthusiasm has subsided in victory. Those are the people, he says, who accept the victory and then remake it "in the likeness of the former world they knew." Lawrence warns: "Youth could win, but had not learned to keep, and was pitiably weak against age. We stammered that we had worked for a new heaven and a new earth, and they thanked us kindly and made their peace. When we are their age no doubt we shall serve our children so."[37] This resembles the distrust of the Official Irish Republican Army's theorists for the less defined goals of the Provisionals. On this basis, disastrous struggles developed between the two IRAs.

Somewhere between the extremes of status quo maintainers and revolutionaries are other analysts and strategists who believe that social change—even drastic change—can come, has come, and can best come through nonviolent procedures. To support their positions, they cite especially the tremendous modifications and even revolutions that technological changes have occasioned in all aspects of society including the distribution of controls over social power. They contend that all wars, especially internecine ones, scar and handicap a people for generations after the fighting ceases. They also claim that elites now in power are more ready than their predecessors to accept even costly compromises with demands from the increasingly literate, informed, organized, and active masses. They take the viewpoint that a constantly more participant society—presumably under such intelligent guidance as they or their kind would provide—can come into being without resort to the uncontrollable and unpredictable risks of armed conflict. These social analysts and strategists thus also offer themselves as essential policy makers.[38] Again these people seem to say: Cherish us or else!

These nonviolent theorists exhibit at least two polar positions, those of token reform or appeasement and of planned, forceful aggression for social modification. The former seek alternatives to violence with little attention to the costs in terms of continued abuses or other maladjustments. They want "peace." The latter preoccupy themselves with the attainment of social change goals; they may risk and sometimes even invite retaliatory violence in order to dramatize their struggle for those goals with their willingness to sacrifice themselves to attain such gains. Several important Northern Ireland organizations have this orientation.[39]

Establishment ideologists accuse nonviolent reformists of being naive tools of revolutionaries. Revolutionaries perceive reformers as obnoxious compromisers in behalf of controlling elites, as people dedicated to propping up a sagging way of life or "social system." Nonviolent reformers brush aside such characterizations with the counter-contention that neither of the other groups is free to work for social change "objectively" or, for that matter, effectively. They claim that establishment social scientists are in organizational straitjackets and that revolutionaries suffer from being "true believers" in untested and untestable canons of faith.

In probing efforts at revolution and at rapprochement in Northern Ireland, it is well to bear in mind all three orientations toward revolution and their variations. Intellectuals of many sorts oversell their potential to aid or frustrate revolution and thus underrate other significant factors. A person free of vocational bias—if such there be—might come to a different and possibly a more tenable and useful perspective.

In spite of the violence since 1968, there appears to be a long-time drift in Northern Ireland toward the third, or nonviolent, orientation. Since the nineteenth century, this has been due to a whole complex of developments. Of the complex, the following may well be stressed: (1) increasing popular literacy and breadth of social and political awareness; (2) the expansion of a compromise-minded professional and business class within Northern Ireland communities; (3) social experimentation by many groups with the efficacy of nonviolent confrontations and mass communication in the achievement of social change; (4) disillusionment with the possibility of net gains from violence; (5) the diminishing prevalence of the violence-prone among the upper and lower classes; (6) the raising of minimum available subsistence levels so that, while deprivation for many persists, there are no longer the frequent periods of actual famine formerly experienced[40]; (7) the decline in opportunities to emigrate and also in the pressing need for emigration until the present conflict broke out; (8) the rising tide of mass media, especially the tendency for mass media in the British Isles to substitute an entertaining fun world of sports and sensationalism for concern with politico-economic problems[41]; (9) the ideological influence of clerics, some of it conservative and some radical; and (10) the overwhelming presence of British-controlled police and the army. Whether appeasers or nonviolent aggressors can predominate remains to be seen. The extent to which either or both can minimize the continuing costs of insurgent and offical terrorism is still difficult to predict.

Notes

1. W. F. Buckley, Jr., "Attack the Symptoms First in the Crime Epidemic," *New York Post,* 11 August 1977, p. 26.
2. Antonio Gramsci, *Il Risorgimento* (Torino: Einaudi, 1950), pp. 199–200; Franco Ferrarotti, *Alle Radici della Violenza* (Milano: Rizzoli, 1979) and *L'Ipnosi della Violenza* (Milano: Rizzoli, 1980).
3. W. D. Whitney and B. E. Smith, eds., *The Century Dictionary,* rev. ed. (New York: Century, 1914), p. 6249.
4. Laurence Urdang, ed., *The Random House Dictionary of the English Language* (New York: Random House, 1968), p. 1357.
5. J. B. S. Hardman, "Terrorism," *Encyclopaedia of the Social Sciences* (New York: Macmillan, 1934), 14:575–80, pp. 575–76 quoted.
6. Paul Wilkinson, *Terrorism and the Liberal State* (New York: Wiley, 1977), p. 49.
7. J. B. Bell and T. R. Gurr, "Terrorism and Revolution in America," in *Violence in America,* ed. H. D. Graham and Gurr, rev. ed. (Beverly Hills: Sage, 1979), pp. 345n., 330.
8. Joseph Conrad, *The Secret Agent* (New York: Doubleday, Page, 1907), p. 69.
9. Central Intelligence Agency, National Foreign Assessment Center, "Patterns of International Terrorism: A Research Paper, " (PA81-10163U, June 1981), p. ii; Warren Hinkle, "The Irish Inquisition," *Inquiry* 4, no. 5 (23 February 1981).
10. Max Lerner, "Political Offenders," *Encyclopaedia of the Social Sciences* (New York: Macmillan, 1934), 12: 199–203, p. 203 quoted.
11. M. D. Blumenthal, R. L. Kahn, F. M. Andrews, and K. B. Head, *Justifying Violence* (Ann Arbor, Mich.: Institute of Social Relations, 1971).
12. Frank Kitson, *Low Intensity Operations* (London: Faber & Faber, 1971), p. 17.
13. C. D. MacDougall, *Understanding Public Opinion* (New York: Macmillan, 1952), chaps. 4, 16.
14. A. McC. Lee, "Such Was the Dawn of the American Daily," *Quill* 31, no. 5 (May 1943): 6–8, 14; idem, *The Daily Newspaper in America,* new ed. (New York: Octagon Books, 1973), pp. 30, 41, 48–49.
15. A. L. Lorenz, *Hugh Gaine* (Carbondale, Ill.: Southern Illinois University Press, 1972); Bernard Bailyn and J. B. Hench, *The Press and the American Revolution* (Worcester: American Antiquarian Society, 1980).
16. R. V. Harlow, *Samuel Adams* (New York: Holt, 1923); J. C. Miller, *Sam Adams, Pioneer in Propaganda* (Boston: Little, Brown, 1936).
17. Lewis Einstein, *Divided Loyalties* (London: Cobden-Sanderson, 1933), p. 47.
18. R. W. Emerson, "Concord Hymn," *The Complete Writings of Ralph Waldo Emerson* (New York: William H. Wise, 1929), p. 880.
19. J. G. Leyburn, *The Scotch-Irish: A Social History* (Chapel Hill: University of North Carolina Press, 1962), p. 305.

20. A. McC. Lee, *How to Understand Propaganda* (New York: Rinehart, 1952); A. McC. and E. B. Lee, *The Fine Art of Propaganda,* new ed. (New York: Octagon Books, 1972), esp. pp. vii–xv.
21. See Chaps. 6–9.
22. Robert Moss, *Urban Guerillas* (London: Temple Smith, 1972), chap. 1; J. A. Schellenberg, *The Science of Conflict* (New York: Oxford University Press, 1982), pt. 3.
23. Crane Brinton, *The Anatomy of Revolution,* rev. ed. (Englewood Cliffs, N.J.: Prentice-Hall, 1965), p. 2; Lawrence Stone, "Theories of Revolution," *World Politics,* 18 (1966): 159–75; Anthony Oberschall, *Social Conflict and Social Movements* (Englewood Cliffs, N.J.: Prentice-Hall, 1973), pp. 81-84; A. T. Turk, *Political Criminality: The Defiance and Defense of Authority* (Beverly Hills, Calif.: Sage, 1982), chap. 3.
24. Friedrich Engels, "On Authority," pp. 481–85 in Karl Marx and Engels, *Basic Writings on Politics and Philosophy,* ed. L. S. Feuer (Garden City, N.Y.: Doubleday, 1959), p. 485 quoted.
25. Louis Kriesberg, *The Sociology of Social Conflicts* (Englewood Cliffs, N.J.: Prentice-Hall, 1973), chap. 8.
26. Karl Marx, letter to Sigfrid Meyer and August Vogt, pp. 292–95 in Marx and Fredrick Engels, *Ireland and the Irish Question,* ed. R. Dixon (New York: International Publishers, 1972), p. 294 quoted.
27. Karl Marx, "From Confidential Communication," pp. 160–63 in ibid., pp. 162–63 quoted.
28. V. I. Lenin, "The Irish Rebellion of 1916," pp. 31–35 in *Lenin on Ireland,* 2nd ed., ed. A. Raftery (Dublin: New Books Publications, 1974), pp. 33–35 quoted.
29. A. McC. Lee, *Multivalent Man* (New York: George Braziller, 1966), chaps. 14–16; idem, *Toward Humanist Sociology* (Englewood Cliffs, N.J.: Prentice Hall, 1973), chaps. 3, 7.
30. Frank Kitson, *Bunch of Five* (London: Faber & Faber, 1977), p. 283.
31. Frank Kitson, *Low Intensity Operations* (London: Faber & Faber, 1971), pp. 29, 9.
32. L. P. Edwards, *The Natural History of Revolution* (Chicago: University of Chicago Press, 1927); Brinton, *Anatomy of Revolution;* Stone, "Theories of Revolution."
33. James Connolly, *Labour in Ireland* (Dublin: At the Sign of the Three Candles, n.d.), p. 8.
34. Regis Debray, *Revolution in the Revolution?* (New York: Grove Press, 1967); idem, *Strategy for Revolution* (London: Jonathan Cape, 1970); Ian Greig, *Assault on the West* (Moscow: Foreign Affairs Publishing House, 1969); E. C. Guevara, *Reminiscences of the Cuban Revolutionary War* (New York: Grove Press, 1968); idem, *Guerilla Warfare* (New York: Random House, 1969); Mao Tse Tung, *On Guerilla Warfare,* trans. S. Griffiths (New York: Praeger, 1961); idem, *On Revolution and War,* ed. M. Rejai (Garden City, N.Y.: Doubleday, 1969).
35. Abbie Hoffman, *Revolution for the Hell of It* (New York: Dial Press, 1968); idem, *Woodstock Nation* (New York: Random House, 1969); Jerry Rubin, *Do It! Scenarios for Revolution* (New York: Simon & Schuster, 1970).
36. Provisional Irish Republican Army, *Freedom Struggle* (1973), pp. 94–96.
37. T. E. Lawrence, *The Letters of T. E. Lawrence,* ed. David Garnett (Garden City, N.Y.: Doubleday, 1939), p. 262.
38. C. M. Case, *Non-Violent Coercion* (New York: Century, 1923); Richard Gregg, *The Power of Non-Violence,* rev. ed. (New York: Schocken, 1960); Staughten Lynd, ed., *Nonviolence in America: A Documentary History* (Indianapolis: Bobbs-Merrill, 1966); Adam Roberts, *Civilian Resistance as National Defense* (Baltimore: Penguin, 1969); David Dellinger,

Revolutionary Nonviolence (Indianapolis: Bobbs-Merrill, 1970); Gene Sharp, *The Politics of Nonviolent Action* (Boston: Porter Sargent, 1973); idem, *Social Power and Political Freedom* (Boston: Porter Sargent, 1980).

39. See chap. 9.

40. R. N. Salaman, *The History and Social Influence of the Potato* (Cambridge, England: University Press, 1949), chap. 16, App. I; R. D. Edwards and T. D. Williams, *The Great Famine* (New York: New York University Press, 1957); Cecil Woodham-Smith, *The Great Hunger* (New York: Harper & Row, 1962); W. L. Langer, "Europe's Initial Population Explosion," *Harvard Today*, Spring 1964, pp. 2-10.

41. Richard Hoggart, *The Uses of Literacy* (Harmondworth, Middlesex: Penguin, 1963); Steve Chibnall, *Law-and-Order News* (London: Tavistock, 1977), chap. 2.

CHAPTER 1

Interethnic Conflict in the British Isles

Until the 1960s, educated English are reported to have asserted, "The British people, as you no doubt know, have absolutely no history of racialism."[1] In order to be at all plausible at any time in British history, that statement requires as delusory an interpretation as does a similar English claim that their traditions and government assure equal justice to the members of all groups in those islands.

The English writer J. B. Priestley points out that not only have the dominant amalgam called English "contrived for centuries to be prickly with prejudices" among their own classes and to the disadvantage of other ethnic groups, but the "ordinary citizen suffers from serious disadvantages ... [for he/she] rarely understands what rights he enjoys, having no written constitution or definite code to which he can appeal."[2] Or, as two English legal experts put it, "English judges tend to treat equality before the law ... as a formal concept concerning equal access to the courts, legal procedures and remedies, not as a principle which entitles them, within the narrow compass of a legal system, to restrain a stronger party from oppressing a weaker one." More specifically on racism, they note that, "apart from their disapproval of slavery, English judges have never declared that acts of racial discrimination committed *in this country* are against public policy."[3]

The understanding of this general interethnic and interracial situation in the British Isles is a necessary prerequisite to the attempt in the present book to describe and analyze the revolt in Northern Ireland that has flared since 1968.

This situation in the British Isles continues to reflect remnants of ancient tribal beliefs and practices that are far from unique to this area. Its persistent hold on members of so many British groups is stimulated by the centuries-long use of geneticist or racist rationalizations to justify class and ethnic differences and especially upper-class English efforts to control the other peoples of the British Isles and, in recent centuries, of a broader empire. In these efforts, the upper-class English have not sought an anglicizing assimilation of ethnic minorities. They have tried to maintain their political, economic, religious, and social-class hegemony over their subject classes and colonial peoples.

Notable in these efforts at control have been the uses to which the English upper-class has put the military and police, the legal rationalizers and implementers, the educators and the mass media, and the clergy of the established church (Roman Catholic until the time of Henry VIII and then Anglican Catholic or Episcopalian, the Church of England). Notable in minority resistance to such domination have been a variety of guerrilla and smuggling activities, ethnic survivals and revivals, sporadic political movements, and religious cults and denominations with strong ethnic and class ties, especially the Roman Catholic, Presbyterian, Methodist, Jewish, and Quaker.

Viewed historically as well as contemporaneously, how are such changing social constructs as ethnic groups, status groups and social classes, mythical ties of nationality, and political forms such as the state and devolved substates related to one another in interethnic competition and/or conflict in the British Isles? What are the feelings common to group members on which such changing social constructs are based? How deeply resistant to change are those feelings among both the dominant upper-class English and the lower classes and less favored ethnic groups in England and elsewhere? How do such feelings and their related social constructs change?

These opening remarks are not meant to suggest that the English were inventive about intergroup prejudice or the racist rationale for it. A reaction of snobbishness or antipathy to differences in sex, class, and area of habitation, as well as in physical appearance and ethnic and/or religious identification, is in many times and places a common block to interpersonal and intergroup understanding and cooperation. It is also a common basis for strivings for personal identity and dignity through invidious distinction.

Until recent centuries, few writers contested the notion that "blood," "stock," or "race" had "an exclusive importance, determining the social status, both of individuals and of groups."[4] Plato and Aristotle, for example, projected their elitist notions about innate inequalities among individuals onto their interpretations of what they would now call "racial" differences. Aristotle contended that such contrasts make it "meet ... that barbarous peoples should be governed by the Greeks—the assumption being that the barbarian and slave are by nature one and the same."[5] On the contrary, as the classicist Hans Kohn points out, during the same period—the fifth and fourth centuries B.C.—the Sophists taught that "the differences between free men and slaves were set by human convention, that slavery has been established by force and was therefore unjust."[6] The enlightened environmentalist contention of the humanist Sophists has been all too rare in human discourse and policy making. Racist and class-serving geneticist ideas similar to those of Plato and Aristotle have dominated in varying degrees too much of both popular and academic thought.[7]

The fourteenth-century Arab social historian Abd-al-Rahman ibn-Khaldûn (1332-1406) takes a view similar to that of the Sophists in providing some general answers to the questions raised above: "It should be known," he contends, "that differences of condition among people are the result of the different ways in which they make their living. Social organization enables them to co-operate toward that end." Ibn-Khaldûn sees "group feeling" (*asabîyah*) as basic to such organization. He asserts that this can best be derived from presumed blood ties but that it can also grow out of practical relations with clients and allies.[8]

During the nineteenth century, many theorists provided pretentious intellectual formulations for popular racist prejudices. They identified cultural with racial traits and thus contended that some peoples have a genetic basis for being superior to others. The French Comte J. A. de Gobineau[9] (1816-82) tried to glorify Teutonism, called by some Gobinism. The English Sir Francis Galton[10] (1822-1911) founded the alleged "science" of eugenics as a way of breeding the more fit and competent, an advocacy in which he was succeeded by Karl Pearson[11] (1857-1936) and many others. The Englishman Houston S. Chamberlain[12] (1855-1927), who became a naturalized German, served as a notorious publicist for such racist views.

Of a more acceptable scientific sort are some other contributions. Ludwig Gumplowicz[13] (1838-1909) introduced widely used terms for group feeling that are usually attributed to others. It was he who suggested the two terms anglicized as syngenism and ethnocentrism.

Syngenism refers to togetherness arising from a common place of birth and manner of living. It is a blend of egoism and sympathy on the part of its members for a limited group rather than more broadly.

Ethnocentrism is a related but broader conception. It places the emphasis for like-mindedness, mutual sympathy, and invidious distinction on ethnic similarity or common group membership rather than on early socialization processes. As Gumplowicz somewhat too categorically concludes: "Every stronger ethnic or social group strives to subjugate and make serviceable to its purposes every weaker element which exists or may come within the field of its influence."[14] W. G. Sumner (1840-1910), to whom the term ethnocentrism is often attributed, wrote similarly twenty-three years after Gumplowicz that the group-centric or ethnocentric view is that "in which one's group is the center of everything, and all others are scaled and rated with reference to it ... Opprobrious epithets are derived from these differences."[15] Like Gumplowicz, Sumner neglected the multivalent character of ethnocentric participation in more than one group (often ethnic, status, peer, and familial). He did not neglect the changing influence of the overall historical and societal context on ethnocentric tendencies.[16]

Cultural heritages and their accompanying ethnocentric identities and viewpoints offer psychological rewards and satisfactions—at a price. Their adherents often do not realize how frozen in time and how romanticized may be their conceptions of what are relics of their ethnic past. Social processes continue. Social institutions either find ways to cope with or adapt to changing conditions, means of livelihood, and survival or suffer degradation. Inhabitants of underprivileged provinces and members of minority ethnic groups in a modern state can continue to get some sense of security and dignity from their traditional identities and practices. On the other hand, if skin color does not present a factor regarded as an indelible barrier to assimilation, they can commingle with and then get lost in the larger society's class structure on whatever terms may be available to them. By thus making common cause with others in a broader social class and on more practically defined issues and objectives, they may learn that they can help themselves and others struggle to cope with problems besetting their class members. That promises to give them greater gains than dissipating their energies working to resurrect and raise to statehood an ancient tribal entity seen in idealized terms.

As far back as chroniclers recount the peopling of the British Isles, there have been successive invasions by Celts (including Goidels or Gaels, Cymry, and Brythons), Romans, Picts, Jutes, Angles, Saxons, Scandinavians (especially Norse and Danes), and Normans, among others. There have also been infiltrations throughout the centuries and today by people with still other ethnic backgrounds. Thus have ethnic as well as social-class differences become an integral part of British internecine conflict and politics, business, and social life. Even in the case of the recent immigrations of middle-class and lower-class nonwhites from parts of the decaying empire, class and ethnic cultural differences are most often seized upon as the basis for invidious distinction, but they are interpreted as being evidences of genetic inferiority. Whether the culturally deviant are nonwhite, Celtic, Cockney, Jewish, or Indian, their characteristics are typically associated by the English with slight or striking physical differences and are interpreted overall as racial, as the result of inferior "breeding," "strain," or "lineage," and hence as unalterably genetic. That even apparent physical differences other than color might owe much to differences in nutrition, in living and working conditions, and in class mannerisms of expression and action rather than to genetic differences is typically disregarded. Until the ethnically different blend into dominant loyalty and class groups, to the degree that they can and do, with appropriate modifications in names, in language and dialect, and in other behavior patterns, outgroups remain subject to exclusion, conflict, exploitation, even at times extermination.

Organized chiefly by the succession of Roman, Anglo-Saxon, Danish, and then Norman conquerors, a mixture of peoples emerged as a nominally homogeneous English nation in control of most of the lowlands of Great Britain. The mixed tribal remnants that had lived in the Welsh and Scottish highlands and the Scottish lowlands or had fled there rather than be oppressed by invaders came to constitute, together with the occupants of Ireland and the smaller islands, the so-called Celtic fringe of the British Isles. In their areas, they were taken to be relatively homogeneous peoples. Their separate ethnic traditions to the contrary notwithstanding, however, the population of England and the Celtic fringe—except for more recent nonwhite immigrants—were and are only slightly different blends of similar human stocks. Languages, dialects, religious sectarianisms, class characteristics, and nationalistic mythologies exaggerate differences. At the same time, physical similarities have been furthered through the centuries by the drift of soldiers and workers from the fringe to English jobs and marital arrangements, by the anglicization and intermarriage with the English of upper-class and middle-class Celts, and the licit and illicit sexual activities of English exploiters of the Celtic areas.

By A.D. 43, the Romans had laid the basis for the romanization and to some degree the organization of England, but the Roman conquest of Wales in 48 to 79 was only nominal, and their arrival in Scotland at the end of that century made no permanent impression. They did not invade Ireland. The Roman legions remained about four centuries and withdrew in 442. By the end of two more centuries, the Jutes, Angles, and Saxons were in control of what is now called England. Then, about 250 years later, in the latter half of the ninth century, came the Vikings and especially the Danes, who eventually—on the eve of the Norman conquest—made England and Ireland substantially parts of a Danish empire. With their superior military and administrative organization, the Normans were able to gain control of England in a comparatively few years following 1066. The so-called Celtic fringe remained a chain of problems to the English for centuries thereafter—even until the present. Like England, that fringe also continued to absorb migrants with a variety of ethnic backgrounds.

As these events took place, tribal identifications tended to become more broadly and inclusively ethnic. Then they began to merge into those of broader social classes and nationality. At the same time, tribal controls yielded to broader units of local governance under aggressive local chieftains or the most recent conquerors. An overarching state form grew out of the more comprehensive hegemony established through federations of such chieftains in the cases of Ireland and Scotland and through repeated conquests by monarchs and their armies in England and Wales.

As a state form became entrenched in England after each major invasion, the currently ruling ethnic group's upper-class used it as a powerful lever with which to try to orient the popular notions of social legitimacy and nationality toward the acceptance of their influence, language, and traditions. Those efforts to place people under the control of the invaders' class structure and to prevail upon them to accept the dominant class's myths of social status and hegemony only partly succeeded, even after the Norman invasion. The Normans did not establish a mythology in which Englishness and later Britishness admittedly and proudly derived from a synthesis of traditions and cultures. The bias that became anglicization laid a basis for the internal colonial exploitation of the ethnically different. It also assured recurrent agitations by the various Celtic nationalities to achieve autonomy.

Domination worked fairly well under feudalism and under an aristocratic and later a more and more plutocratic empire. Then the decay of empire and rising social awareness among the British masses mandated new initiatives in state form. These initiatives, to achieve some broad acceptance, moved toward more devolved or decentralized authority—at least in appearance. They have also exhibited greater dependence upon the largely American-centered multinational corporations.[17]

The Welsh and Scottish derivations of the English Tudor and Stewart dynasties and of the recent prime ministers, David Lloyd George and Ramsay MacDonald, might give the impression that England has more than a little interest in its multiethnic heritage, character, and United Kingdom interrelationships. On the contrary, Welsh and Scots who were given opportunities in England as a result of such expedient developments were soon absorbed into English social classes as "English people." At the same time, this assimilation did not offset or modify the treatment of Celts in their homelands and in English slums as crude, exploitable colonials. It did not mitigate the use of anglocentric British history and policy in the mass media, in government-controlled education, and in decision making. Instead of attempting to create a cosmopolitan state in which Britishness—like contemporary Americanism—would wear many garbs, the dominant English elites long tried to create a state culturally expedient for themselves with the lower classes divided against themselves by ethnic differences.

The long process through which Anglo-Normans conquered Wales was typical of their approach to the rest of the Celtic fringe as well as to overseas colonies. As two Welsh historians recount it, "at points conveniently situated near the more fertile lands, and most suitable for military defense or operations, a castle was built and garrisoned. Gradually the Cymry [Welsh] were ousted from the cultivated area, or else became, on some terms or other, the tenants of the Norman lord." The invader thus gradually forced the Welsh "further and further into the less desirable areas of the country ... [and] extended his power. ... In time towns began to spring up under the shelter of the castle walls, settlement from England was encouraged, charters conferring municipal privileges were from time to time conferred upon the settlers, and most of the early charters of the Welsh boroughs, drawing, as they do, an acute distinction between Englishmen and Welshmen, mark the nature of the struggle which went on during these years."[18] The intensity of that struggle rises and falls with changing technological, economic, and political conditions. It still continues in the principal areas of English-Celtic confrontation.

From the standpoint of the English, it is fortunate that localized tribalism long kept the Welsh, Scots, and Irish from becoming integrated nation-states. The Celts glory in their localisms and their ideological and especially religious differences. They have thus made it all the easier for their better organized and more powerful exploiter to benefit from their confusion and internecine feuding.[19]

The next major step after the domination of the Celts became the clearance of them from their lands and their use as soldiers and colonizers abroad and workers on farms and in factories in British cities. The population of Celtic rural regions was thus drained not only by forced migration through land clearances but also by "voluntary" migration in search of sustenance and by uncontrolled famine and disease.

To illustrate the clearance process, the Scottish Duchess of Sutherland, with the aid of British troops, "appropriated to herself *seven hundred and ninety-four thousand acres of land,* which from time immemorial had belonged to the [Sutherland] clan." In doing so, she transformed the whole into twenty-nine sheep walks, "each of them inhabited by one single family, mostly English farm-labourers." From 1814 to 1820, she thus "systematically expelled" 15,000 people, or some 3,000 families. "All their villages were demolished and burned down, and all their fields converted into pasturage." In return, the Duchess allowed her fellow clan members to purchase two acres for each family. "These 6,000 acres had been lying waste until then, and brought no revenue to the proprietors." She assessed the clan members an average of two and one-half shillings an acre for this favor. "Other Scottish noblemen went further. Having superseded human beings by sheep, they superseded sheep by game, and the pasture grounds by forests."[20] A Scottish historian summed up the consequences of the clearances thus: "In the long run the net result was extensive depopulation, the concentration of wealth in fewer hands, and an implacable resentment which is as fierce today [1968] as it was at the time of the actual Clearances. However regarded, however palliated, it is not a pretty story."[21]

Through several centuries, periodic crop failures combined with a laissez-faire governmental policy to provide brutal checks upon the overpopulating tendencies of the poor rural Celts. In the case of the Irish, this policy of ignoring the people's miseries had been stimulated by such conflicts as the Irish "rising" of 1798, which the English crushed with spectacular savagery. It had also been nourished by a biased interpretation of the nonviolent agitations of Daniel O'Connell during the 1820s and later. Such developments supported the English view of Ireland as an unruly conquered province with uncouth inhabitants and not as an assimilable part of the United Kingdom. Thus the deliberate land clearances in Ireland were tremendously stimulated by the greatest in a long series of famines, that of 1845-48, without the English making any substantial effort to offset its destructiveness. As a consequence of those years of blight and neglect, Ireland lost about 1.5 million people through starvation and famine-related epidemics and lost another million through emigration.[22]

Just prior to the 1845-48 famine, O'Connell, who had already gained political rights for Roman Catholics by his nonviolent methods, held in 1843 a series of some forty peaceful "monster" rallies. They were organized to urge the repeal of the 1801 act of political union of Ireland with England. Individual rallies attracted as many as 250,000 people. The reaction to these gatherings by the English Lord Chancellor of Ireland in 1843 was: "The peaceable demeanour of the assembled multitudes is one of the most alarming symptoms."[23] As a historian commented on this statement: "An Irish people united was an ominous spectacle, and the British Government, seized with something near panic, began to prepare 'as if in hourly expectation of civil war.' "[24]

Such events provide background for the ready persistence of an English laissez-faire policy toward the sufferings of the Irish people during the great famine. What if food was continually exported to England from

Ireland in 1845-48 while hundreds of thousands of people were starving? The Irish had to learn their place.

"How do you govern it [Ireland]?" Thomas Babington Macaulay asked the House of Commons in 1844 and then told his fellow members: "Not by love but by fear ... not by the confidence of the people in the laws and their attachment to the Constitution but by means of armed men and entrenched camps."[25] It was and is an old and customary relationship between the English and their minority and colonial peoples.

What about the Jewish role in English interethnic conflict? It is an old one. England expelled its Jews, then numbering some 17,000, in 1290. They were not officially readmitted to the British Isles until Cromwell's time in the 1650s. Cromwell took the view that Jewish industriousness and involvement in business would fit in well with his followers' type of Protestantism and would help to counteract what he considered the less desirable influences and tendencies of the Roman Catholics, especially in Ireland.[26]

As a result of O'Connell's agitation, the Roman Catholics had won greater political rights in 1829. This agitation also stimulated liberal concern for Jewish rights, but the Jews gained their rights only through a series of enactments in 1858-78. A detailed account of the Jewish lot in the British Isles would chiefly indicate the extent to which the Jews of various social classes—except during the expulsion period—had and still have much the same problems as the Celts and nonwhites. That means that the well-to-do are tolerated or assimilated, and the others rate as outsiders or second-class citizens until and if they are assimilated. A Benjamin Disraeli, whose well-to-do Jewish father had him baptized into the Anglican church, could become prime minister. The subtleties of anti-Jewish prejudice and the responding Jewish reactions to it can only be suggested here.[27]

Overseas imperialism, beginning with Ireland, strengthened English racism all the more, to the extent that that was possible. It gave exaggerated training to both aristocrats and rank-and-file soldiers and colonists in the oppression and exploitation of controlled peoples. Finally, with the decay of the militarily dominated empire, the immigration of quantities of nonwhite colonials of middle- and lower-class status began at least by the 1950s to make British "racialism" even more overt and admitted.

English historical and social writing, literature, and even "science" are stained, popularly at least, by genetic snobbishness. They contain elaborate efforts at justification of what some critics call the English "premise" and others designate as the English "religion" of inequality.[28] These writings have become more sophisticated and cosmopolitan during the past century, in part at least. The story is a long and many-stranded one that includes

William Shakespeare's *The Merchant of Venice* (1596) and Rudyard Kipling's poem, "The White Man's Burden" (1899). Think of Disraeli, whose Jewish background was just mentioned, having a character in one of his novels attribute to the genetic superiority of the "Saxon race" England's erstwhile role as "the arbiter of the world," and having a group agree: "All is race; there is no other truth" (1847).[29] Clerical and so-called "scientific" apologies for classism, imperialism, and even racism persistently echo such themes.[30]

The influential Francis Galton (1822-1911), for example, looked upon as the founder of the dubious but popular "science" of eugenics, claimed that "England has certainly got rid of a great deal of refuse, through means of emigration. She has found an outlet for men of adventurous and Bohemian natures, who are excellently adapted for colonizing a new country, but are not wanted in old civilizations; and she has also been disembarrassed of a vast number of turbulent radicals and the like, men who are decidedly able but by no means eminent, and whose zeal, self-confidence, and irreverence far outbalance their other qualities."[31] It was Galton's contention that, since "man's natural abilities are derived by inheritance, under exactly the same limitations as are the form and physical features of the whole organic world,"[32] this process of weeding the British human stock by emigration was solving a lot of the United Kingdom's actual and potential problems. The British Isles nevertheless continued to produce much the same social types, and social scientists came to point to the persistence of social, cultural, and other environmental influences as probably more formative of them than the genetic. The shipping abroad of so many of its more venturesome people also helps to account for the United Kingdom's loss in adaptability to changing life conditions.

In this century, the formerly respected and influential writings of the English psychologist Cyril Burt (1883-1971) similarly did much to support class-oriented and racially segregated systems of education, as well as racially restrictive immigration legislation, not only in the United Kingdom but also in the United States and elsewhere. After Burt had become the first knighted psychologist in England, and the American Psychological Association had given him its 1971 Thorndike award, he was shown to have based his elitist theories in large part upon rigged and faked data.[33] As one way of accounting for the popularity of Galton's and Burt's extreme genetic determinism, the psychologist Leon Kamin sarcastically notes: "Every professor knew that his child was brighter than the ditch-digger's child, so what was there to challenge?"[34]

That there are genetic differences among individuals is scarcely to be denied, even though it is difficult or impossible to sort out genetic from environmental influences. That various human groups have somewhat different genetic backgrounds is also not to be denied, but to erect this generalization into a sweeping claim as to the genetic superiority or inferiority of an ethnic or so-called racial group overlooks the extent to which all human groups come of mixed stock and exhibit within them highly diverse qualities, including levels of competence and accomplishment.[35]

It is now possible to confront and discuss objectively the frightful German persecution and genocidal destruction of Jews and Poles. On the contrary, after more than a millenium of contempt, genocidal persecution and extermination, and exploitation of such so-called racial minorities as the Welsh, Scots, and Irish, England still believes itself and claims the reputation of being historically "a country that has been largely free of domestic racial prejudice."[36]

Serious English students of their country's parliament still speak of its "uninterrupted history of protecting the freedoms of the people" without evidencing any need to place a modifier before "people."[37] It can be said with equal accuracy about both Germans and English—not to mention the many other examples of arrogant ethnic domination around the world—that "a people who have marked a minority as a separate people to be despised and hated have opened the way to something which infects the whole of their national life."[38]

Individuals of Welsh, Scots, Irish, and lower-class English background have managed to achieve positions of power and prestige in the English establishments, but this does not alter the foregoing statements. Such *arrivisti*, or at least their carefully schooled and intermarried children or grandchildren, are looked upon as "English." For all their racist Anglo-Saxon mythology and their demands for ethnic and class conformity, the English (and, for that matter, all the British) are of exceedingly mixed backgrounds, both biologically and ethnically, as we have seen. Only bigoted advocates of a racist Anglo-Saxonism or Celticism can make a case for anything but the highly cosmopolitan derivation and nature of all classes and ethnic segments of British society. If one has a "nice English" family name, powerful personal connections and wealth, and such an evidence of genteel schooling as an upper-class accent, one can be part of the "racially" elect "English" upper class, suitable to participate in imperial exploits, fun, and games.[39]

This combination of apparent rigidity with actual adaptability makes the "premise of inequality"—with its racist rationalizations—have the quality of a "cement of English social life."[40] As it was worded by the English economist John Stuart Mill (1806-73), liberty is only for those "capable of being improved by free and equal discussion," and "despotism is a legitimate mode of government in dealing with barbarians, provided the end be their improvement, and the means justified by actually effecting that end."[41] This viewpoint, as a piously expressed hope, has always figured in public declamations by the English as they went about their business of dominating and exploiting British society and their imperial connections. It is part of noblesse oblige.

The foregoing deals primarily with aspects of the backgrounds of interethnic conflict in the British Isles rather than with the current situation. The political and cultural activities of the nationalist Plaid Cymru and other groups in Wales, of the Scottish National Party and other Scottish organizations, of various nationalistic bodies such as the two wings of the Irish Republican Army and the related Sinn Féin parties in Northern Ireland and the Republic of Ireland, as well as more limited efforts in such other parts of the Celtic fringe as Cornwall and the Isle of Man, present a very complex picture. They and the tense situation surrounding nonwhite immigrants highlight the persistence of the general conflict tendencies in the exploitative relationships outlined.

England's recent "problems" with nonwhites from its colonies and former colonies actually differ little from those it has had down through the centuries with its white minorities. The so-called racial differences of the white minorities were more clearly, in any significant sense, cultural and mythological and not biological, but they were and are used to justify exploitative conduct similar to that exhibited toward nonwhites. As an informed student of English reactions to the current Northern Ireland rebellion observes, "the campaign against the war in Vietnam, which England could do *nothing* to affect, was far larger than the opposition to the war in Ireland. Deepseated racism underlies this apathy."[42]

Despite the similar deprivations suffered by the ethnically identifiable or religiously distinguishable Celts and other ethnic minorities, customary attitudes do not permit those groups to make common cause with one another and especially with the nonwhites.[43] Thus, fragmented nationalistic radicalism rather than efforts at integrated class action has been the predominant development.[44] Not only in Cornwall and the Isle of Man but even in Yorkshire and East Anglia have there been stirrings of home rule agitation, of a kind of nationalism.[45]

What groups are responsible for all this divisiveness and its attendant woes? The word "responsible" distorts the situation. It suggests a degree of conscious plotting that goes beyond the intellectual competence available in such traditionally entrenched and custom-bound conspiracies as the English, the various Protestant, and the Roman Catholic. The English power elite is an invidious conspiracy in the sense that its class-conscious mores provide a necessary modus operandi that calls for a recognition of the special rights of their kind of people, rights not conceded to those in other classes or ethnic groups. As we have seen, that identity is one reinforced in England, as elsewhere, by a racist conception of "good breeding," taken to be a select genetic distillation from choice tribal stock. Especially in Northern Ireland, the Roman Catholic and Protestant ethnic conspiracies are at least as binding, but they are popularly given nontheological and nonecclesiastical reinforcements that are racist, based on Celticism and Anglo-Saxonism and their poetic mythologies.

Both in the English power structure and in the churches, elites are cohesive, competing, and to a degree cooperating, and they possess strong and growing international and supranational ties. The sociologist C. Wright Mills defines power elites as "those political, economic, and military circles which as an intricate set of overlapping cliques share decisions having at least national consequences."[46] As these circles tend to become more narrow and more integrated in modern society, actions for which their members are responsible become more significant, but they continue to involve compromise among conflicting or competing interests and viewpoints. In spite of the emergence of tremendously powerful conglomerate corporations and their use of sophisticated "think tanks," their planning in any country or group of countries is still subject to possible opposition, to inaccurate social diagnoses, and thus to ill-advised actions.

Imperialism consists of lopsided controls over international trade made possible by military as well as economic domination. For its maintenance, imperialism requires the exploitative and often destructive use of military personnel and hardware. It entrenches itself through treaties among nations, through regional and worldwide politico-economic federations, through the burgeoning of multinational conglomerates, and through supranational cartel deals. Imperialism refers to ways to minimize (for the enterprisers) the costs of exploiting other people's raw materials and human resources. As Mills notes, "That the facilities of power are enormously enlarged and decisively centralized means that the decisions of small groups are now more consequential."[47]

As we have seen, enterprisers in the English upper stratum assured themselves centuries ago of their class control of their "racially inferior" domestic "barbarians," in other words of their own lower class of workers and soldiers. With the aid of middle-class apologists, technicians, and other functionaries, the English aristocracy participated in the development of an elaborate traditional scenario of social statuses, social-class identities, education and educational deprivation, class-oriented games and propaganda media and ideologies in order to preserve its class control. That very persistent federative conspiracy seized and milked a huge empire. Beginning with Wales, Scotland, and Ireland and then going clear around the world, those enterprisers expanded as far as they could their supplies of workers and soldiers, of "racially inferior barbarians," as well as of raw materials.[48]

During all this, the English upper stratum has modified time and again to meet changed conditions of national and international power structurings. It has absorbed the children of aggressive upstarts. It has managed spectacular continuity. When these enterprisers took control of a country, they both installed their own managerial surrogates and induced local people to serve as assistant managers.

In such cases as Ireland, the American colonies, Australia, and New Zealand, they also blunted local agitation in Great Britain by shipping abroad troublesome "rabble" to become what they hoped would be dependable resident instruments of empire. Presented with the alternative of staying in prison for debt, religious dissent, politico-economic agitation, or theft, or of being shipped abroad in crowded, fever-ridden, and vermin-infested vessels, many men and women chose the latter and became founders of colonial families.

English enterprisers apparently hoped that their own lower classes, when exported from England, would have more commitment to the crown than would conquered "natives." This exportation had the added advantage—still notable in Northern Ireland—of providing a lower class divided against itself, with "privileged" immigrants who were made all the more dependent on an English elite by the competitive threat to their livelihood from "foreigners." In Ireland, many Scottish Dissenters and English Protestants remain "West Britons" even after hundreds of years. Through dress, mannerisms, affectations of speech, and admiration of things English and upper-class, aspiring Roman Catholics have also willingly gotten themselves labeled as "West Britons" even though they are Irish in background.

Thus, in the traditional, socially irresponsible scenario of the imperialist, as intellectualized by middle-class functionaries, the unemployed and underemployed in the colonies are not wasting their lives. They are potential workers, men or parents of men available for the army, spurs to the efficiency of workers identified with the more privileged group, depressors of wages and working conditions. After all, generations in the ranks of the royal armies came "from Ireland, the Highlands [of Scotland],

and the poorest classes in England, whose refuge from pauperism it was in youth as the workhouse was in age."[49] As an American social analyst concludes, "More attention should be paid to the similarities between Anglo-Saxon images of Irishmen, African or American Negroes, and their own [English] working classes, not to mention such equally 'subordinate' categories as women and children."[50] This recalls the statement of the eighteenth-century Anglo-Irish Bishop George Berkeley, "the negroes, in our plantations, have a saying: 'If a negro was not a negro, Irishmen would be negroes.' "[51]

It is now relevant to present a summary of recent efforts by the British government to cope with interethnic conflicts. This section focuses especially on how domestic and multinational corporations are sheltered from loss as a result of interethnic conflict and, for that matter, are encouraged to profit from it.

Governmental moves are of three kinds in particular: (1) modest and largely cosmetic steps toward granting rights to minority members; (2) exclusion or deportation of "undesirables," especially those "racially" different; and (3) the continued use of force to "restore law and order." The character and purposes of these moves become clearer when one views the extent to which industrial and financial corporations benefit from ethnic oppression and from lower classes stimulated to be divided against themselves.

As viewed from an American perspective, the most successful ideological straddlers in the world are the English. With little effort to rationalize raw force with their publicly avowed morality, the English often appear to accept violent repression of the social rights of others because they regard themselves as, de facto, the final arbiters of social control and justice. An English clergyman, for example, recently explained his parishioners' quiet acceptance of the death of a local soldier in Ireland by asserting that "the British have long regarded themselves as policemen of the world."[52] In each case, English policy makers try to give the impression that they are unwillingly forced to use violence and suspend civil liberties, as various official investigation reports on Northern Ireland violence consistently assert or imply. The most common other characteristics of those reports are their apparently candid recounting of events and their constructive suggestions. Typically, they all promise more in subsequent actions to counteract abuses by public authorities than those authorities then implement.[53]

This is not to imply that there is much that is deliberate about English ideological straddling or hypocrisy. It does not have to be a consciously calculated folk or class conspiracy, as we have said, even though it amounts to a folk or class conspiracy to dominate so far as its effects are concerned. It does not need to be consciously calculated. It is inherent in multivalent English culture and class subcultures.[54] It is a complex of tribalistic cultural relics nurtured by entrepreneurial circumstances and opportunities.

In assessing governmental moves in relation to ethnic minorities, three significant points need to be born in mind: (1) the lack of a bill of rights, (2) the pervasive power of a patrician traditionalism, and (3) the need for going beyond legal recourses.

In the first place, then, the United Kingdom has no written constitutional bill of rights comparable to the first ten amendments to the U.S. Constitution. "Consequently rights in the UK are based on the negative concept that anything is lawful unless it is expressly forbidden by Act of Parliament or [by judicial interpretation of] common law." This lack of positive assurance is exacerbated by "a wide gap between principle and practice [in the administration of justice], which seriously inhibits the rights of individuals." Notably, "the defects of the judicial system provide formidable obstacles for the accused."[55] In consequence, to illustrate, "East African Asians with British passports are helplessly shuttlecocked from one continent to another" and "black people suffer discrimination in housing, employment and education."[56]

The second significant point to bear in mind concerning the United Kingdom government—its patrician traditionalism—is to be seen thus: The government represents "the containment of capitalism within a patrician hegemony which never ... actively favoured the aggressive development of industrialism or the general conversion of society to the latter's values and interests."[57] Lacking "the leadership of a militant radicalism, the masses are unable to break the system," and thus "the working class became negatively reconciled to the same Old Corruption, to elite hegemony, class distinctions, and deference to tradition." Thus the United Kingdom is often termed the most bourgeois state. In the current industrial crisis, therefore, "bourgeois radicalism" emerges in the form of Northern Irish, Scottish, Welsh, and other nationalisms. There is little evidence of a proletarian "class struggle in the metropolis, although this may soon change."[58] In other words, patrician traditionalism cloaks administrators and judges and assures them a degree of social distance from popular pressures and social invisibility to popular inspection. As a part of this, mass media exhibit "a systematic tendency to reproduce definitions of reality derived from the political elites" rather than more directly and naively from firsthand observation.[59]

The third point to be held in mind about governmental action is perhaps overstated by an English civil libertarian. He insists that "we should not expect too much of the law. Nor should we put too much effort into changing it." As he sees it, "The law enshrines general standards of acceptable behaviour but ultimately racialism in all its forms can only be beaten by economic and social improvements, education and propaganda, and political action."[60] He apparently does not see how useful in economic, educational, and political action it can be to work to obtain more egalitarian legislation. Nor does he appear to be aware of how useful subsequent efforts can be to try to assure the implementation of such legislation once it is law.

The first British legislation against racial discrimination is contained in clause 87 of the Government of India Act of 1833. It set forth the principle that no Indian native or other British subject resident in India "shall, by reason only of his religion, place of birth, descent, colour, or any of them, be disabled from holding any place, office or employment" in the East India Company then governing India. By customary practice and through subterfuge, this clause was inoperative in all but low-level positions. After all: "England has a destiny to rule other people less favoured and less competent than Englishmen."[61]

From 1950, various race relations bills were considered in Parliament, but none was enacted until 1965. "The black migrants who began to come to Britain to relieve the labour hunger of the 1950s had been taught they were British, sharing with all citizens of the Commonwealth and empire an indivisible allegiance to the crown." This "fiction copied from the ancient Roman empire"[62] is congruent with British upper-class faith in their class and ethnic superiority as the viable basis for social domination. The Notting Hill race riots of 1958 and subsequent incidents stimulated the eventual enactment of the 1965 Race Relations Act, to be supplemented by the acts of 1968 and 1976. These acts made it a civil and not a criminal offense to treat a person less favorably than another because of color, race, nationality or citizenship, or ethnic or national origin. They do not take into consideration discrimination on the grounds of religion, language, sex, political belief, or status. Certain other laws, such as the Sex Discrimination Act of 1975, help with some of these matters.

This campaign from the 1950s for legislation and action against discrimination lacked substantial voter support, and "there was little public awareness of the nature or extent of racial discrimination." Lacking an "ideal of equality, embodied in a written constitution or elsewhere, to which the lobbyists could turn in support of their case for using law to combat racial discrimination," the agitation "was radical and without precedent" in the United Kingdom.[63]

Under all these acts, implementation remains a serious problem. For example, the House of Lords, acting in its capacity as the court of final appeal, even went so far in 1971 as to interpret the 1965 and 1968 acts as permitting a housing authority to require an applicant for accommodations to be British. That decision again suggests the greater power of English patrician traditionalism than of governmental enactment.

The 1976 Race Relations Act does not apply to Northern Ireland, but the Fair Employment (Northern Ireland) Act of 1976 establishes a Fair Employment Agency (FEA) entrusted with power to investigate complaints and prosecute firms guilty of religious or political discrimination. The first report of that FEA noted "that Catholics were massively under-represented in almost all of the North's industries and accounted for the vast majority of the unemployed." As a result, "the letters column of the Belfast *Newsletter* was filled for three weeks with outraged unionist [Protestant Loyalist] correspondence." The pressure of organized Protestantism against the FEA's implementation of its legal mandate became effective when one of FEA's decisions favoring a Roman Catholic was reversed by a court. For example, Michael Farrell, well known as an anti-Loyalist writer and political activist, was denied promotion by the Belfast College of Technology. He vented his frustration by asserting: "This demonstrates once again the irreformability of the Northern State. However well intentioned the FEA may be, one intimidating court decision has reduced it to toothless impotency."[64]

The race relations acts made incitement to racial hatred a criminal offense on the same grounds as the civil discrimination provisions. Here again, implementation is a crucial problem. "The main difficulty is that 'hatred' is a very strong word and it is extremely difficult to persuade juries to convict."[65] In the case of printed material, too, it is not easy to ascertain the individual who may have been responsible for leaving a racist item in a letterbox. As a manual of the National Council for Civil Liberties advises: "In practice, the law has failed to halt the continuous flow of racialist literature and speeches directed against the black community." At the same time, the legislation "has been used on more than one occasion to imprison and fine black 'militants' who have complained of white oppression."[66] As a disillusioned former community relations officer notes: "It is a long time since West Indians in England felt confidence in the willingness of the police to protect them, and Pakistanis interviewed in the East End [of London] after the first reports of Paki-bashing stated that it was no use for them to call the police to their aid; they said that the police, when called, were slow to arrive and frequently seized upon Pakistanis who had been attacked rather than upon their attackers."[67]

More effective than these modest steps toward granting some rights to minority-group members have been steps to exclude or deport the racially different and to use force to suppress civil rights agitations. Immigration rules, prior to the Immigration Act of 1971, distinguished between aliens and Commonwealth citizens. That distinction opened the door to many nonwhite colonials, and the Act of 1971 therefore made the distinction one between "patrials" or ones with the "right of abode" and others. Without going into the complicated legal definition of who is or who is not a patrial, it is enough to note that certain Commonwealth citizens who are white, for example those from Australia and Canada, can often establish patrial status through having had a parent or grandparent who was a resident United Kingdom citizen. East African Asians are unlikely to be able to do so. Nonpatriality gives immigration and police officials much greater control over immigrants; in extreme cases, they can exclude them or deport them.

The 1981 British Nationality Act limits British citizenship with full right of residence to those who are already legally settled in Britain or one of whose parents was a citizen and whose claim on citizenship was registered at birth abroad. Under this act, citizens of dependent territories can no longer take up residence in Britain.

Another legislative device for handling "undesirables" was the Prevention of Terrorism Act of 1974, "which was rushed through Parliament after the pub-bombings outrage in Birmingham in November 1974." Replaced by the Prevention of Terrorism (Temporary Provisions) Act of 1976, the legislation "gives the police the power to arrest and question suspects and detain them for up to seven days; to search people and places; it also allows the Secretary of State to make an exclusion order removing someone from Great Britain or Northern Ireland (or in some cases, from the UK entirely); to ban terrorist organizations."[68] This legislation has been used particularly against Irish and nonwhite agitators, whether violent or not.

The government action that remains the one upon which most dependence is placed is not gestures toward granting rights to minority members or the exclusion or deportation of "undesirables." It is the continued use of force throughout the British Isles to "restore law and order." As a British specialist on insurgency advises, "the simplest method of all" for the suppression of even nonviolent subversion is "the ruthless application of naked force," even though he contends that "it is most unlikely that the British government, or indeed any Western government, would be politically able to operate on these lines even if it wanted to do so."[69] On the contrary, that is just what British soldiers did under orders in Northern Ireland when they killed thirteen unarmed nonviolent marchers and fatally wounded a fourteenth in Derry in a civil rights demonstration on 30 January 1972, "Bloody Sunday."[70] Other less spectacular examples are numerous.[71]

With the replacement of their empire by politico-economic arrangements in which multinationally controlled corporate networks become the major instruments of social control, the English stance toward the British Celtic fringe began to change. The English establishment's experiences with the politically "free" Irish 26-county state appear to help convince financiers and their politicians that plutocratic relationships might effectively enough control such an entity without their having to retain overt responsibility for the official selection of its political leadership. As the Irish socialist James Connolly had warned in 1897, political independence would not be enough to free the Irish people from British control, from the hegemony of "the whole army of commercial and industrial institutions she has planted in this country."[72] The example of the Irish state makes pressures from Scotland and Wales toward at least nominal "devolution" amount to the proposal of a "democratic" facade behind which the current capitalistic military-industrial "system" might continue to flourish.

From another perspective, an English writer regards it as plausible to state that "the sense of fair play on which the English still pride themselves seems to demand that if the Scots and the Welsh believe that they can govern their own countries without being a nuisance to their neighbours, they should be allowed to do so." He does not define what the English—popularly or from an establishment viewpoint—might mean by "being a nuisance to their neighbours." Those who live within the Celtic fringe or in the Celtic slums of English cities have had experiences in depth with anglocentric interpretations of such a formula.

The same author goes so far as to claim that many of the contemporary English "in their heart of hearts would themselves now prefer to be just English, instead of continuing to be British."[73] He is in effect implying that perhaps "devolved" or quasi-independent substates can be useful units in a corporately controlled military-industrial state. In contrast, the Northern Ireland Orange dictatorship and its recurrent civil disorders in 1920–72 did not provide an encouraging model. Thus patrician traditionalists as well as conservative corporate executives question strongly the utility of devolved substates as units of control. Sentimental attachment to a substate's "national" identity attracts them as an alternative to class conflict, but it is no cure-all. Why experiment with new and untried sets of power brokers until one is forced to do so? All power brokers tend to be or to become "undependable," in other words to overestimate their "proper" share of the "take."

Whether viable or not, such nationalist efforts as those symbolized by the Scottish National Party and the Welsh Plaid Cymru continue to make their play for support. Offshore oil in Scottish waters has given their nationalism a new urgency, and Scotland does have a separate church and legal system and rather distinctive educational and journalistic traditions. The Welsh are especially concerned with depopulation and economic problems.

Celticism and Anglo-Saxonism serve too easily the manipulative and exploitative purposes of those in control. They are bases—like skin color and religious denominationalism—for dividing the middle and especially the lower classes against themselves. As long as imperial armies provided careers for aggressive proletarians and as British industry and commerce had adequate markets, the British of all classes tended to become more and more content with their class status. With the shrinking of empire, with participation in the polyglot European Economic Community, with the decline of markets and decay of productive facilities, interethnic conflict within British cities becomes more common and the proletarians gradually lose what satisfaction they had with their statuses.

Notes

1. C. E. Lincoln, "The British Say They Aren't Prejudiced," *New York Times,* 14 November 1965, p. 64.
2. J. B. Priestley, *The English* (New York: Viking, 1973), pp. 11, 13.
3. Anthony Lester and Geoffrey Bindman, *Race and Law in Great Britain* (Cambridge, Mass.: Harvard University Press, 1972), pp. 24–25; cf. Lawrence Grant et al., *Civil Liberty: The NCCL Guide to Your Rights,* 3rd ed. (Harmondsworth, England: Penguin, 1978).
4. Pitirim Sorokin, *Contemporary Sociological Theories* (New York: Harper & Row, 1928), p. 219.
5. Aristotle, *Politics,* trans. Ernest Barker, rev. ed. (Oxford: Clarendon Press, 1948), p. 3; cf. Plato, *The Republic,* trans. Allan Bloom (New York: Basic Books, 1968), pp. 94, 150.
6. Hans Kohn, "Race Conflict," *Encyclopaedia of the Social Sciences* (New York: Macmillan, 1934), 13:36–41, p. 36 quoted; Walda K. Fishman and Irving Wainer, "A History of the Concept of Race," *Science for the People* (Cambridge, Mass.) 14, no. 2 (March/April 1982): 6–9, 31–33.
7. Gilbert Murray, *Ancient Greek Literature* (1897, re-issue Chicago: University of Chicago Press, 1956), pp. 163–64; H. E. Barnes, *An Intellectual and Cultural History of the Western World,* 3rd rev. ed. (New York: Dover, 1965), 1:131–33.
8. Abd-al-Rahman ibn-Khaldûn, *The Muqaddimah: An Introduction to History,* 3 vols., trans. Franz Rosenthal (New York: Pantheon, 1958), 1:249, 263–64.
9. J. A. de Gobineau, *The Inequality of Human Races,* trans. from part of 1853–54 French version by A. Collins (London: Heineman, 1915).
10. Francis Galton, *Hereditary Genius* (New York: D. Appleton, 1870).
11. Karl Pearson, *National Life from the Standpoint of Science* (London: A. & C. Black, 1901).
12. H. S. Chamberlain, *The Foundations of the Nineteenth Century,* trans. from the 1899 German version by John Lees (London: John Lane, 1911).

13. Ludwig Gumplowicz, *Der Rassenkampf* (Innsbruck: Verlag der Wagner'shen Univ.-Buchhandlung, 1883), pp. 240–53.
14. Gumplowicz, "The Mechanistic Interpretation of Society," pp. 346–48 in R. E. Park and E. W. Burgess, *Introduction to the Science of Sociology*, 2nd ed. (Chicago: University of Chicago Press, 1924), p. 347 quoted.
15. W. G. Sumner, *Folkways* (Boston: Ginn, 1906), p. 13.
16. A. McC. Lee, *Multivalent Man* (New York: George Braziller, 1966), pp. 153–56.
17. R. M. MacIver, *The Web of Government* (New York: Macmillan, 1947); Michael Hechter, *Internal Colonialism: The Celtic Fringe in British National Development: 1536–1966* (Berkeley: University of California Press, 1975), chaps. 8–10; Tom Nairn, *The Break-Up of Britain* (London: NLB, 1977), chaps. 1, 9.
18. John Rhys and David Brynmor-Jones, *The Welsh People*, 4th ed. (London: T. Fisher Unwin, 1906).
19. R. I. Jack, *Medieval Wales* (Chicago: University of Chicago Press, 1973); Rosalind Mitchison, *A History of Scotland*, (London: Methuen, 1970); Edmund Curtis, *A History of Ireland*, 6th ed. (New York: Barnes & Noble, 1950).
20. Karl Marx, "The Duchess of Sutherland and Slavery" (1853), pp. 142–48 in Marx and Frederick Engels, *Articles on Britain* (Moscow: Progress Publishers, 1971), pp. 145–47 quoted; cf. Mitchison, *History of Scotland*, pp. 377–78.
21. William Ferguson, *Scotland: 1689 to the Present* (New York: Praeger, 1968), p. 277; cf. G. S. Pryde, *Scotland from 1603 to the Present Day* (London: Thomas Nelson and Sons, 1961), p. 158.
22. R. E. Kennedy, Jr., *The Irish* (Berkeley: University of California Press, 1973), chap. 2.
23. Edward Sugden, quoted by Cecil Woodham-Smith, *The Great Hunger: Ireland 1845–1849* (New York: Harper & Row, 1962), p. 17.
24. Woodham-Smith, ibid.; cf. R. D. Edwards and T. D. Williams, eds., *The Great Famine* (New York: New York University Press, 1957).
25. T. B. Macaulay, quoted by Woodham-Smith, ibid., p. 18.
26. Bernard Shillman, *A Short History of the Jews in Ireland* (Dublin: Cahill, 1945), p. 13.
27. H. S. Q. Henriques, "The Jewish Emancipation Controversy in Nineteenth-Century Britain," *Past and Present* (Oxford, England), no. 40 (July 1968); Colin Holmes, *Anti-Semitism in Britain, 1876–1939* (London: Edward Arnold, 1978); Geoffrey Alderman, "Not Quite British: The Political Attitudes of Anglo-Jewry," *British Political Sociology Yearbook* 2 (1975): 188–211.
28. Matthew Arnold, "Lecture on 'Equality,' " pp. 48–97 in his *Mixed Essays* (New York: Macmillan, 1903); R. H. Tawney, *Equality*, 4th ed. (London: Unwin Books, 1964), chap. 1; J. S. Mill, *Autobiography*, ed. Roger Howson (New York: Columbia University Press, 1924), pp. 120–21, 165; idem, *Principles of Political Economy*, ed. J. M. Robson, based on 7th ed. (Toronto: University of Toronto Press, 1965), 3:752–57; J. J. Maquet, *The Promise of Inequality in Ruanda* (London: Oxford University Press, 1961).
29. Benjamin Disraeli, *Tancred* (New York: Collier, n. d., originally issued in 1847), p. 134. Cf. Jacques Barzun, *Race: A Study in Superstition*, rev. ed. (New York: Harper Torchbooks, 1965), chap. 6.
30. L. P. Curtis, Jr., *Anglo-Saxons and Celts* (Bridgeport: University of Bridgeport, 1968), chaps. 2, 5, 6; T. F. Gossett, *Race: The History of an Idea in America* (Dallas, Texas: Southern Methodist University Press, 1963), chaps. 1–8; Barzun, *Race*, esp. chap. 2; Christine Bolt, *Victorian Attitudes to Race* (Toronto: University of Toronto Press, 1971).
31. Francis Galton, *Hereditary Genius* (New York: D. Appleton, 1870), p. 361.

32. Ibid., pp. 1 et seq.

33. A. R. Jensen, "Kinship Correlations Reported by Sir Cyril Burt," *Behavior Genetics* 4 (1974): 1–28.

34. L. J. Kamin, quoted by Nicholas Wade, "IQ and Heredity: Suspicion of Fraud Beclouds Classic Experiment," *Science* (Washington), 194 (1976): 916–19, p. 918 quoted; Kamin, *The Science and Politics of I. Q.* (New York: Wiley, 1974).

35. Marvin Harris, *Culture, Man, and Nature* (New York: Crowell, 1971), pp. 87–88, 96.

36. Simon Abbott, ed., *The Prevention of Racial Discrimination in Britain* (New York: Oxford University Press, 1971), p. xi.

37. Kenneth Bradshaw and David Pring, *Parliament and Congress* (London: Constable, 1971), p. 137.

38. Philip Mason, *Race Relations* (London: Oxford University Press, 1970), p. 3.

39. Tawney, *Equality*, p. 247; D. V. Glass, ed., "Introduction," pp. 3–28, to *Social Mobility in Britain* (Glencoe: Free Press, 1954); J. B. Montague, Jr., *Class and Nationality: English and American Studies* (New Haven: College and University Press, 1963), p. 149.

40. Mason, *Race Relations*, p. 165.

41. J. S. Mill, *Dissertations and Discussions: Political, Philosophical, and Historical*, 5 vols. (London: Longmans, Green, 1867), 3:167.

42. Russell Stetler, "IRA: Beyond the Barricades," *Ramparts* (Menlo Park, Calif.), March 1972, pp. 9–12, 14–16, p. 15 quoted. Cf. Alvin Shuster, "British Are Indifferent to Ulster Crisis," *New York Times*, 3 May 1972, p. 2.

43. Edwin Eames and Howard Robboy, "The Wulfranian and the Punjabi: Conflict, Identity and Adaptation," *Anthropological Quarterly* (Washington) 51 (1978): 207–12.

44. Tom Nairn, *The Break-Up of Britain: Crisis and Neo-Nationalism* (London: NLB, 1977), p. 39.

45. William Greenberg, *The Flags of the Forgotten* (London: Clifton Books, 1969), p. 137.

46. C. W. Mills, *The Power Elite* (New York: Oxford University Press, 1956), p. 18.

47. Ibid., p. 23.

48. V. G. Kiernan, *The Lords of Human Kind* (Boston: Little, Brown, 1969), chap. 1.

49. Ibid., p. 59.

50. L.P. Curtis, *Anglo-Saxons and Celts*, p. 121; see G. W. Allport, *The Nature of Prejudice* (Cambridge, Mass.: Addison-Wesley, 1954), chap. 12.

51. George Berkeley, quoted by Stetler, *"IRA"*, p. 11.

52. Quoted by Shuster, "British Are Indifferent."

53. See, for example, evidence of this given in H. G. Bennett, chair, *Report of The Committee of Inquiry into Police Interrogation Procedures in Northern Ireland* (London: HMSO, Cmnd. 7497, March 1979).

54. Lee, *Multivalent Man*, chaps. 14-17.

55. Grant et al. *Civil Liberty*, pp. 13–14.

56. Anna Coote and Lawrence Grant, eds., *Civil Liberty: The NCCL Guide*, 2nd ed. rev. (Harmondsworth, England, Penguin, 1973), p. viii.

57. Nairn, *Break-Up of Britain*, p. 32.

58. Ibid., p. 39.

59. Steve Chibnall, *Law-and-Order News* (London: Tavistock, 1977), p. 3.

60. Roger Darlington, "Are Anti-Racism Laws Working?" *Rights* (London) 3, no. 1 (September-October 1978): 11–12, p. 12 quoted.

61. Ann Dummett, *A Portrait of English Racism* (Harmondsworth, England: Penguin, 1973), p. 49.
62. Lester and Bindman, *Race and Law*, p. 148.
63. "Relating Britain's Races," *Economist* (London), 24 April 1982, pp. 45–46, p. 46 quoted.
64. Joe McConnell, "The Michael Farrell Case," *Hibernia* (Dublin), 21 December 1978, p. 8; cf. R. J. Spjut, *The Fair Employment (Northern Ireland) Bill* (London: National Council for Civil Liberties, n.d.), Farrell, *Northern Ireland*, 2nd ed. (London: Pluto Press, 1980).
65. Darlington, *"Anti-Racism Laws,"* p. 11.
66. Coote and Grant, *Civil Liberty*, p. 268.
67. Dummett, *English Racism*, p. 12; cf. E. J. B. Rose et al., *Colour and Citizenship* (London: Oxford University Press for the Institute for Race Relations, 1969); Chris Collins, "Ireland and Racism," *Hands Off Ireland!* (London), no. 7 (April 1979): 16–18.
68. Grant et al., *Civil Liberty*, pp. 534–35.
69. Frank Kitson, *Low Intensity Operations* (London: Faber and Faber, 1971), p. 87.
70. Lord Widgery, chair, *Report of the Tribunal Appointed to Inquire into the Events on Sunday, 30th January 1972* (London: HMSO, H.L. 101, H.C. 220, April 1972).
71. "Northern Ireland 1968–1978: A Decade of Strife," *Hibernia* (Dublin), 21 December 1978, pp. 15–26; see esp. chap. 8 below.
72. James Connolly, "Nationalism and Socialism," *Shan Van Vocht* (Belfast), as quoted on p. 50 in Samuel Levenson, *James Connolly* (London: Quartet Books, 1977).
73. Greenberg, *Flags of the Forgotten*, p. 137.

CHAPTER 2

The Stuff of History

When did the Northern Ireland struggle begin? As with everything else in this current conflict, even the selection of such a date becomes a propaganda contest. An enticing date from an Irish nationalist viewpoint is 1172, the year that Henry II of England assumed dominance over Ireland, or 1607-9, the years the Tudors confiscated large areas of the northern province of Ulster and began a program of planting there English and more Scottish settlers. Spokespeople for the present Northern Ireland loyalists prefer to speak of the "popish" threat to their status that led in 1912 to some 471,000 of them signing a pro-British "Solemn League and Covenant" and in 1920-21 to the establishment of the "Orange State," the Protestant-controlled six-county province at that time separated within the United Kingdom from the other twenty-six Irish counties.

These dates suggest ancient but ever fresh tensions among Irish separatists, pro-British unionists, and British surrogates. That the separatists or nationalists tend to be ethnically Roman Catholic and the unionists, ethnically Protestant (Episcopalian) and Dissenter (Presbyterian, Methodist, etc.) suggests labels that caricature the participants by overstressing the religious dimension. Many active in this struggle have little regard for the teachings of any church.

Historical references and symbolism constantly recur in the propaganda of the current struggle. From what sources come the historical myths, rhetoric, and fantasies employed in terrorizing actions and counteractions? To what extent have they been created by scholars and professional propagandists? How deeply are they embedded in the popular traditions, in the cultural patterns of thought that influence possible behavior among the opposing groups?

For our purposes here, there is no need more than to outline briefly aspects of the eight-century conflict of the Irish with the British invaders for the control of Ireland and more especially Northern Ireland. Some relevant details about precursors of the present struggle will suffice.

Irish history is an inexhaustible warehouse of materials propagandists use for almost any purpose, but, as a Northern Ireland historian points out, "the most widespread, and most erroneous, assumption made about the [present] Ulster crisis is that it is created entirely by Irish history, by the inability, that is, of Ulster people to free themselves from the problems of the past and address themselves to those of the present and of the future."[1] Those directly involved in the fighting have been and are too young to have experienced previous Irish troubles. All that is available about the past to all three sides is sentimentalized and brutalized folk symbols, customs, and myths with which to clothe their aspirations and their efforts.

For the two groups of Irish partisans, stimuli come overwhelmingly from the more immediate pressures of their contemporary world. It is no accident that the nationalists borrow, for example, the song of the American blacks, "We Shall Overcome," and use it frequently in their demonstrations. On the other hand, the poorly informed British soldiers try to implement a colonial policy that bred bitterness and failed in colonies around the world.

Those contemporary stimuli nevertheless are translated many times into terms of the events, personages, and sayings of many yesterdays. This practice provides a lethal mixture for today's struggles. Let us look at some of that background, especially in Northern Ireland.

The separation of the Anglican church (including the Church of Ireland) from Rome in 1534 under Henry VIII (1491-1547, king from 1509) strengthened the hold of the suppressed Roman Catholic church on the Irish as their ethnic defense body. It became even more crucial to the Irish than the dissenting churches were to become to the lower-class English. As the historian W. E. H. Lecky asserts: "Anglicanism was from the beginning at once the most servile and the most efficient agent of tyranny." With "the assistance of temporal authority and by the display of worldly pomp," that church "naturally flung herself on every occasion into the arms of the civil power."[2] Thus the utilization of the established Church of Ireland by the English as an instrument of domination had primarily political and class rather than religious significance. Lecky adds, "the English cared much more for the suppression of the Irish race than for the suppression of its religion."[3] They did not even have the Anglican Book of Common Prayer translated into Irish. On the contrary, they did all they could to discourage the use of the Irish language and other Irish customs. The evident purpose was genocide, the absorption of the Irish into the British lower class.

During the reign of the daughter of Henry VIII, Elizabeth I (1533-1603, queen from 1558), a series of wars against the Irish "broke the force of the semi-independent chieftains, crushed the native population to the dust, and established the complete ascendency of English law." Systematic slaughter and starvation of men, women, and children and the destruction of houses were carried so far that Elizabeth was told that she "had little left to reign over but ashes and carcases" in much of Ireland. "It is easy to imagine what feelings it must have planted in the minds of the survivors."[4] This holocaust and the ones in subsequent centuries rankle in Irish traditions much as do the Russian pogroms and the Nazi holocaust among the Jews.

With the seventeenth century, the Tudors systematically confiscated land from the native Roman Catholics in the northern province of Ulster and gave control of it to Scottish and English Protestants (Anglicans) and Dissenters (chiefly Presbyterians). These were termed "plantations." As the historian Owen Dudley Edwards points out, the Scots in particular "introduced the factor of a Presbyterian proletariat, peasantry and bourgeoisie into an Ireland where Protestantism had hitherto been an upper-crust religion. Very quickly they came into conflict with the dispossessed Irish Catholics, and also became increasingly embroiled with Government, established church and landowning class."[5] As the historian F. S. L. Lyons adds, "Because it [Ulster] was the last part of Ireland to be colonised, and because the previous population were not wiped out when they lost their land and their status, and because the newcomers included both Episcopalians and Presybyterians, the triangular friction with which we are familiar became an integral part of Ulster history."[6] Thus was laid the general basis for the threefold—West English, Orange, and Green—ethnic siege mentality, a kind of frontier insecurity, now to be found especially in the six of the nine Ulster counties making up Northern Ireland. As a joint Irish Council of Churches (Protestant and Dissenter) and Roman Catholic Working Party states: "Britain, like most imperial powers, whether Protestant or Catholic, frequently used religious division as an instrument of imperial policy. Down to the middle of the nineteenth century, there was religious discrimination and denial of political rights and economic opportunities to Roman Catholics and to dissenters."[7] More objective commentators would date that: "down to the present time," not just "to the middle of the nineteenth century."

The intergroup terrorism stimulated by the Ulster plantation continued and became the second great Irish holocaust. In 1641-49, Roman Catholic peasants tried to regain their lands and in the process slaughtered thousands of Protestant settlers. In August 1649, an English Puritan army won a victory near Dublin, and two weeks later Oliver Cromwell landed with more Protestant troops. His visit of a little more than nine months is especially remembered for the general massacres he directed of the inhabitants following his successful siege of Drogheda and his storming of Wexford. As a historian notes, "what shocks the modern conscience nearly as much as the actual details of the carnage is the complacency and sanctimoniousness with which Cromwell contemplated the massacres and sought to justify them in the sight of God and man."[8]

All in all, it is estimated that in 1641-52, more than one-half of the Irish—some three-quarters of a million people—either died or emigrated. Those not slaughtered by Roman Catholics or Protestants died of starvation or disease. Other thousands were forced to go to the Continent. Then in 1689 came the unsuccessful Roman Catholic siege of Protestant Derry in which the storied Apprentice Boys helped save the city and in 1690 the defeat at the Boyne river of the troops of the deposed Roman Catholic King of England, James II, by those of his Protestant successor, William of Orange. These are events constantly recalled in Orange propaganda. Their rehearsal helps maintain the siege mentality.

The holocausts of the later sixteenth century and of the 1640s had their parallels in the third and fourth major Irish holocausts, those in the 1740s and 1840s. Those events similarly arose from the bitter theme of inequality and exacerbated the deeply felt siege mentality of both Protestants and Roman Catholics. The dependency of the Irish peasantry on the potato grew steadily after its introduction late in the sixteenth century. Notable failures of that crop, attended by famine, disease, and emigration, occurred in 1726-29, 1739-41, 1756-57, 1800, 1807, 1816-17, 1822, 1839, 1845-48, 1863, and 1879.

The failure of 1739-41 sent thousands to England and the Continent and, especially from Ulster, to the American colonies. The latter emigration, largely of middle-class farmers and artisans, is said to have provided much of the backbone for Washington's army. The disaster of those years took about one-third of the island's population.[9]

Then another outflow "apparently began after the potato failure and typhus epidemic of 1817 and increased after the 1822 famine."[10] It peaked in 1845-48, and those years are the ones to which reference is most often made,[11] the fourth great Irish holocaust. As in the case of the other disasters, the problem was not a food shortage in the British Isles or even in Ireland; it was inequitable food distribution. In speaking of the 1845-48 famine, an English historian asserts that it was a problem "of destitution rather than food shortage. There was sufficient food in Ireland to feed the population, if they had been able to buy it." Each year, Irish grain was shipped to England.[12] In that disaster, Ireland lost more than 2 million of its 8.5 million people and began a century of population decline, a decline due chiefly to emigration.

In brief compass, one cannot more than suggest the complicated, continuing, and all-pervasive ramifications of the bitter theme of inequality. At least since the middle of the eighteenth century, both Roman Catholic and Protestant peasants and laborers formed defensive and retaliatory organizations to try to cope with oppressive landlords and opposing sectarian groups. They burned houses and hayricks and disabled cattle as well as fought each other. As the historian Giovanni Costigan states, "of necessity all were local or regional—since because of the poverty and want of education of their leaders, they lacked a disciplined national organization."[13] Roman Catholic bodies included the Defenders and the Whiteboys; Protestants had, among others, the Steelboys, Oak-Boys, and Peep-o'-Day Boys.

The long standing feud between the Defenders and the Peep-o'-Day Boys peaked 21 September 1795 in the Battle of the Diamond in Armagh in which twenty to thirty were killed. That became the celebrated birthday of the Orange Society, later called the Orange Order and the Loyal Orange Institution. This was predominantly a lower-class society controlled by upper- and middle-class Protestants. The body "simply channeled a vast flow of fervent feeling which already existed into one enormous reservoir of partisan and religious ardour (or bigotry, according to how you view it)."[14] As an interclass, anti-Roman-Catholic conspiracy, it was "productive of class peace." At the same time, to help keep the lower-class Protestants quiet, it also permitted that "certain forms of class conflict could be expressed."[15]

The egalitarian doctrines of the American and French revolutions and especially the writings of Thomas Paine helped stimulate an effort at a joint Protestant and Roman Catholic revolt in 1796-98 led by Wolfe Tone. According to the historian J. C. Beckett, Tone's "plans were foiled not so much by the strength of England and the hesitation of France [to help] as by the deep-seated division among the people of Ireland." The revolt had middle-class Protestant and Roman Catholic support, but it lacked lower-class backing. Nevertheless, although defeated, Tone "established, and later came almost to personify, a tradition of revolutionary violence that has never wholly died out of Irish politics."[16]

Two Roman Catholic bodies launched on 17 March 1858 came to provide a term, Fenian, somewhat comparable to Orange in political significance. The Irish Revolutionary Brotherhood, later called the Irish Republican Brotherhood, appeared in Dublin. Its slogan was "Soon or

Never," with the reference to the replacement of British rule with an Irish republic. The Fenian Brotherhood took shape in New York City and recognized the Supreme Council of the IRB as the provisional government of the Irish republic. Both organizations advocated a violent course of action. With the failure of an attempted rising in 1867, Clan na Gael became its successor as the Irish-American advocate of a revolutionary course. It was eventually helpful in the agitations during World War I and the subsequent separation from England.

Two leaders in particular characterize political struggles of the nineteenth century: Daniel O'Connell and Charles Stewart Parnell, a Roman Catholic and a Protestant, and both often referred to popularly as "uncrowned kings of Ireland." O'Connell (1775–1847), also called the "Liberator," utilized the Roman Catholic clergy to organize a successful nonviolent struggle for the emancipation of the Roman Catholics and also, incidentally, of the Dissenters. With similar tactics, climaxed by "monster meetings" of as many as several hundred thousand people, he tried to gain a reestablishment of a separate Irish legislature, but in that he failed. Parnell (1846–91) also used nonviolent tactics of a spectacular sort—particularly the boycott[17]—to achieve land reforms that brought about more widespread land ownership. His efforts gave a powerful impetus to Irish attempts eventually to obtain self-government.[18]

James Connolly (1868–1916), an outstanding socialist labor leader and theoretician, similarly characterizes the struggles of the early part of the twentieth century. After extensive labor organizing, he joined in the planning of the 1916 rising against English rule and became military commander of the Republican forces in Dublin. Like other leaders of that crushed but significant rebellion, he became one of those executed by the English. An unanticipated consequence of that series of executions was the manner in which it publicized to the world the Anglo-Irish struggle and dramatized to the Irish of all social classes possibly attainable aspirations.[19]

The four major Irish holocausts and the reputations and sayings of Tone, O'Connell, Parnell, and Connolly still live in the struggles of the Northern Irish. Selectively and appropriately interpreted, they persist in the folklore, annual celebrations, and paranoid distrusts and hatreds of both Orange and Green people. They also help to account for the "racial" rejection of the Irish by the English and for the lack of empathy for Irish people and their problems.

Efforts to account for the persistence of nationalist resistance on "racial" grounds are not only irrelevant but absurd. Cultural and politico-economic differences there surely are among the ethnic and pressure groups involved, but reference to "Anglo-Saxon" or "Scotch-Irish" or "Celtic" genetic characteristics as causative can be brushed aside on many bases. One need not go any further than to note the similarities of the peoples who invaded Great Britain and Ireland from time to time through the centuries and then the vast extent to which they have intermingled.[20] Nonetheless, racist epithets and "explanations" are deeply imbedded in English and Irish popular discussions and in the more trashy mass media.[21]

Protestants provided some of the notable leadership in the nineteenth century for efforts to obtain unified home rule for Ireland, even though other and more numerous Protestants organized powerful opposition to the movement. A Protestant lawyer, Isaac Butt, formed the Home Rule League in 1873. The "uncrowned king of Ireland," the Protestant Parnell, did what he could to support the idea as a popular orator and in the Westminster Parliament. The English Liberal politician, W. E. Gladstone, also a Protestant, sponsored home rule bills for Ireland in 1886 and 1892–93. The first bill was defeated in Commons, and the second was adopted by Commons and then rejected by the House of Lords.

In opposition, orators for the Protestant Orange Order—a society dedicated to "the Protestant ascendency"[22]—popularized such slogans as "Ulster will fight, and Ulster will be right."[23] It organized extensively and intensively against the movement for island-wide home rule. Efforts in Ulster to prepare armed resistance to a possible Dublin parliament for all Ireland began in the nineteenth century.[24] In 1911 this started to take the shape of an Ulster citizens' army. Stimulated by the introduction of the third home rule bill in 1912, the paramilitaries became integrated in 1913 into an Ulster Volunteer Force. As mentioned above, this Protestant agitation led on 28 September 1912 to some four or five hundred thousand men and women signing "Ulster's Solemn League and Covenant." This was directed against "the present conspiracy to set up a Home Rule parliament in Ireland."[25]

Similar agitations in favor of home rule under the crown or of complete independence centered at Dublin. The Irish Republican Brotherhood, mentioned above, persisted as a secret organization that insisted on complete Irish independence. The Irish National Volunteers (later to become the Irish Republican Army) came formally into existence 25 November 1913. In reaction to partition pressures from pro-unionist politicians, membership in the National Volunteers soared from 10,000 to 100,000 in six months, approximately the same size as the Ulster Volunteer Force but not as well equipped.

The socialist labor organizer James Connolly made himself the principal ideologist for those to whom home rule of any sort under the crown was unacceptable. His most frequently quoted statement is the following:

> If you remove the English army tomorrow and hoist the green flag over Dublin Castle, unless you set about the organization of the Socialist Republic your efforts would be in vain. England would still rule you. She would rule you through her capitalists, through her landlords, through her financiers, through the whole array of commercial and individualist institutions she has planted in this country and watered with the tears of our mothers and the blood of our martyrs.[26]

With regard to the Protestants of the north and their continuing efforts to maintain island-wide union with England or divide Ireland for the purpose of continuing partial union, Connolly wrote in 1914:

> It is the trusted leaders of Ireland that in secret conclave with the enemies of Ireland have agreed to see Ireland as a nation disrupted politically and her children divided under separate political governments with warring interests. ...
>
> Let us remember that the Orange ... Order was not founded to safeguard religious freedom, but to deny religious freedom, and that it raised this religious question, not for the sake of any religion, but in order to use religious zeal in the interests of the oppressive property rights of rack-renting landlords and sweating capitalists.[27]

Connolly is still the favorite radical theoretician in Ireland for the nationalist political parties and paramilitary organizations. Such pressures did not prevent a nominal victory for those opposing partition, for such home rule compromisers as "trusted leader" John Redmond and "enemy of Ireland" Prime Minister H. H. Asquith.

In 1914, after the Lords had been stripped in 1911 of their conclusive veto power, the third home rule bill was enacted over the Lords' opposition through being adopted by Commons in three successive sessions. Then the act was laid on the shelf by special legislation until World War I should end. It reserved to Westminster control not only of external relations but also of fiscal affairs. In other words, it did not go nearly so far in granting self-government as did the 1907 grant to the dominions of Australia, Canada, and South Africa.[28] In any event, the act never became operative.

Nationalists welcomed this legislation as a possible step, a gain, but an inadequate one on the way to autonomy. The unionists were outraged by its specification of a single government for the whole island. Unionists thus made further plans to establish a Provisional Ulster Government to take charge at the time home rule of any kind should come into force. Especially as a result of successful gun-running and evidences of support from British army officers, the Ulster Volunteer Force encouraged unionists in their continuing struggle. The outbreak of World War I, on the other hand, convinced nationalists that Britain's preoccupation in Europe would make complete political independence for Ireland a possibility. As a result, even though as many as 100,000 Irishmen were serving in the British army, the secret Irish Republican Brotherhood and the open Irish voluntary military organizations created a situation that was met by the British with strengthened military control of the island.

The Irish Republican Brotherhood and the Irish National Volunteers it had inspired required the first two years of World War I to organize an insurrection. The miseries of exploitative industrialization and the accompanying urban slums, the failure of recent strikes against the British-controlled corporations, and rising social possibilities and expectations born of the wartime economy and military experiences all combined to make for greater dissatisfaction. Even though the Irish nationalist leader John Redmond was supporting the war effort in effect to assure home rule under the crown, Irish agitators for independence were encouraged by the more privileged separatist actions taking place in the north and by the promise and hope of German assistance in the form of arms, perhaps of invasion, and of keeping the English preoccupied.

Militarily the Easter Rising of 1916 failed. Only fifteen hundred rebels participated in it, but it was a significant turning point in the history of the two separating parts of Ireland. "Although the rebellion had come as a shattering surprise to ninety-nine per cent of Irishmen of all classes and political beliefs, being unexpected even by most of those who carried it out, such an event could not leave any nationally-minded Irishman's attitude to events in the future unaffected."[29] It was a great stimulus to the independence movement, to the independence political party, Sinn Féin, to the Irish paramilitary groups, and to the northern unionists.

On the first day of the Easter Rising, 24 April, P. H. Pearse read the proclamation of the Irish Republic at the occupied General Post Office in Dublin. This document "guarantees religious and civil liberty, equal rights and equal opportunities to all its citizens." It is "oblivious of the differences carefully fostered by an alien government, which have divided a minority from the majority in the past."[30]

The seven signers of that proclamation and other leaders of the insurrection were tried and executed by the British. The spacing out of the executions did much to help the media dramatize the martyrdoms; it enlisted both Irish and American support for the republican movement. As Connolly told the court-martial that condemned him to death: "We succeeded in proving that Irishmen are ready to die endeavouring to win for Ireland those national rights which the British Government has been asking them to die to win for Belgium."[31]

Throughout the war, there had been talk of conscripting the Irish in the same manner as other inhabitants of the United Kingdom. The great German offensive of March 1918 finally brought the Westminster government to announce on 9 April that it was going to do so. Lloyd George so misinterpreted the Irish as to promise in return the backing of a home rule bill establishing partition. "Never perhaps had British insensitiveness to Ireland been more blatantly illustrated. The effect was to add insult to injury on a gigantic scale."[32] The promise was not trusted.

The republican Sinn Féin party responded to this and other evidences of increasing British military repression by issuing a "Manifesto to the Irish People" for circulation during the election campaign of December 1918. In it, four moves were outlined to convert the election of representatives to the British Parliament into a revolt against British control. The moves were to secure the establishment of the republic:

> 1. By withdrawing the Irish Representatives from the British Parliament and by denying the right and opposing the will of the British Government or any other foreign Government to legislate for Ireland.
> 2. By making use of any and every means available to render impotent the power of England to hold Ireland in subjection by military force or otherwise.
> 3. By the establishment of a constituent assembly comprising persons chosen by Irish constituencies as the supreme national authority to speak and act in the name of the Irish people, and to develop Ireland's social, political and industrial life, for the welfare of the whole people of Ireland.
> 4. By appealing to the Peace Conference for the establishment of Ireland as an Independent Nation.[33]

When the election results were announced on 28 December, Sinn Féin had won 73 of the 105 seats. Twenty-four of the 32 counties elected only republicans. The Unionists scored 26 seats, but they polled a majority only in 4 northern counties: Antrim, Derry, Down, and Armagh. The other 6 seats went to the Irish Nationalist Party, which, in the previous election, had controlled 68 constituencies. It had continued to stand for home rule under the crown.

Sinn Féin tried to implement all four of its proposals, but the fourth confronted the problem that the doctrine of self-determination for minority peoples applied only in countries that had lost the war!

On 7 January 1919, twenty-six of the Sinn Féin candidates who had won seats in the British parliament met in Dublin to make plans for the establishment of the Dáil Éireann (Irish Constituent Assembly). They invited all elected representatives to an organizing meeting of the Dáil to be held in Dublin on 21 January, three days after the Paris Peace Conference convened. The Unionists and Nationalists boycotted the meeting. Thirty-six Sinn Féiners were in jail. The meeting took place, adopted a provisional constitution, a "Declaration of Independence," and a "Democratic Programme." The constitution merely vested "full power to legislate" in itself, "composed of Delegates (Teachtaí) chosen by the people of Ireland from the present constituencies of the country," and provided for five ministers and their duties. The declaration stressed that "the Irish electorate has in the General Election of December, 1918, seized the first occasion to declare by an overwhelming majority its firm allegiance to the Irish Republic." Here are some excerpts from the "Democratic Programme":

> In return for willing service, we, in the name of the Republic, declare the right of every citizen to an adequate share of the produce of the nation's labour.
> It shall be the first duty of the government of the Republic to make provision for the physical, mental and spiritual well-being of the children, to secure that no child shall suffer hunger or cold from lack of food or clothing or shelter, but that all shall be provided with the means and facilities for their proper education and training as citizens of a free and Gaelic Ireland.

After those actions in "two of the most momentous hours in Ireland's history," the meeting adjourned.[34]

The Dáil Éireann and the Irish Republican Army, supported by the Irish Republican Brotherhood, thus became an alternative governmental structure throughout Ireland other than Ulster's most Protestant and unionist counties. As President Eamon de Valera of the Dáil asserted on 30 March 1921, "From the Irish Volunteers we fashioned the Irish Republican Army to be the military arm of the Government."[35] At the same time, the British strengthened the Royal Irish Constabulary with Black and Tans and Auxiliaries, "two volunteer forces recruited in England from misfits unable to settle down in post-war Britain; ... the British were reluctant to use the military because it would have meant admitting that a state of war existed between the British and the IRA."[36]

The Ulster Unionist Council, formed in 1905 as the federation of unionist and Orange organizations, furnished backing for the British, who in turn supported their position. The Unionist Party grew out of the Council. At first it opposed any home rule for any part of Ireland and then came around to the more expedient possibility of maintaining union for a part of the island. The Ulster Special Constabulary, maintained by the crown, and the Ulster Volunteers were in constant conflict with the Roman Catholics and especially with the IRA in the northeastern separating counties—Antrim, Armagh, Down, Fermanagh, Londonderry (called by the Irish Derry), and Tyrone—and especially along the border with the twenty-six other counties.

The home rule act of 1914 could not now become operative, and therefore David Lloyd George as British prime minister backed enactment of a new Government of Ireland Act, introduced in Commons 25 February 1920, and given royal assent 23 December. The act authorized two dependent governments in Ireland within the United Kingdom. It also hopefully defined a federating Council of Ireland and specified steps that could be taken toward a unifying and integrating Irish government. The alternative Irish Provisional Government ignored this act and continued to operate and enjoy wide support—accompanied by guerrilla warfare. The act therefore took effect only in Northern Ireland. Under it, King George V formally opened Northern Ireland's first parliament on 22 June 1921.

The fifth part of this 1920 act contains an inconsistency pertinent to the continuing three-sided struggle. On the one hand, it specifies that the government shall not "either directly or indirectly ... establish or endow any religion, or prohibit or restrict the free exercise thereof, or give a preference, privilege, or advantage, or impose any disability or disadvantage, on account of religious belief or religious ceremony," etc. On the other hand, it indicates that schools receiving public money can offer religious instruction. Significantly enough, the court system in the United Kingdom and especially in Northern Ireland is such that that section of the 1920 act has not served as the basis for litigation to counteract religious discrimination.[37]

Even though the 1920 act became the basis of the Northern Ireland government, the civil war continued there and in the twenty-six counties.

An agreement by Irish Provisional Government and British representatives, a controversial "treaty" signed 6 December 1921, became the first constitution for the Irish Free State. It was a step to end the Anglo-Irish conflict. The Dáil Éireann accepted it 7 January 1922, under armed pressure.[38] Westminster's Irish Free State (Agreement) Act of 31 March 1922 gave the "treaty" further sanction. In effect, the document legitimated the Dáil within the United Kingdom as a dependent legislature, and it therefore ushered in an internecine Irish Civil War between the "pro-treaty" and "anti-treaty" Irish forces.

The possibility outlined in this act of a Free State government for all Ireland was meaningless. Both houses of the Northern Ireland Parliament agreed unanimously to reject that option. Similarly, the specifications for a boundary commission and a Council of Ireland also became inoperative. The boundary line indicated in the Government of Ireland Act, 1920, was further ratified by the Ireland (Confirmation of Agreement) Act, 1925, at Westminster and by resolutions the same year in the parliaments of the Free State and Northern Ireland.

Another agreement, the so-called Craig-Collins agreement among representatives of the Irish Provisional Government, the Government of Northern Ireland, and the British Government on 30 March 1922, began with the statements "Peace is to-day declared" and "From to-day the two Governments undertake to co-operate in every way in their power with a view to the restoration of peaceful conditions in the unsettled areas." This meant especially Belfast. The agreement dealt with integrating Roman Catholics into the Belfast police, with setting up a bipartisan committee to investigate complaints of "intimidation, outrages, etc.," and with funds and arrangements for aid to expelled and otherwise unemployed workers.[39] The pact failed. The Northern Ireland government, acclaimed as a "Protestant parliament for a Protestant people," imposed its control by force of arms upon the one-third of the population belonging to the Roman Catholic minority.

Thus came into existence the "Orange state." The Irish labor leader James Connolly predicted its general character in 1913 when he pointed out: "According to all Socialist theories North-East Ulster, being the most developed industrially, ought to be the quarter in which class lines of cleavage, politically and industrially, should be the most pronounced and class rebellion the most common. As a cold matter of fact, it is the happy hunting ground of the slave-driver and the home of the least rebellious slaves in the industrial world."[40] Oversimply, but in terms of major social-historical realities, Connolly accounts for this situation by recalling "how the land was stolen from Catholics, given to Episcopalians, but planted by Presbyterians; how the latter were persecuted by the Government, but could not avoid the necessity of defending it against the Catholics, and how out of this complicated situation there inevitably grew up a feeling of common interests between the slaves and the slave-drivers."[41]

In different terms but much to the same point, both church leaders and radical activists agree with Connolly's implication that the current conflict there is not basically religious, even though its propagandists in part use religious themes as alleged justifications for their nonviolent and violent actions against one another.[42] It is in this confusing as well as confused manner that the stuff of history is employed.

The Public Broadcasting System presented many people in the United States in 1982 with a major television example of the British use of the stuff of Irish history. The British Broadcasting System had developed a 13-part series entitled "Ireland: A Television History." Robert Kee, an English television personality and historian, wrote its scenarios and directed it.[43] PBS extended each segment with comments by polite and largely Irish-American students of history and current affairs.

The whole series is carefully sanitized, but, to give it credibility, it is more accurate about British roles in the remote past. The material on the recent past is quite slanted. Irish Republican objectives are portrayed as either vicious or confused and not motivated by oppression and discrimination. The mounting unemployment rates and their ethnic inequality are not reported.

As an English law professor, David R. Lowry, formerly of Belfast's Queen's University and now of New York's Pace University, characterizes Kee's work: "BBC knew their man. Mr. Kee exhibits just the right amount of pro-British paternalism in a highly entertaining and technically proficient manner."[44]

Notes

1. A. T. Q. Stewart, *The Narrow Ground: Aspects of Ulster, 1609–1969* (London: Faber & Faber, 1977), p. 183.
2. W. E. H. Lecky, *History of the Rise and Influence of the Spirit of Rationalism in Europe,* 2 vols. (1865, re-issue: London: Watts, 1910), 2:64–65.

3. Lecky, *A History of Ireland in the Eighteenth Century*, 5 vols. (1892, re-issue: London: Longmans, Green, 1902), 1:11.
4. Ibid., pp. 5, 7, 10.
5. O. D. Edwards, "Ireland," pp. 1–209 in Edwards, Gwynfor Evans, Ioan Rhys, and Hugh Mac Diarmid, *Celtic Nationalism* (New York: Barnes & Noble, 1968), p. 50.
6. F. S. L. Lyons, *The Burden of Our History* (Belfast: Queen's University, 1978), p. 19.
7. C. B. Daly and R. D. E. Gallagher, chairs, *Violence in Ireland: A Report to the Churches*, rev. ed. (Dublin: Veritas Publications, 1977), p. 13.
8. Giovanni Costigan, *A History of Modern Ireland* (New York: Pegasus, 1969), p. 78.
9. R. N. Salaman, *The History and Social Influence of the Potato* (Cambridge: University Press, 1949), pp. 604–7.
10. R. E. Kennedy, Jr., *The Irish: Emigration, Marriage and Fertility* (Berkeley: University of California Press, 1973), p. 27.
11. Cecil Woodham-Smith, *The Great Hunger* (New York: Harper & Row, 1962).
12. Hugh Shearman, *Modern Ireland* (London: George G. Harrap, 1952), p. 99.
13. Giovanni Costigan, *A History of Modern Ireland* p. 106.
14. Tony Gray, *The Orange Order* (London: Bodley Head, 1972), p. 57; cf. Peter Gibbon, *The Origins of Ulster Unionism* (Manchester: University Press, 1975).
15. Henry Patterson, *Class Conflict and Sectarianism* (Belfast: Blackstaff Press, 1980), p. xi.
16. J. C. Beckett, *The Making of Modern Ireland: 1603–1923* (New York: Knopf, 1966), pp. 266–67.
17. N. D. Palmer, *The Irish Land League Crisis* (New Haven: Yale University Press, 1940).
18. Robert Kee, *The Green Flag* (New York: Delacorte, 1972), pts. 3-4.
19. Samuel Levenson, *James Connolly, A Biography* (London: Martin Brian & O'Keefe, 1973); C. D. Greaves, *The Life and Times of James Connolly* (London: Lawrence & Wishart, 1961); Beckett, *Making of Modern Ireland*, p. 441.
20. E. A. Hooton and C. W. Dupertuis with Helen Dawson, *The Physical Anthropology of Ireland*, 2 vols. (Cambridge, Mass.: Peabody Museum of Archeology and Ethnology, Harvard University, 1955); K. H. Connell, *Irish Peasant Society* (Oxford: Clarendon Press, 1968), chaps. 2, 4.
21. Lecky, *History of Ireland*, vol. 1, esp. chap. 1; L. P. Curtis, Jr., *Anglo-Saxons and Celts* (Bridgeport: University of Bridgeport, 1968); idem, *Apes and Angels: The Irishman in Victorian Caricature* (Washington, D.C.: Smithsonian, 1971); Edmund Leach, "The Official Irish Jokesters," *New Society* (London), 20/27 December 1979, pp. vii-ix.
22. Hereward Senior, *Orangeism in Ireland and Britain: 1795-1836* (London: Routledge & Kegan Paul, 1966), p. 298.
23. Edmund Curtis, *A History of Ireland*, 6th ed. (New York: Barnes & Noble, 1950), p. 383.
24. David Boulton, *The UVF: 1966-73: An Anatomy of Loyalist Rebellion* (Dublin: Torc Books, 1973), chap. 2.
25. Ronald McNeill, *Ulster's Stand for Union* (London: John Murray, 1922), p. 10.
26. James Connolly, "Socialism and Nationalism," reprinted from *Shan Van Vocht* (Belfast), January 1897, pp. 121-24, in Connolly, *Selected Writings*, ed. P. B. Ellis (Harmondsworth, England: Penguin, 1973), p. 124 quoted.
27. Ibid., p. 274.
28. *Public General Acts*, 1914, pp. 406-51; Edmund Curtis and R. B. McDowell, eds., *Irish Historical Documents: 1172-1922* (London: Methuen, 1943), pp. 292-97.

29. Kee, *Green Flag*, p. 572.
30. "The Proclamation of the Republic," pp. 317-18 in Curtis and McDowell, *Irish Historical Documents*.
31. James Connolly, quoted by Desmond Ryan, *The Rising: The Complete Story of Easter Week* (Dublin: Golden Eagle Books, 1966), pp. 262-63.
32. Kee, *Green Flag*, p. 618.
33. "Manifesto to the Irish People," pp. 919-20 in Dorothy Macardle, *The Irish Republic,* rev. American ed. (New York: Farrar, Straus & Giroux, 1965), p. 919 quoted.
34. Quotations from constitutional documents, ibid., pp. 923, 273, 275-76.
35. Eamon de Valera, quoted in ibid., p. 437.
36. Gray, *Orange Order*, p. 181.
37. Harry Calvert, *Constitutional Law in Northern Ireland* (Belfast: Stevens, 1968), pp. 334-35; Kevin Boyle and others, *Law and State: The Case of Northern Ireland* (London: Martin Robertson, 1975), pp. 9-13.
38. Macardle, *Irish Republic*, pp. 955-56.
39. Ibid., pp. 966-67.
40. James Connolly, "North-East Ulster," reprinted from *Forward* (Glasgow), 2 August 1913, pp. 263-67, in Ryan, *Rising,* p. 263 quoted.
41. Ibid., p. 264.
42. Daly and Gallagher, *Violence in Ireland;* Provisional Irish Republican Army, *Freedom Struggle* (1973); in contrast, see Ian Paisley, *The Dagger of Treachery* (Belfast: Puritan Printing, 1972).
43. Kee, *Green Flag,* and *Ireland: A History* (London: Weidenfeld and Nicolson, 1980). The latter is described as "The book of the major BBC/RTE Television Series." RTE stands for Radio Telefis Eireann or Irish Radio-Television.
44. D. R. Lowry, "Mr. Robert Kee's Saxon Squint," Boston *Irish Echo,* July 31, 1982, p. 7.

CHAPTER 3

Human Rights in the Orange Statelet

A man in his sixties and his two sons in their thirties saunter each morning to a street corner. There they stand and talk. When they can, they grab a cigarette from somebody or a few pennies and run "to a bookmaking shop to place a bet on the longest shot of the day." In their whole lives, only one of these three able-bodied men—the father—has had a continuing job. For two years (1942-44), he worked as a common laborer at an American military base. "In two generations of this family there had been only one job, and it took a World War to get them the one." A well-placed and well-meaning American got the thirty-seven year-old son a job in 1972 driving a taxi, but the never-employed man could not bring himself to take it. The demands of a novel routine and the fear of failure made him shrink from the opportunity. His joblessness was "a disability that was every bit as real as a broken leg." [1]

These men could be blacks in an American urban ghetto.[2] They could be some of *gli ultimi* (the lowest) in the poverty-stricken west of Sicily.[3] They might be French Canadians.[4] They might just as well be some of the many such people in Bangladesh, India, Syria, Lebanon, Libya, Rhodesia, South Africa, or Latin America. They actually belong to an ethnic group called Roman Catholic Irish, and they live on the British dole in the Bogside, a "Green" ghetto in what they call Derry and what the English term Londonderry in Northern Ireland. They contribute to the unemployment that, since the separation of the twenty-six counties to the south, has been the highest of any section of the United Kingdom. As Jimmy Breslin puts it, "Once you teach a person to remain on welfare for all his adult life it is very hard to tell him, 'You have a job.' " His experiences in Northern Ireland made him "understand the street corners of Harlem a little more," and he also realized that "today the men are behind barricades at these street corners. For as it had to be, now they fight."[5]

This sort of situation thus became an integral part of the social scene in the "Orange state." For this and for many other reasons, a senior social servant with twenty years' experience there wrote in 1939,

In Northern Ireland we claim that we have the biggest shipyard, the biggest ropeworks, the biggest linen manufacturers and the biggest tobacco factory in the world; I am afraid there is one other factory in which we could probably claim that we or the Free State [the 26 counties] are the largest manufacturers—namely the factory of grievances. I am not at all sure that this particular factory isn't the most paying one in the province.[6]

In commenting on this statement, the historian Patrick Buckland says that this "jaundiced view ... fairly summed up Northern Ireland's experience of regional government in the inter-war [1921-39] years." He adds that those grievances included not only those of the nationalist minority but also those "of its supposed supporters, who were far from united behind and contented with their Unionist government."[7]

As we have noted, agitation for separation by Irish nationalists and against it by British loyalists, especially in the northeastern counties, climaxed in the civil war of 1919-21 and the separation of the twenty-six counties of the "Free State" from the six counties that became the United Kingdom province of Northern Ireland.

When the first six-county government was announced in 1921 by Sir James Craig, its prime minister, it consisted entirely of wealthy Protestant landowners, merchants, and manufacturers. The overwhelming majority of the members of the provincial Senate and House of Commons were also Protestants.[8] Similar people continued to rule with the help of the Unionist Party, the Protestant Orange Order, repressive "emergency" legislation, and carefully cultivated anti-Roman Catholic prejudices. They gave substance to the latter through providing invidious privileges in employment, housing, education, and personal safety to the thus less underprivileged but still oppressed lower-class Protestants. This provincial upper-class gradually changed from the traditional land-based aristocracy toward becoming a class of entrepreneurial plutocrats at first centered in Northern Ireland and then more and more in England. The provincial upper-class hold persisted until it was destabilized by increasing popular political sophistication, modern violence technology, and the shrinking of the world under the influence of the mass media, the alternative media, and politico-economic imperialism.

Arising out of England's wartime struggle from 1914 to hold Ireland and at least Northern Ireland, a series of laws had been applied, enacted, and implemented for the purpose of striking fear into the minds of dissidents. These laws granted unusual powers to the military, the police, and the judiciary. They began especially with the United Kingdom Defense of the Realm Act of 1914 as applied to Ireland. They were made even more sweepingly repressive by the Restoration of Order in Ireland Act of 1920. The latter authorized the military to imprison any Irish man or woman without charge or trial for an indefinite period of time. Through secret courts, "political offenders were to be tried by their opponents ... while prisoners of war could be tried by their enemy captors and sentenced on the charge of 'murder' to be hanged."[9]

In order to localize such terrorizing powers, the Northern Ireland government very quickly after its institution enacted a piece of emergency legislation to cope with the continuing violence in its area: the Civil Authorities (Special Powers) Act of 7 April 1922. It was the first of a series of reenactments and modifications. The Irish nationalists called them "flogging acts." They help more than any other legislation to explain the continuing struggle there. With the aid of the London-based National Council for Civil Liberties (NCCL), of governmental bodies, and of legal specialists, let us look in more detail at that legislation and its significance in operation:

A special commission of the NCCL to study the Special Powers Acts came to these major conclusions in 1936:

> *Firstly*, that through the operation of the Special Powers Acts contempt has been begotten for the representative institutions of government.
>
> *Secondly*, that through the use of Special Powers individual liberty is no longer protected by law, but is at the arbitrary disposition of the Executive. This abrogation of the rule of law has been so practised as to bring the freedom of the subject into contempt.
>
> *Thirdly*, that the Northern Irish Government has used Special Powers towards securing the domination of one particular political faction and, at the same time, towards curtailing the lawful activities of its opponents. The driving of legitimate movements underground into illegality, the intimidating or branding as law-breakers of their adherents, however innocent of crime, has tended to encourage violence and bigotry on the part of the Government's supporters as well as to beget in its opponents an intolerance of the 'law and order' thus maintained. The Government's policy is thus driving its opponents into the ways of extremists.

> *Fourthly*, that the Northern Irish Government, despite its assurances that Special Powers are intended only against law-breakers, has frequently employed them against innocent and law-abiding people, often in humble circumstances, whose injuries, inflicted without cause or justification, have gone unrecompensed and disregarded.[10]

G. B. Hanna, a member of the Northern Ireland government opposing this legislation, accurately characterized it more simply when he said: "The Home Secretary shall have power to do whatever he likes or let someone else do what he likes for him."[11]

In coming to its conclusions, the NCCL commission insisted that it was not dealing with a "temporary" or "emergency" measure. It "stressed that the Special Powers Acts have become part of the *permanent law of Northern Ireland*. Whatever the nature of the legislation upon its introduction in 1922, it is now clear beyond any doubt that the Commission has to deal with no mere temporary or emergency measure."[12]

At the time that this was written, in 1936, the NCCL commission was happy to note:

> The fact that the Government's opponents have not been driven to adopt a policy of systematic violence, but rather to repudiate such course, is one of the hopeful features in the present state of Northern Ireland. But at the same time there can be no doubt that large numbers of persons, particularly amongst the youth, who would normally owe allegiance to the constitutional Nationalist party, are being driven into the Republican movement.[13]

At the moment there was little violence, but those "being driven into the Republican movement," the Irish Republican Army and the Sinn Féin political party, were a rising threat.

For the further implementation of the special powers legislation, the Emergency Powers (Northern Ireland) Act 1926 gave "the Governor power to declare a state of emergency if it appears to him that any action has been taken or is likely to be taken in the immediate future whether in Northern Ireland or elsewhere the result of which would be to endanger essential services." The state of emergency would "continue until the proclamation is revoked."[14]

The Civil Authorities (Special Powers) Act (Northern Ireland) had to be renewed annually until 1928 to remain in force. Then it was extended for a five-year period. In 1933 the legislation was amended to include this statement: "The Act of 1922 shall continue in force until Parliament otherwise determines." It thus became a "part of the peace preservation legislation in force"[15] until it was broadened in 1972-73 with more grants of arbitrary powers under pressures of the stepped-up conflict of the time.

Leading spokespeople for the government of Northern Ireland claimed:

> The operation of the Civil Authorities Act in no way interferes with the liberty of anyone who is prepared to obey the law and who does not seek by unconstitutional means to subvert the Constitution.
>
> No law-abiding citizen in the whole of the North of Ireland is subject to-day to any harassment by reason of the existence of the Act. It does not affect the law-abiding citizen; it only operates against the law-breakers.[16]

Such spokespeople place great confidence in the wisdom and affiliations of the Home Minister. As the NCCL commission notes, "The most cursory examination of the Special Powers Acts makes it apparent that they purport to effect an almost *complete delegation of law-making power to the Executive,* and that this delegation covers a considerable portion of the sovereignty conferred upon the Northern Irish legislature by the Act of 1920." The commission had "doubts as to the constitutional validity of the Special Powers Acts in their entirety."[17] This did not keep the acts from remaining on the books and being implemented. As three Northern Ireland legal specialists point out, "the fundamental legal rights of all citizens against arbitrary arrest and imprisonment were effectively annulled by the provisions" of the acts. They add that, even though the legislation was "not formally directed against Roman Catholics and Republicans, ... it was common knowledge that it was against them and them alone that it was directed and used."[18]

The enactment of the 1922 act "was quickly followed by the issue of a series of Statutory Rules and Orders whereby the Home Minister supplemented the Schedule [of offenses specified in the act] with powers far more stringent than those assented to by the legislature, not without much controversy, a few months previously."[19]

Examples of the regulations in force under the act are the following:
- *Regulation 4* empowers any member of the constabulary to go into any house or building on suspicion; "there is power to use force to effect entry, and upon entry having been made, to search."

- *Regulation 5* permits any police officer to stop, search, and seize any vehicle on a public road on suspicion.
- *Regulation 6* grants similar power with regard to any person suspected of carrying arms or anything else "in any way prejudicial to the preservation of peace or maintenance of order."
- *Regulation 7* requires persons stopped by the police on suspicion to answer a police officer's questions.
- *Regulation 8* grants "power to suppress the publication of literature prejudicial or likely to be prejudicial to the preservation of peace or the maintenance of order."
- *Regulation 10* permits arrest without warrant and detention for not more than 48 hours for the purpose of interrogation.
- *Regulation 24A* outlaws membership in "any unlawful association or seditious conspiracy." It originally listed the Irish Republican Brotherhood, Irish Republican Army, Irish Volunteers, and "certain other organizations of a nationalist kind." In 1966 it added the Ulster Volunteer Force, a Protestant paramilitary organization, "or any division or branch thereof." In 1967 it began to include " 'republican clubs' or any like organization however described."[20]

Subsequently, even though the Home Minister had wide powers already conferred on him by the Special Powers Acts, cases arose in which he even expanded their interpretation after a new problem had arisen:

> Illustrative of this type of *ad hoc* rule-making is the case of Regulation 22B. In October 1933, shortly prior to the local elections, the Government carried out a 'round-up' in which forty or fifty persons were arrested. No reasons were given for the arrests and no charges were, or, apparently, could be, laid against the men. After they had been detained for some time the Government promulgated Regulation 22B, under the terms of which the men were privately examined. On declining to answer certain questions put to them by the Resident Magistrate conducting the examinations they were charged with 'refusal to answer questions,' and the Magistrate's certificate of such refusal sufficed to secure their conviction and sentence to terms of imprisonment for an offence which was created subsequent to their arrest.[21]

This sort of thing was possible because the 1922 act provided as follows:

> If any person does any act of such a nature as to be calculated to be prejudicial to the preservation of the peace or maintenance of order in Northern Ireland and *not specifically provided for in the regulations,* he shall be deemed to be guilty of an offence against the regulations.

In commenting upon this, the NCCL commission notes:

> The possibilities presented by this section defy enumeration. Not only does it give the Executive *carte blanche* to prosecute any person, however innocent of crime, whose activities may not be to their liking, but it violates the fundamental principles of public law. *In countries where the rule of law prevails, it is recognised by all jurists that no man may be prosecuted and punished unless for the contravention of some specific provision of the criminal law.* [The section quoted], by stretching the limits of guilt beyond certainty or definition, strikes at the very root of the rule of law, since it permits criminal activity being defined in accordance with the day-to-day whim or convenience of the Executive.[22]

Under the Special Powers Act of 1922, offenders could not claim trial by jury. They could be tried by two or more "Resident Magistrates." As the NCCL commission asserts, "By a stroke of the pen the Northern Irish Government has abolished what hitherto has been regarded as a fundamental right of every Briton." Under Regulation 22B, too, persons could be examined privately by a Resident Magistrate if they are "believed to be capable of giving material evidence or information" with regard to a suspected offence. Neither offenders nor examinees are entitled to legal assistance. *"In certain cases such right is in fact excluded."*[23] Even though it "is axiomatic in English criminal law that an accused man is presumed to be innocent until the contrary is proven," the 1922 act states: "Where under the regulations any act done without lawful authority or excuse is an offence ... the burden of proving that the act was done with lawful authority ... shall rest upon the person alleged to be guilty of the offence."[24] As a part of all this, the act succeeds in setting aside habeas corpus by: "(*a*) exposing persons to peril and incarceration without charge or limit at the whim of the Executive *and (b)* depriving such persons of the right to test the legality of their detention by application to the Courts." The NCCL commission is thus led to say, "*This fact, coupled with the dissestablishment of the rule of law in the Six Counties puts the Executive in a position paralleled only by continental dictatorships.*"[25]

Here are some excerpts from the NCCL commission report having to do with practices under the acts up to 1936:

> Frequently when the meetings of left-wing political organisations have been rendered impossible by Orange rowdyism the police have stood by and tolerated such conduct. Again, there is abundant material to indicate that favouritism is displayed by the police to Orange processions and demonstrations on occasions when clashes between them and Catholic or left-wing sympathisers have eventuated. To some extent this apparent partiality may be due to a feeling of impotence rather than to a desire (particularly on the part of the ordinary rank and file of the R.U.C. [Royal Ulster Constabulary]) to show favouritism, for there is no doubt that Orange hooliganism often reaches such a pitch as to require the most drastic use of force to suppress it.[26]

> Persons arrested and detained, whether under charge or not, have been subjected to interrogation, frequently of many hours' duration, by large numbers of police. ... During interrogation the prisoner is surrounded by his questioners, and unsatisfactory replies may produce blows. These interrogations are often held late at night and are carried on until the prisoner's strength is well nigh exhausted. Information furnished in such circumstances would be so notoriously unreliable that such interrogations cannot be regarded as genuine attempts to elucidate facts.[27]

> Whilst there are, no doubt, cases in which a search [of a house] is conducted in an orderly manner, in the bulk of instances brought under the Commission's notice searches were made by bodies of armed police who have on occasions threatened inhabitants with their firearms. It appears to be recognised that such searches, which are of constant occurrence, should take place in the dead of night and should be marked with

brutality and violence. ... Perhaps the most remarkable feature of the searches under Special Powers described to the Commission has been the fact that in almost every case the police departed empty handed and that the occupants of the houses searched were never charged under Special Powers or otherwise.[28]

The fact that *detenus* [detainees] under Special Powers have no right to be brought before a Court tends to facilitate any tendency toward physical ill-treatment by lessening the chances of its discovery.[29]

The close relations maintained by the Government's leading members with the Orange Order, coupled with the little use made of Special Powers against activities notoriously productive of disorder, provides some show of reason for the view that the Government permits the perpetuation of, rather than seeks to quell, sectarian troubles. ... The widespread allegations of 'placing' in Government offices, the fact that important judicial and official positions (e.g. County Court Judgeships) are largely withheld from practising Catholics, the maintenance of the 'B' Specials [part-time special police], the personal ties between the Executive and the Orange Order, and the frankly sectarian speeches made even by Ministers, are all disquieting features of the political life of the Six Counties. Coupled with the electoral 'reforms' introduced by the Government some years ago—i.e. the abolition of proportional representation and the rearrangement of the constituencies—these tendencies make it difficult to contradict the assertion that the Unionist Government's policy has resulted in the inflammation of religious bigotry and the aggravation of sectarian differences amongst the Northern Irish community.[30]

Not only have important incidents such as the October 1932 strike seen the use of Special Powers [against the strikers] in their full force and measure, but there is abundant evidence of the daily use of such powers against individuals active in the working-class movement, particularly on its left wing. Domiciliary visits, searches, interrogations, detentions and Exclusion Orders appear, in this way, to have been freely employed.[31]

The serious disorders of July 12th–18th 1935 arose directly from the 'Orange' celebrations of the Battle of the Boyne Anniversary, which the Government not only omitted to take steps to ban or control, but facilitated by the raising of an existing ban on all processions. It is not without importance that before this ban was raised the Grand Master of the Orange Order, Sir Joseph Davison, a prominent Unionist, indicated the intention of the Order to defy the ban if it were not raised before the '12th.' The actual celebrations were supported by the presence and participation of all the leading members of the Government, including the Home Minister who had raised the ban.[32]

Lord Craigavon [Prime Minister 1921–40] speaks of a 'Protestant Parliament for a Protestant people' while Sir Basil Brooke (Minister of Agriculture) in a public address on July 12th, 1933, said: 'Many in this audience employ Catholics, but I have not one about my place. Catholics are out to destroy Ulster with all their might and power.' In March 1934, referring to his former statement, Sir Basil said: 'When I made that declaration on last Twelfth I did so after careful consideration. What I said was justified. I recommended people not to employ Roman Catholics, who are 99 per cent disloyal. ... I will continue to criticise and take what action I can.'[33]

It was Craigavon who abolished proportional representation because "the people did not understand the danger of making mistakes under it."[34] The "mistakes" led to some minority representation.

While the developments suggested by the foregoing were taking place in the six counties, the twenty-six began to modify their Free State dominion status that had been set up under the 1922 constitutional agreement or "treaty." Eire's relations with the crown became eroded by the following series of steps:

In the first place, the Statute of Westminster 1931 constituted a grant of equality to all Dominions. Under it, "no Act of Parliament of the United Kingdom passed after the commencement of this Act shall extend, or be deemed to extend, to a Dominion as part of the law of that Dominion, unless it be expressly declared in that Act that that Dominion has requested, and consented to, the enactment thereof."[35] Subsequently, under Eamon de Valera's leadership, the oath of allegiance to the crown by governmental officials was eliminated in the Free State in 1933. In 1936 he abolished the office of governor general, a royal appointee. The year following, Eire adopted a constitution republican in form but not in name; it still retained its British Commonwealth status. It defined Ireland as "a sovereign, independent, democratic state," and it asserted that the "national territory consists of the whole island of Ireland, its islands and the territorial seas." It did admit, however, that, "pending the re-integration of the national territory," the Irish government would control only twenty-six counties.[36]

The ties with the United Kingdom became even more tenuous when de Valera as president declared Ireland's neutrality during World War II. The next logical and actual step then was the Irish Republic of Ireland Act 1948, agreed to by the United Kingdom's Ireland Act of 1949, that severed formal connections with the United Kingdom as of Easter Day 1949. Significantly enough, the British act "declared that, notwithstanding that the Republic of Ireland is not part of His Majesty's dominions, the Republic of Ireland is not a foreign country for the purposes of any law in force in any part of the United Kingdom ... and references ... to foreigners, aliens, foreign countries ... shall be construed accordingly."[37]

Westminster's 1949 Ireland Act that recognized the Irish Republic also sought to reassure those in control of Northern Ireland of their continued hold on status within the union. It stated "that in no event will Northern Ireland or any part thereof cease to be part of His Majesty's dominions and of the United Kingdom without the consent of the Parliament of Northern Ireland."[38]

These actions in the twenty-six counties were paralleled by others in the six that gradually built more and more of a wall between the two sections. Those who led the Northern Ireland parliament from 1921 to 1972 represented principally the interests of industry and the landed gentry. They were preoccupied with problems associated with the long twenty-six county border, with not becoming a minority in an all-Ireland republic, with fighting socialistic tendencies, and with opposing possible encroachments of Northern Ireland Republicans upon their perquisites. For popular support, they depended upon the Orange Order and the Unionist Party to keep the lower class enthusiastically divided against itself and upon the arbitrary powers of a procapitalist police establishment to prevent consolidated lower-class social action. The controlling class finally ran into difficult problems born of the growing Roman Catholic middle class, of broadening popular perspectives, and of renewed minority agitation and violence.

Violence against and in favor of minority agitation continued sporadically in Northern Ireland in spite of and also because of the efforts to control it outlined above. Similar emergencies in England have been less frequent, but they have occurred and have resulted in legislation applicable to Northern Ireland as well as Great Britain. For example, the British Union of Fascists precipitated the passage of the Public Order Act of 1936 through its Cable street battle and its Mile End Road anti-Jewish pogrom.[39] While inspired by the "black shirts," this legislation was also used against North Irish agitators. It "prohibited the wearing of uniforms signifying connection with a political organization or object," and it barred "quasi-military" organizations.[40] The fascist enthusiasm had even invaded the twenty-six counties in the form of the Irish Army Comrades Association, or "Blueshirts," who were especially active in 1933-35.[41]

As World War II approached, Irish leaders became preoccupied with their country's neutrality, and Northern leaders worried about their security in the face of possible opportunistic efforts by the IRA. This resulted in detention without trial in Northern Ireland under the Special Powers Acts in 1938-45. As Loyalist and Republican veterans returned from military service, they represented pools of trained guerrilla fighters who were faced with employment problems. Northern politicians were also edgy because of the movement in the twenty-six counties that resulted in Eire's full republican status as of 1949. In 1951, therefore, the Stormont legislature supplemented the United Kingdom Public Order Act of 1936 with its own enactment. This legislation required prior notice of intended processions and gave police control of their routing. The Minister of Home Affairs was authorized to ban all or specific types of processions and meetings. The police could prevent the obstruction of businesses and of public meetings and could arrest without warrant upon "reasonable suspicion."[42]

The postwar boom ended for Northern Ireland in 1951. Except for some improvement in general economic conditions in 1954 and 1955, the trend of industrial and agricultural employment was downward on into the 1960s and beyond. Projects for coping with unemployment did more to help the increasingly mechanized and rationalized production units than to absorb workers. In the midst of these problems, the Irish Republican Army in 1956 began another attempt to eliminate British "occupation" of the North. The fighting was chiefly along the border, reached a peak in 1957-59, cost 19 lives, and was expensive in terms of surveillance to both parts of Ireland.

IRA's publicity bureau issued a statement on 26 February 1962, the significance of which was apparently not immediately clear. It said: "The Leadership of the Resistance Movement has ordered the termination of 'The Campaign of Resistance to British Occupation.' " It added that "all arms and other materials have been dumped and all full-time active service volunteers have been withdrawn." According to the historian Tim Pat Coogan, this decision was prompted especially by steps being taken in Eire to terminate both the campaign and the IRA. Quite prematurely, the *New York Times* published this obituary:

> The original I.R.A. and Sinn Fein came in like lions ... and now they go out like lambs. ... Partition is resented but the present generation know that if Partition is ever to be ended it must be by peaceful arrangements. The ... Irish Republican Army belongs to history, and it belongs to better men in times that are gone. So does the Sinn Fein. Let us put a wreath of red roses on their grave and move on.[43]

Rather than the death of the IRA and its political party affiliate, Sinn Féin, the formal end of the resistance campaign was symptomatic of a developing division that became open in the IRA in December 1969 and in Sinn Féin in January 1970. As we shall see, the division resulted from a revolt of actionist Provisionals against the Marxist-Leninist-oriented Officials who had controlled both the army and the party. The Official IRA turned more and more toward political methods both in Northern Ireland and in the twenty-six counties. Less ideologically guided, the Provisional IRA built its strength primarily on physical protection for nationalist areas, on dramatic events, and on money-raising activities.

Patricia McCluskey and her husband, Dr. Con McCluskey, of Dungannon, County Tyrone, started a Campaign for Social Justice in January 1964 that also emphasized a political approach. It collected data, publicized its findings widely, and helped stimulate from 1965 a London-based Campaign for Democracy in Ulster participated in by as many as one hundred Westminster Labour MPs. Both organizations concerned themselves with discrimination in housing, public appointments, electoral practices, boundaries, and employment.

The Campaign for Social Justice also gave birth in February 1967 to the Northern Ireland Civil Rights Association (NICRA). This Belfast-centered body was modeled after the National Council for Civil Liberties of London. As an official British investigation commission discovered, "These organisations concern themselves with immediate social reforms, such as opposition to job and housing discrimination by Unionists, support for universal adult franchise in local government elections and fairer electoral boundaries in local government." The commission found that these two associations "are not concerned, as organisations, with altering the constitutional structure of Northern Ireland, and in this sense represent a quite new development among Catholic activists." Loyalist misinterpretation of and lack of sympathy with the goals of these bodies as expressed in nonviolent processions and confrontations led directly to the renewal and expansion of the Northern Ireland struggle in violent terms.

The same investigating commission outlines the background for this significant development as follows:

> A much larger Catholic middle-class has emerged, which is less ready to acquiesce in the acceptance of a situation of assumed (or established) inferiority and discrimination than was the case in the past. ... We were impressed by the number of well educated and responsible people who were and are concerned in, and have taken an active part in, the Civil Rights movement, and by the depth and extent of the investigations which they have made, or caused to be made, to produce evidence to vouch their grievances and support their claims for remedy.[44]

Unfortunately, the fact that the civil rights movement enlisted mostly—even though not exclusively—Roman Catholics made it easy for Loyalists to assume that it was an attack on their privileges. As the commission report continues: "Officially the [Northern Ireland Civil Rights] Association campaigned only on civil rights issues, but in practice its activities tended to polarise the Northern Ireland community in traditional directions. It was bound to attract opposition from many Protestant Unionists who saw or professed to see its success as a threat to their supremacy, indeed, to their survival as a community."[45]

The movement's efforts at change through nonviolent confrontations were thus met with both vigilante and official violence. Inevitably then, organizations so subjected to repression, as the commission points out, "attracted the attention and support of certain left-wing extremists, some of whom by infiltration gained positions of influence within the movement, and their readiness to provoke and profit by violence was crucial at various stages in the disturbances, although their activities and influence were condemned and opposed by many of the movement's leaders and supporters."[46]

Terence O'Neill as Northern Ireland prime minister in 1963–69 made efforts at rapprochement both with the minority community and with leaders of the twenty-six county state. As a commentator noted, however, "If Terence O'Neill is going to move politics into the central plains, he has got to overcome the Orange and the Black."[47] These are two principal Protestant secret societies, the Loyal Orange Institution and the Royal Black Institution, the Orange's senior and prestigious branch. These bodies had traditionally depended for political clout upon appearing to be basically "a labouring and poorer artisan class Protestant movement."[48] But that tie was weakening, and the Unionist—intimately Orange-related—Party was dividing. Thus O'Neill in 1968–69 faced, as the commentator pointed out, "his hardest struggle." That was "to ensure the survival of the Unionist Party in an age when the Protestant working man's vote won't be cast according to his faith. This is the Orange nightmare."[49] Neither he nor the party succeeded in this, and the divisions accompanied even greater Loyalist extremism.

The situation in the Orange statelet on the eve of renewed or stepped-up disorders can be summarized rather accurately by quoting official conclusions of the before-mentioned governmental commission. Those investigators called the following "the immediate and precipitating causes of the disorders" discussed in the next chapter:

> (1) A rising sense of continuing injustice and grievance among large sections of the Catholic population in Northern Ireland, in particular in Londonderry and Dungannon, in respect of (i) inadequacy of housing provision by certain local authorities (ii) unfair methods of allocation of houses built and let by such authorities, in particular, refusals and omissions to adopt a "points" system in determining priorities and making allocations (iii) misuses in certain cases of discretionary powers of allocation of housing in order to perpetuate Unionist control of the local authority. ...

> (2) Complaints, now well documented in fact, of discrimination in the making of local government appointments, at all levels but especially in senior posts, to the prejudice of non-Unionists and especially Catholic members of the community, in some Unionist controlled authorities. ...

> (3) Complaints, again well documented, in some cases of deliberate manipulation of local government electoral boundaries and in others a refusal to apply for their necessary extension, in order to achieve and maintain Unionist control of local authorities and so to deny to Catholics influence in local government proportionate to their numbers. ...

(4) A growing and powerful sense of resentment and frustration among the Catholic population at failure to achieve either acceptance on the part of the Government of any need to investigate these complaints or to provide and enforce a remedy for them. ...

(5) Resentment, particularly among Catholics, as to the existence of the Ulster Special Constabulary (the 'B' Specials) as a partisan and paramilitary force recruited exclusively from Protestants. ...

(6) Widespread resentment among Catholics in particular at the continuance in force of regulations made under the Special Powers Act, and of the continued presence in the statute book of the Act itself. ...

(7) Fears and apprehensions among Protestants of a threat to Unionist domination and control of Government by increase of Catholic population and powers, inflamed in particular by the activities of the Ulster Constitution Defence Committee and the Ulster Protestant Volunteers, provoked strong hostile reaction to civil rights claims as asserted by the Civil Rights Association and later by the People's Democracy which was readily translated into physical violence against Civil Rights demonstrators.[50]

It is unfortunate that these conclusions were not faced and acted upon clearly and quickly. Westminster was still following the traditional Tory line that "it is convention not to interfere in Northern Irish affairs."[51] The conclusions still represent an unfinished and haunting agenda. As an investigative reporter summed it up on the eve of stepped-up disorders, "I talked to Catholics and Protestants in Ulster involved in the struggle for civil rights. Everywhere I found despair which can, without exaggeration, be compared with the South in the United States. The same phrases about 'ghetto housing,' gerrymandering and 'the fight for votes' are used."[52] At the same time, a British minister with a special responsibility for Northern Ireland asserted at a news conference: "The point I want to get over is that you ... are British and to be British is the greatest heritage you could have." A reporter said that the reply from the Northern Irish in the audience might well have been: "How long, O Lord, until we come into thy Kingdom and see our heritage?"[53]

Notes

1. Jimmy Breslin, statement, pp. 79–82, in House of Representatives, Committee on Foreign Affairs, Subcommittee on Europe, *Northern Ireland* (Washington, D.C.: Government Printing Office, 1972), p. 81 quoted.
2. K. B. Clark, *Dark Ghetto* (New York: Harper Torchbooks, 1965), chap. 3; Elliot Liebow, *Tally's Corner* (Boston: Little, Brown, 1967), chap. 2.
3. Danilo Dolci, *Waste*, trans. R. Munroe (New York: Monthly Review Press, 1963); Jerre Mangione, *The World Around Danilo Dolci*, 2nd ed. (New York: Harper & Row, 1972).
4. Pierre Vallieéres, *White Niggers of America*, trans. Joan Pinkham (New York: Monthly Review Press, 1971), chap. 1.
5. Breslin, statement, p. 81.
6. "Sir Wilfred Spender's Financial Diary, 1939–40," quoted by Patrick Buckland, *The Factory of Grievances* (New York: Barnes & Noble, 1979), p. 1.
7. Buckland, ibid., pp. 1–2.
8. Michael Farrell, *Northern Ireland: The Orange State*, 2nd rev. ed. (London: Pluto Press, 1980), pp. 67–69.
9. Dorothy Macardle, *The Irish Republic*, rev. American ed. (New York: Farrar, Straus & Giroux, 1965), p. 381.
10. National Council for Civil Liberties, *Report of a Commission Appointed to Examine the Purpose and Effect of the Civil Authorities (Special Powers) Acts (Northern Ireland) 1922 & 1933* (London: NCCL, 1936, reissued 1972), pp. 39–40. (Hereinafter referred to as NCCL Commission.)
11. G. B. Hanna, quoted by ibid., p. 13.
12. NCCL Commission, ibid., p. 7.
13. Ibid., footnote, pp. 39–40.
14. Lord Cameron, chairman, Commission Appointed by the Governor of Northern Ireland, *Disturbances in Northern Ireland* (Belfast: HMSO, Cmnd. 532, September 1969), p. 108. (Hereinafter referred to as Cameron Commission.)
15. Ibid., p. 104.
16. Viscount Craigavon and Sir Dawson Bates, respectively, quoted by NCCL Commission, footnote, p. 40.
17. NCCL Commission, ibid., p. 9.
18. Ibid., pp. 9–10.
19. Kevin Boyle, Tom Hadden, and Paddy Hillyard, *Law and State: The Case of Northern Ireland* (Amherst: University of Massachusetts Press, 1975), p. 7.
20. Cameron Commission, pp. 105, 107.
21. NCCL Commission, p. 11.
22. Ibid., pp. 14–15. Words in act italicized by NCCL Commission.
23. Ibid., p. 16. In 1973, in response to a recommendation in the Diplock report, for major Scheduled Offences, "trial by judge alone should take the place of trial by jury for the duration of the emergency." As we shall see later, these became called "Diplock courts." Lord Diplock, chairman, Commission to Consider Legal Procedures to Deal with Terrorist Activities in Northern Ireland, *Report* (London: HMSO, Cmnd. 5185, December 1972), p. 18.
24. NCCL Commission, pp. 17–18; Section 2(6) of the 1920 act.
25. Ibid., p. 21.

26. Ibid., pp. 26-27.
27. Ibid., p. 27.
28. Ibid., pp. 27-28.
29. Ibid., p. 28.
30. Ibid., pp. 31-32.
31. Ibid., p. 32.
32. Ibid., footnote, p. 31.
33. Ibid.
34. Henry Boylan, *A Dictionary of Irish Biography* (Dublin: Gill and Macmillan, 1978), p. 73.
35. Roger Hull, *The Irish Triangle: Conflict in Northern Ireland,* new ed. (Princeton: Princeton University Press, 1978), p. 95.
36. Basil Chubb, *The Government and Politics of Ireland* (London: Oxford University Press, 1970), p. 65.
37. Chubb, ed., *A Source Book of Irish Government* (Dublin: Institute of Public Administration, 1964), p. 28.
38. Ibid.
39. R. Benewick, *Political Violence and Public Order* (London: Allen Lane, Penguin, 1969), chaps. 10, 11.
40. Cameron Commission, p. 107.
41. Maurice Manning, *The Blue Shirts* (Dublin: Gill and Macmillan, 1970).
42. Cameron Commission, pp. 107-8.
43. Tim Pat Coogan, *The I. R. A.* (London: Pall Mall Press, 1970), pp. 343-44; cf. rev. ed. (Douglas, Isle of Man: Fontana Paperbacks, 1980), p. 418.
44. Cameron Commission, p. 15.
45. Ibid.
46. Ibid.
47. Jeremy Bugler, "The House of Orange," *New Society* (London), 19 December 1968, pp. 905-6, p. 906 quoted.
48. S. E. Long, "The Union: Pledge and Progress: 1886-1967," pt. 3 in M. W. Dewar, John Brown, and Long, *Orangeism: A New Historical Appreciation* (Belfast: Grand Orange Lodge of Ireland, 1967), p. 149.
49. Bugler, "House of Orange."
50. Cameron Commission, pp. 91-92.
51. Quoted by Mary Holland, "Northern Ireland: The Homeless, Voteless Catholics," London *Observer* Service from Londonderry, 9 October 1968, p. 7.
52. Ibid.
53. Quoting Lord Stonham, minister at the Home Office, ibid.

CHAPTER 4

Revolt Renewed

Even major social adaptations can be achieved without bloodshed in a country that has both constitutional guarantees of civil rights and popularly supported freedom to protest and to demonstrate. Despite the much vaunted civil libertarian traditions of the United Kingdom, the ruling Loyalists in Northern Ireland made "a fatal error. ... It was to mistake the Civil Rights movement of the sixties for an attack on the State of Ulster [Northern Ireland] itself. Thus, by choice of the ruling elite, the energy of the reformist impulse has been made to shake the foundations of society,"[1] to quote the 1972 report of an "insight team" of the London *Sunday Times*. Stated a little differently but to the same point, even at a price of continuing civil violence and bitterness, those ruling Northern Ireland were not about to permit their province to become something resembling a democratized community.

The preceding chapter indicates the repressive character of the social situation in Northern Ireland, but its nature is not clearly understood in other parts of the United Kingdom. Here, as in other connections, popular oversimplifications and distortions are not at all unusual. Fantasies blind the English as much to the brutal practices they permit or support in Ireland as do similar notions of Americans to similar practices against exploited Filipinos, Koreans, Vietnamese, and a long list of other foreigners, especially in Latin America, and concerning deprived Amerinds, Chicanos, blacks, poor whites, prisoners, mental patients and sexual deviants in this country. While the dossiers on our police, prison guards, soldiers, and hospital orderlies are surely mixtures of kindness and savagery, they include reports that match in brutality anything the British are doing in the streets and private homes of Derry and Belfast and in interrogation centers and prisons.

All too many people everywhere are unaware of their unwitting participation in violence and try to protect themselves from being informed. They do not perceive their responsibilities in the social ramifications of terror until they accidentally learn of disastrous consequences of their racist firing or denial of an important privilege or opportunity. Should their city have a riot, a violent strike, or even civil war, they have ready rationalizations for the situation: Members of some vicious or pathological group are said to be the irresponsible perpetrators. Without reference to causative factors, "law and order" must be restored immediately by the wielders of official violence at any "necessary" cost to the revolting deprived. Even now the British shrink from recognizing how their shortsighted policies are increasing the threat of the class and ethnic powder kegs on which they are sitting.

The purpose of this book is not to provide a detailed history of the current Northern Ireland conflict. As a part of this effort to clarify and interpret its nature, however, it should be helpful in this chapter to narrate its opening phases. To begin with, let us see how an official commission appointed by the royal governor of Northern Ireland recounts the incident in 1968 at Caledon that appears to have lit the fuse to renew civil war in Northern Ireland. Such commissions, as we shall see, are often rather candid in some of their factual admissions; they depend for their points on their recommendations and their rationalizations of them. This Cameron Commission report suggests in subdued tones something of the whole internecine and anti-imperialist struggle:

> It was the Caledon squatting incident which was the starting point for the disturbances which followed. Caledon is a village in Dungannon Rural District, which is in Co. Tyrone. The village is mainly Protestant, and under the prevailing system the local Unionist Councillor had effective responsibility for allocating Council houses in the area.
>
> There had been squatting in two new houses at Kinnard Park, Caledon, during the previous months, encouraged by Mr. Austin Currie, M.P. (N.I.) and others. No. 11 was occupied by the Goodfellow family and No. 9 by the McKenna family. These families came from another district in the area of the Rural District Council, where the Unionist Councillor had, in effect, opposed the building of houses for Catholic tenants. The McKennas eventually left and their house was allocated to a Miss Emily Beattie. Miss Beattie took possession of her house on the 13th June. She was 19 years old, a Protestant, and secretary to the local Councillor's Solicitor, who was also a Unionist Parliamentary candidate living in Armagh. The Councillor's explanation for giving her the house was that in effect he was rehousing her family who lived in very poor conditions; also he

Revolt Renewed 79

had expected her to be married before she took possession of the house. In fact she did marry soon afterwards.

In concentrated form the situation expressed the objections felt by many non-Unionists to the prevailing system of housing allocations in Dungannon Rural District Council. By no stretch of the imagination could Miss Beattie be regarded as a priority tenant. On 18th June, within a few days of Miss Beattie taking possession, the Goodfellow family, squatting next door, were evicted with full television coverage. Mr. Currie had protested at all levels against the allocation to Miss Beattie, and raised the matter on the adjournment in the Northern Ireland House of Commons on 19th June 1968. He received no satisfaction, and accordingly formally occupied Miss Beattie's house with two others on 20th June, until in the presence of policemen, a few hours later they were evicted by Miss Beattie's brother who, himself a policeman, was to become a resident of the same house. Quite apart from the real merits of Mr. Currie's case against the allocation, he scored thereby a major propaganda success.[2]

Currie, as a member of the Northern Ireland (Stormont) parliament, had managed by this act to dramatize in the media the plight of Roman Catholic families in search of housing.[3]

Agitation for the relief of the nationalist minority had been taking the form of civil rights fact-gathering, discussions, and complaints. The expanding middle-class nationalist professionals were attempting to focus policy-making attention on the contrasts between United Kingdom libertarian pretentions and Northern Ireland realities. As the previous chapter mentions, leadership in this movement was from 1964 provided by the McCluskeys of Dungannon through the Campaign for Social Justice and then from 1967 by the Northern Ireland Civil Rights Association and some related bodies.

The Caledon affair turned this agitation toward more activist methods. The same Cameron Commission report gives this account of the next significant step toward open conflict:

The next event was the Civil Rights march in Dungannon on 24th August [1968]. This occurred because of the feelings aroused by the much publicized Caledon incident and was intended mainly as a protest against housing policy in the area.

This had been under close scrutiny for several years by the Campaign for Social Justice, and extensive surveys of housing policy in Dungannon Rural District Council and Dungannon Urban District Council had been carried out. These had shown what would appear to be a strong pattern of political influence in the location and allocation of houses in the area. Mr. Currie now persuaded members of this group to organise a march from Coalisland to Dungannon.

About 18 months previously the Northern Ireland Civil Rights Association had begun to become active. Its original purpose had been mainly to provide support for individual complaints against authority, on the lines of the National Council for Civil Liberties in Great Britain. Its activities had so far been limited and had attracted little publicity. Dr. McCluskey in Dungannon, of the Campaign for Social Justice, was a member and through him a meeting with the Northern Ireland Civil Rights Association executive was arranged. This was held on 27th July at Maghera. The Civil Rights Association had doubts about getting involved in housing agitation and mass processions, but eventually agreed to a march on 24th August.

After the march had been announced at the end of July the police originally raised no objection in principle. The route was to be from Coalisland to Market Square, Dungannon. ... However, there was soon a move in extreme Unionist circles to oppose the march, on the grounds that Market Square was Unionist territory. Senator Stewart (Chairman of the Urban District Council and a prominent resident) told the police that there would be trouble if the march entered the Square and proposed a re-route by Quarry Lane to Anne Street. Mr. John Taylor M.P. also told the police that there would be trouble if the procession entered the Square. We think it is to be inferred from their own evidence that whether these local Unionist leaders would have organised, they at least would not have discouraged, the organisation of a counter demonstration if the march had been allowed to enter Market Square. Such a counter demonstration, if organised, would almost certainly have led to an outbreak of violence—as persons occupying positions of such responsibility cannot have failed to appreciate.

Faced with these representations the police decided that the threat of counter demonstration should be taken seriously, the more so as the Ulster Protestant Volunteers advertised a public meeting to be held in the Market Square on the evening of 24th August. Late on 23rd August the march was accordingly re-routed, and arrangements were made to halt it near Quarry Lane at Thomas Street, Dungannon, and divert it to Anne Street.

The march took place on the evening of 24th August as arranged, but halted at the police barrier. At least 2,500 people marched from Coalisland and a much larger number gathered at Thomas Street. Mr. [Gerard] Fitt M.P. and Mr. Currie were among the speakers, and Miss [Betty] Sinclair of the Northern Ireland Civil Rights Association presided. Beyond the police were a miscellaneous crowd of at least 1,500 people, some of whom were potential counter demonstrators.

The march and the meeting aroused a good deal of feeling. Opponents noted the presence of several prominent Republicans among the marchers, and there was some regrettable and irresponsible abuse of the police by Mr. Fitt. The police calculated that about 70 of the stewards were Republicans, and of these some 10 were members of the Irish Republican Army. On the other hand the organisers prevented the public display of any banners except the Civil Rights banner. ... There was a hope among many participants that something new was taking place in Northern Ireland, in that here was a non-violent demonstration by people of many differing political antecedents and convictions, united on the common platform of reform. Miss Sinclair closed the proceedings by leading those present in singing "We Shall Overcome." ...

It is significant that this first Civil Rights march, unaccompanied by any provocative display of weapons, banners, or symbol was carried out without any breach of the peace. It attracted considerable public attention and was also regarded as proof in certain circles that many elements in the society of Northern Ireland whose ultimate political purpose differed in very marked degree could co-operate in peaceful and lawful demonstration in favour of certain common and limited objectives.

There is little doubt that it was this demonstration which suggested to certain bodies and persons in Londonderry to draw public attention to their claims for relief and remedial action by way of similar action, which originally at least they intended to be non-violent. The atmosphere in Londonderry was however highly charged for reasons arising out of political, social and economic conditions in the city and an explosion of violence could easily be detonated.[4]

This was a mild prologue to events that were violent and have often been violent since. As one analyst puts it, "The revival of the IRA campaign could only have been avoided if the aims of the Civil Rights Movement had been gained immediately and completely."[5]

The focus of action quickly moved from Dungannon to Derry. On 27 August, an effort to substitute a committee for the mayor in control of housing allocation was defeated in the Derry Corporation meeting. Then, on 2 September, the Northern Ireland Civil Rights Association (NICRA) issued a statement that it planned to hold a meeting in Derry shortly to protest not only the housing situation but also unemployment and to demand local government reform and the rights of free speech and assembly. On 8 September, it informed the Royal Ulster Constabulary (RUC) that it proposed to hold a march Saturday, 5 October. The General Committee of the (Protestant) Apprentice Boys of Derry objected to the Minister of Home Affairs, William Craig, about the NICRA march. It claimed, and Craig agreed, that the march would actually be a Republican/Nationalist rally. The Apprentice Boys then came up with an announcement that they planned to march over the same route as NICRA on the same day.

Craig banned both marches. To prevent possible disorders, he forbade "all public processions or meetings in any public place within or on the Walls [of Derry], and in the Waterside." Eddie McAteer, as head of the Nationalist Party, called the Apprentice Boys' announcement Craig's excuse. David Smylie of the Ulster Shankill Protestant Volunteers claimed that now NICRA could easily set aside Loyalist rights to march through threatening to march![6] As the Cameron Commission recounted:

> The route proposed on behalf of the Civil Rights Association was one commonly followed by "Protestant" and "Loyalist" marches in Londonderry. ... This route traversed certain Protestant districts and ended within the city's ancient Walls, which have major significance in Orange tradition because of the successful defence of Londonderry [in 1689] against James VII and II. The proposal to follow this route was designed to symbolise the claim of the Civil Rights Association to be non-sectarian, and neither Unionist nor Nationalist.[7]

Revolt Renewed

NICRA proceeded with its march plans in order to demonstrate its civil right to protest in that manner, and the police anticipated trouble. Two platoons of "riot police" were brought in together with two water wagons. Thus about 130 police sought to block 2,000 demonstrators who assembled east of the River Foyle and hoped to march across the Craigavon Bridge into the walled part of Derry. The police barred access to the bridge, and the Cameron Commission admitted:

> The procession marched straight up to the police, and it appears to us established on the evidence that at this stage batons were used by certain police officers without explicit order, although this is denied by the police. We regret to say that we have no doubt that both Mr. Fitt and Mr. McAteer were batoned by the police, at a time when no order to draw batons had been given and in circumstances in which the use of batons on these gentlemen was wholly without justification or excuse.[8]

For about half an hour, a meeting was held in the street in front of the police barricade with pleas for the right to hold nonviolent processions. When the leaders of NICRA then advised the assembled people to disperse, the police claimed that members of the "Young Socialists Alliance" tossed their placards and banners and some stones at them. At any rate, when marchers tried to retreat, they found themselves confronted in the rear as well as in front by lines of police. Both lines made baton charges, and the crowd was sprayed with water from the wagons. Further outbreaks continued for three days in Derry, and sympathetic demonstrations were also held elsewhere in the province. With respect to "the police handling of the demonstrations in Londonderry on 5th October 1968," the Cameron Commission concluded:

> There was use of unnecessary and ill controlled force in the dispersal of the demonstrators, only a minority of whom acted in a disorderly and violent manner. The wide publicity given by press, radio and television to particular episodes inflamed and exacerbated feelings of resentment against the police which had already been aroused by their enforcement of the ministerial ban.[9]

A group of Queen's University students on 9 October confronted the politicians in Belfast's City Hall with demands for human rights and against the police brutality in Derry. Then, on 16 October, after Nationalist M.P.s had withdrawn from the Stormont parliament, 1,300 students marched to the Belfast City Hall in another demonstration for civil rights. In consequence, these protests became "transformed into the People's Democracy," called by the Cameron Commission "an unnecessary adjunct to the already existing and operative Civil Rights Association. People's Democracy provided a means by which politically extreme and militant elements could and did invite civil disorder, with the consequence of polarising and hardening opposition to Civil Rights claims."[10] Since the civil rights movement, in spite of its nonviolent stance, had already had violence directed at it by both vigilantes and police, the commission's contention appears partisan.

The level of tension made the Prime Minister of Northern Ireland, Terence O'Neill, assert to the Stormont House of Commons that "unless the Province returns to sanity, future progress is gravely at risk."[11] In spite of previous praise for some of O'Neill's liberalizing efforts, the British Prime Minister, Harold Wilson, impatiently asserted on 21 October: "I do not think that anyone in this House [of Commons] is satisfied with what has been done, and in particular the feeling that Captain O'Neill is being blackmailed by any of the thugs putting pressure on him is something which the House could not accept."[12] It is always easier to blame someone else's actions rather than basic British policies.

Demonstrations continued throughout the province and especially in Derry. In spite of the existing ban on parades and meetings, some 3,500 took part on 19 October in a peaceful sit-down demonstration in Derry. On 2 November, 2,000 marched to the Diamond in the center of Derry's walled section and listened to a reading of the U.N. Declaration of Human Rights. An effort by the Loyal Citizens of Ulster to block this march was prevented by the police.

A leader in these Derry civil rights marches was a Protestant, a Unionist, Ivan A. Cooper. In response to a further ban by Craig on 13 November of all noncustomary processions and meetings within Derry's walls, Cooper as president of the Derry Citizens' Action Committee joined hands with fourteen other members of the committee on 16 November in

> ... spear-heading 15,000 marchers on a journey that could have ended in a bloodbath. Its conclusion was a victory for nonviolence but, as they set out on that sunny Saturday afternoon singing, "We Shall Overcome," Cooper and his aides somehow looked frail and naive as they moved against the monolithic power of Stormont, represented by the steel barricades and un-

smiling policemen who blocked their path at Craigavon Bridge. They did overcome that day but the struggle for fundamental rights goes on.[13]

In spite of the efforts of 400 police, the massive procession succeeded in penetrating the walls and in staging a sit-down in the Diamond area. The next day NICRA praised the people of Derry for maintaining their "right to march in any part of their own city." They also asked O'Neill to get rid of [Minister of Home Affairs] Craig, who was, they said, "leading the provinces on a path of inter-communal strife."[14] Further demonstrations there and elsewhere continued.

The Nationalist Party, the principal antipartitionist factor in Northern Ireland prior to 1968-69, under McAteer's leadership not only withdrew from the Stormont parliament but also on 17 November took the position that it would "support the exercise of non-violent civil disobedience at such times and under such circumstances as may be considered expedient to cleanse a system which has as its basis a deliberate policy of denying equal treatment and equal opportunity to all." In addition, it made these more specific suggestions:

> Declaring its "disappointment and disillusionment with the so-called 'pace of change,'" the party called for: (1) the repeal of the Special Powers and Public Order Acts; (2) the establishment of "one man, one vote"; (3) the introduction of "justice in all areas of local government"; (4) the creation of a Public Appointments Commission; (5) the allocation of public housing authority housing on an equitable points system; (6) the extension to Northern Ireland of the Race Relations Acts; and (7) the appointment of an Ombudsman.[15]

The response of the Northern Ireland government to the civil disturbances and to the Nationalist Party's demands came on 22 November in the announcement of the following reforms:

(1) Allocation of Houses

The Government undertook to ensure that all housing authorities placed need in the forefront in the allocation of houses, and that future housing allocations would be carried out on the basis of a readily-understood and published scheme.

(2)   Investigations of Citizens' Grievances

The Government agreed to consider the need for effective machinery to investigate grievances in an objective way, and in the area of Central Government activity, to introduce legislation to appoint a Parliamentary Commissioner for Administration.

(3)   Implementation of Londonderry Area Plan

The Government announced that it would take all possible steps to ensure that prompt and effective action would be taken to implement a Plan, designed to transform the economic and social life of the City, and to assist this objective by the appointment of a strong, well-qualified and objective Development Commission.

(4)   Reform of Local Government including the Franchise

The Government indicated its firm intention to complete a comprehensive reform and modernisation of the local government structure within a period of three years—that is, by the end of 1971—to review the franchise in the context of the organisation, financing and structure of the new local government bodies, and to abolish the company vote in local government.

(5)   Special Powers

The Government announced that after discussions it had agreed with the United Kingdom Government that—

(i) as soon as the Northern Ireland Government considered this could be done without undue hazard, such of the Special Powers as are in conflict with international obligations would, as in the past, be withdrawn from current use; but

(ii) in the event of the Northern Ireland Government considering it essential to re-activate such powers, the United Kingdom Government would enter the necessary derogation [from the obligations imposed by the European Convention of Human Rights].[16]

The vagueness and the limited nature of these reform proposals blunted their influence. The promise "to review the franchise," for example, only became more palpable the next May, 1969, when additional pressures resulted in an announcement of plans to establish the principle of "one man, one vote."[17]

Agitation continued. On 30 November, NICRA held a march in Armagh that was halted by a Loyalist crowd led by the Reverend Ian Paisley and his lieutenant, Major Ronald Bunting. Violence greeted a civil rights meeting on 4 December at Dungannon. In response to a television appeal by Prime Minister O'Neill, NICRA and Derry Citizens' Action Committee announced that they had discontinued marches at least until 11 January. On 11 December, O'Neill dismissed the controversial Craig. On 16 December, the "N.I. Attorney General announces adjournment until May 1969 of summonses arising from the Civil Rights campaign at Londonderry, Armagh, and Dungannon." Then the next big event was announced by People's Democracy (PD): On 20 December, PD said it would sponsor a march from Belfast to Derry on 1 to 4 January. Major Bunting "warns 'People's Democracy' marchers to avoid 'Loyalist' areas. March is criticised by leading Nationalists."[18]

About forty marchers left Belfast City Hall at nine o'clock on 1 January 1969. Their placards asked for equal voting rights, fair housing allocations, more jobs, and repeal of repressive legislation. Two banners identified the marchers as being members of People's Democracy and devoted to civil rights. From the moment that they started the 75-mile walk, Bunting and his Loyal Citizens of Ulster (numbering at the outset about 70 people) began to harrass the marchers. Bunting announced they would continue to do so throughout the four days.

A NICRA report summarized the four-day march as follows:

> 1969, which was to be a year of violence, began violently. Alarmed that the NICRA one month truce [to 11 January] with O'Neill might lose the impetus of the civil rights campaign, the PD decided to take the initiative and bring their campaign back on to the streets. ... The PD decided on a march from Belfast to Derry through some of the most Loyalist and reactionary rural areas in the North. They left Belfast on January 1, and from their first steps outside the City Hall until their last faltering steps into Guildhall Square in Derry, they were harrassed, manhandled and beaten.
>
> The RUC, despite the appearance of protection, made little effort to prevent attacks on the marchers apart from advising rerouting or cancellation of the march. Attacks were made in Antrim and Toome, outside Maghera, in Dungiven, at Burntollet Bridge and on the way into Derry. As an exercise in marching it was either foolhardy or brave, but as part of an attempt to put political pressure on a Government to grant basic democratic reforms it succeeded only in raising the political temperature. The end result of the march was a heightening of sectarian feel-

ings. The Loyalists, angered by what they regarded as a provocative march, could feel no sympathy towards the civil rights campaign, even though they too could benefit from the same civil rights. They saw civil rights as a threat to the Government, and consequently as a threat to Protestant privilege. The PD march helped to drive the Protestant working class into the arms of Paisley and Bunting.

On the Catholic side the march, particularly the Burntollet ambush, was seen as a Protestant attack on the Catholic students. Civil rights was slowly becoming identified in the Catholic mind with opposition to the Unionist regime, and that meant opposition to the state. A conscious attempt to organise a broad non-sectarian civil rights movement was being gradually identified with a sectarian ideology and the PD's failure to distinguish between political progress and political turmoil hardly helped to reassure the Loyalist population.[19]

The attack on the marchers at Burntollet Bridge, not far from Derry, on the fourth day of the march was an especially disastrous event. Two careful students of the march summarize their findings concerning that attack thus:

The attack was organised locally by representatives of the Orange order and the Special Constabulary, in close collaboration with some members, at least, of the Royal Ulster Constabulary. ... The police force on duty ... were not expected to resist or arrest attackers. ... After the event, no real attempt was made to pursue those involved. Five people were prosecuted. These were victims largely irrelevant to the organisation of the onslaughts.[20]

A participant in the march recalled its end thus:

The battered remnant of the march trudged on to Derry. At Irish Street estate on the outskirts of the city there was another ambush with stones and petrol-bombs, and in Spencer Road the RUC stopped the march while Loyalists pelted it with rocks from a hilltop quarry. But eventually it arrived to the rapturous welcome from a huge crowd in Guildhall Square.[21]

During that evening, drunken Loyalists got into street fights and smashed doors and windows in the Green Bogside area of Derry. In consequence, a local "citizens' army" was formed and a barricaded section called "Free Derry" was set aside as a defensive effort. The RUC kept out of that area for a week.

The Cameron Commission report bears out some of these contentions concerning police relations with the marchers:

> Available police forces did not provide adequate protection to People's Democracy marchers at Burntollet Bridge and in or near Irish Street, Londonderry on 4th January 1969. There were instances of police indiscipline and violence towards persons unassociated with rioting or disorder on 4th/5th January in Londonderry and these provoked serious hostility to the police, particularly among the Catholic population of Londonderry, and an increasing disbelief in their impartiality towards non-Unionists.[22]

Serious riots broke out in Derry on 19 and 20 April 1969, which led to the injury and eventual death of a Catholic. As a result of these riots, the police agreed to leave the Derry Bogside area, a depressed Catholic ghetto, to local control. Then came the "traditional summer parades, particularly those in Londonderry and Belfast. In these circumstances sectarian conflict was to be expected, unless the police were strong enough to prevent it."[23] Whether or not they were strong enough and well enough motivated and trained to control disorders—which is doubtful—they did not do so at all adequately or properly.

The Royal Ulster Constabulary then consisted of 3,200 of whom 240 were in a reserve employed for riot control. The Ulster Special Constabulary, or "B Specials", included about 8,500 part-time civilians who had the reputation of being overwhelmingly Protestant and Loyalist; of them, only 300 were mobilized to work full-time with the RUC. Army detachments were also present, but they were not under the control of the Northern Ireland government.

In its search for events that led to the summer's open conflicts, the Scarman Tribunal—later appointed by the provincial government—discovered:

> On the last day of March and during the month of April there occurred a number of explosions at electricity and water installations in the Province. We are satisfied that, though the perpetrators of these outrages cannot, with one exception, be identified, they were the work of Protestant extremists who

were anxious to undermine confidence in the government of Captain O'Neill. At the time it was widely thought that the explosions were the work of the IRA, though it is quite clear now that they were not.[24]

O'Neill resigned on 28 April and on 1 May James Chichester-Clark took over as provincial Prime Minister. He immediately announced an amnesty for all demonstration offenses since 5 October 1968. Among others, Paisley and Bunting thus got out of jail. NICRA was hopeful because of the amnesty and suspended its current civil disobedience campaign. A somewhat peaceful atmosphere prevailed superficially, with scattered incidents here and there, until the two summer Orange holidays, 12 July and 12 August. These celebrate respectively the victory in 1690 of William of Orange's forces at the Battle of the Boyne and the locking of Derry's gates in 1689 by the Apprentice Boys against the forces of James II, the Roman Catholic English sovereign. According to the Scarman Tribunal, "the traditional marches of the 12th [of July] heightened tension everywhere. Disturbances which arose by way of minority response to Protestant marches occurred on 12 July in Londonderry, Dungiven, and in Belfast in the neighbourhood of Unity Flats and in the Ardoyne."[25]

These events were changing the character of the struggle. Symptoms of this change include the following: The Derry Citizens' Action Committee that had been devoted to civil rights confrontations in association with NICRA changed into the Derry Citizens' Defence Association. It became concerned especially with the defense of the Catholic Bogside. At the same time, in Belfast and elsewhere, mixed housing areas were becoming exclusively either Protestant or Roman Catholic.

The events on 12 August triggered even more serious rioting and might well be called the point at which something resembling overt civil war developed. As the Scarman Tribunal reported the developments:

> On 12 August the traditional Apprentice Boys' Parade was due to take place in Londonderry. The Minister of Home Affairs and his senior police advisers had to decide whether or not to ban it. Believing that all sections of responsible opinion in Londonderry were anxious to keep the peace and that, in particular, the Apprentice Boys on one side, and the Bogside leaders on the other had made arrangements for stewarding, the Minister decided not to intervene, but to allow the parade to proceed. The parade itself was well controlled and orderly but,

as it passed Waterloo Place, some stones were thrown out of William Street in the direction of the police and the parade. The stone-throwers were young hooligans, but their actions released the strong feeling of the Bogside to an extent that the few stewards available were quite unable to control. From this small beginning developed not only three days of disturbance in Londonderry, but the many disturbances elsewhere, including in particular the very serious disorders in Belfast. ...

On the 13th the disturbances spread to other centres. There was serious trouble in the Falls Road area of Belfast. At the same time there were riots in Dungannon, Dungiven, Newry and Armagh. The scale of the riots in Londonderry was such that they were beyond the ability of the police to suppress or control. It became clear to those in authority that the aid of the Army would have to be sought. At five o'clock on 14 August the Army entered Londonderry.

We are satisfied that the spread of the disturbances owed much to a deliberate decision by some minority groups to relieve police pressure on the rioters in Londonderry. ...

On the night of the 14th, the worst violence of the 1969 disturbances occurred in Belfast, notably in the Ardoyne and on the Falls Road. The police, who believed by now that they were facing an armed uprising, used guns, including Browning machine-guns mounted on Shorland armoured vehicles. Four Catholics were shot dead by police fire: one Protestant was killed by a shot fired by a rioter in Divis Street. Catholic houses were burnt by Protestants, especially in the Conway Street area. The only clear evidence of direct IRA participation in these riots occurred at St Comgall's School in Divis Street, where automatic fire was directed against the police. On the same night there was a riot in Armagh, as a result of which a Catholic man was killed by USC [Ulster Special Constabulary] fire.

By the morning of 15 August the police were exhausted. They failed to control the violence which broke out that day on the Crumlin Road and in the Clonard area of the city. Nor did they prevent the burning of factories by Catholics and public houses by Protestants. It has to be admitted that the police were no longer in control of the city. On the evening of the 15th, the Army entered the Falls Road, but not the Crumlin Road, which was the scene of a serious confrontation between Protestants and

Catholics. Two people—one Protestant and one Catholic—died by civilian shooting in Belfast on 15 August. Catholic houses were burnt that night by Protestants at Bombay Street (Falls Road area) and Brookfield Street (Crumlin Road). On the evening of 16 August, the Army entered the Crumlin Road and thereafter the disturbances died away. In some riot areas barricades remained. Defence committees began to exercise *de facto* authority in several Catholic areas. So far as the Falls Road district is concerned we are satisfied that the disturbances produced the committees rather than the committees the disturbances.[26]

Views on the nature of the conflicts varied widely. The provincial Prime Minister, James Chichester-Clark, asserted: "This is not the agitation of a minority seeking by lawful means the assertion of political rights. It is the conspiracy of forces seeking to overthrow a Government democratically elected by a large majority."[27] The Roman Catholic primate, together with the bishops of Derry, Clogher, Dromore, Kilmore, and Down and Connor, disagreed in these terms:

The fact is that on Thursday and Friday of last week the Catholic districts of Falls and Ardoyne were invaded by mobs equipped with machine-guns and other firearms. A community which was virtually defenceless was swept by gunfire and streets of Catholic homes were systematically set on fire.

We entirely reject the hypothesis that the origin of last week's tragedy was an armed insurrection.

We believe that a necessary pre-condition to any restoration of confidence on the part of the Catholic community must be an open recognition of these facts. ...

We ask all concerned to realize that among Catholics belief in the impartiality of the Ulster Special Constabulary is virtually non-existent. The future can hold out no hope whatever unless the whole community is able to trust the forces of law and order.[28]

The Scarman Tribunal disagreed with the Prime Minister about the conspiracy theory. It concluded:

In our judgment there was no plot to overthrow the Government or to mount an armed insurrection. ... While accepting that the major riots that occurred in Londonderry, Belfast, Armagh and Dungannon were not deliberately planned, we are satisfied that, once the disturbances started, they were continued by an element that also found expression in bodies more or less loosely organised, such as the People's Democracy, and various local Defence Associations, and in associating themselves with bodies such as NICRA and the several Action Committees. The public impact of the activities of this element was tremendously enhanced by the coverage given by the mass media of communication. ...

Neither the IRA nor any Protestant organisation nor anybody else planned a campaign of riots. They were communal disturbances arising from a complex political, social and economic situation. More often than not they arose from slight beginnings: but the communal tensions were such that, once begun, they could not be controlled.[29]

It is unfortunate that this judicious view of the tribunal did not carry greater weight in Stormont and Westminster.

The immediate costs of the 1969 summer riots became stimulants to further conflict. In July and August, 8 Catholics and 2 Protestants were killed. The injured totaled 290 Catholics (87 by gunshot), 231 Protestants (61 by gunshot), 2 Ulster Special Constabulary, 366 RUC (6 by gunshot), and 10 in the fire service. Claims for damages to property in the province in July and August totaled 2,737. By 1972, 1,255 awards had been made for those 1969 claims in the amount of £2,293,448. The other 1,482 claims were still outstanding.[30]

The total security statistics before the end of 1969 are somewhat higher. They include one RUC and 12 civilian deaths in 1969. RUC and RUC Reserve injuries were 379 in 1968 and 711 in 1969; of these, the army and the Ulster Defence Regiment had 22 in 1969. The total of civilians injured is not available. The official record of violence in 1969 gives a total of 8 explosions.[31]

In Belfast in July/August 1969, police received 431 complaints of intimidation. In direct consequence of such reported intimidation, 128 homes were vacated. A more comprehensive survey for July to September in Belfast indicates that 1,505, or 5.3 percent, of the Catholic households were displaced, and 315, or 0.4 percent, of the Protestant. According to the Scarman Tribunal, "It is likely that the root causes of this exodus were direct violence, intimidation or general fear due to the disturbances, and isolation from co-religionists."[32] Segregation was proceeding apace. For the same period more generally, the figure is estimated to have been 3,500 displacements (85 percent Roman Catholic).[33]

And so revolt was renewed in Northern Ireland and renewed in a manner and under continuing conditions that have made it quite persistent. It has occasioned the resurrection of the IRA and the organization and reorganization of Loyalist vigilante groups. Its rhetoric and the practices of the mass media have also led to its mischaracterization as being a "religious" struggle, even though widely divergent spokespeople take a contrary view. Before surveying and analyzing aspects of the conflict, let us look at some of those views on what is happening.

D. R. Campion, editor of the Jesuit weekly *America,* asserts that the Northern Ireland war "is not essentially a religious one but unfortunately it is tied in with religious convictions, religious passions." Agitators, he says, exploit "differences that have existed in the past ... [and thus] exacerbate the political and economic situation."[34] Jimmy Breslin, an Irish-American journalist, puts it more categorically: "In my opinion the words 'Protestant' and 'Catholic' in Northern Ireland have virtually no religious meaning at all, they stand for the 'ins' and 'outs' of a political system."[35]

The largest Protestant church in Northern Ireland, the Presbyterian (locally referred to as a "dissenting" church), takes a view similar to that of those Roman Catholic writers in an official statement issued in 1969: "Though the conflicts in our country are continually presented in terms of Protestant versus Catholic, religious differences in fact constitute only a part, though a real part of the causes. Religion commonly is used more as a convenient label or cover for different 'national,' political, social and economic interests. Some of those most militantly engaged, particularly in Belfast, have only nominal Church connection and these conflicts have become for them a kind of substitute for religion."[36] The same church has, however, "supported the use of force by the state and been opposed to all violence against the state" on the grounds that "the government of a country is divinely ordained and has the right to claim the citizens' respect, support and obedience."[37]

Joint statements by leaders of the principal religious denominations of Northern Ireland hopefully but unconvincingly underline the same contentions again and again. As the heads of the Church of Ireland (Anglican), Methodist, Presbyterian, and Roman Catholic bodies jointly averred on 30 May 1970: "We have no wish to deny that there are serious and deep divisions, which we deplore, in the Northern Ireland community, but we wish to assert that these divisions are not primarily of a religious character. They arise from deep and complex causes—historical, political and social—but the religious differences between professing Christians are not a primary cause."[38]

Even the Tory political establishment at Westminster stated through representatives in 1972 that it prefers "to use the labels 'Republican' and 'Loyalist' rather than 'Catholic' and 'Protestant' to describe extremists of the rival factions, for the gulf between them is one of politics rather than one of creeds and the methods used by the extremists are equally abhorrent to Christians of both persuasions."[39]

Thus, at least on this single point of labeling, if no other, entrenched Irish Protestant, Dissenter, and Roman Catholic and British spokespeople talk as though they view the struggle in similar terms. Only a few "Orange" (Protestant) and "Green" (Roman Catholic) ultras deny the labeling. For them, "Papists" and "Prods" are battling for doctrine-related objectives. The extremist head of the Free Presbyterian Church, an organization not affiliated with the regular Presbyterian Church, the Reverend Ian Paisley, its founder, states his position in the current struggle in these terms:

> We are at war in this Province with the hierarchy of the Roman Catholic Church. ... The Jesuits are the Gestapo of the Vatican. Their purpose is to undo the Reformation and bring Protestantism and all other religions of the world under the jackboot of the Papacy. ... The hatred of all things British and Protestant is but the product of the diabolical and soul-destroying doctrines of the Church of Rome. ... The I.R.A. is the armed wing of the Roman Catholic Church.[40]

Exploiting such theories, Paisley has not only built a substantial denomination of ultras outside of the traditional Presbyterian church but has also made himself into a threatening political figure both in Northern Ireland and in the Parliament at Westminster.

Far closer to the realities of the Northern Ireland struggle than the disavowals of leading clerics is the note struck by the American Jesuit editor W. Van E. Casey when he observes:

> It is impossible in Ireland to separate politics and religion. They are the obverse and reverse of the same coin. The Irish are almost one hundred percent Protestant or Catholic—at least nominally. This fact alone raises serious questions about the role and the effectiveness of Christianity in Irish history and on the Irish character. Has Christianity been used only as a cloak to cover the sickness in the Irish soul?

And then Casey accuses:

> If the Irish, all of them over there, are not aware of the grave harm they are doing to the cause of Christianity throughout the world, then they are playing ostrich in their little green ghetto. They are an embarrassment to the Christian world. They make the Irish outside of Ireland ashamed to be Irish.[41]

By confining themselves to idealistic discourse, to some helpful social work practices, and to traditional rituals, denominational leaders at most obscure the contributions their ecclesiastical structures and procedures also make to divisiveness, to intergroup ignoring and ignorance, to intergroup rejection and hatred. As a Working Party appointed by the Irish Council of Churches/Roman Catholic Joint Group on Social Questions admitted in 1977: "The Irish Churches have until recently been slow to recognise that total religious segregation is by no means a necessary nor a desirable consequence of legitimate denominational differences; nor is it an acceptable protection for religious beliefs. ... Lack of contact, lack of dialogue breed an environment of fear, suspicion, ignorance and prejudice, which can rightly be termed sectarian."[42]

On the contrary, as Professor Norman J. Gibson of the New University of Ulster contends: "Both the Catholic and Protestant Churches have believed it essential that they should be heavily involved in education ... as a means of sustaining and perpetuating their religious and moral belief systems." The identification of Roman Catholicism with Irish nationalism and of Protestantism with British imperialism, as Gibson points out, has thus helped to make "church controlled or influenced education ... shape the minds and environment in which mutual ignorance, suspicion and fear may lead to social and political breakdown, violence, death and destruction."[43] As much can also be said about the influence of religious affiliation upon segregation in employment, housing, and all other aspects of Northern Ireland life and about the little that churches have effectively done to offset their contributions to that tinderbox situation.

This all appears quite confusing as one looks at one after another way of perceiving the Northern Ireland struggle. One gets the impression of thousands of well-meaning bystanders and small gangs of criminal guerrillas. The third "side" of the struggle, the police and the military, claim on the whole that they "just do a job." The British soldiers know little about why Orange "paddies" are subversively fighting Green "paddies," and vice versa, and are also against the British government. They are often terrified by the threat that both types of "paddies" represent to them.

Leaders of various sorts—depending on their vocational and political biases—sort all this out to their own satisfaction. They offer their constituencies ways of assessing blame that will hopefully mobilize support for their goals. On the contrary, as this book may make clear, few people in the British Isles are free of "blame" for this festering situation. Few are not involved in one way or another—mostly unwittingly—in this conflict. Let us proceed further in this survey by looking into how the Irish learn to be violent.

Notes

1. London *Sunday Times* Insight Team, *Northern Ireland: A Report on the Conflict* (New York: Vintage, 1972), p. 27.
2. Lord Cameron, chairman, Commission Appointed by the Governor of Northern Ireland, *Disturbances in Northern Ireland* (Belfast: HMSO, Cmd. 532, September 1969), p. 21. Hereinafter referred to as Cameron Commission.
3. Simon Winchester, *In Holy Terror: Reporting the Ulster Troubles* (London: Faber & Faber, 1974), p. 27.
4. Cameron Commission, pp. 21-23.
5. Alan O'Day, "Northern Ireland, Terrorism, and the British State," in *Terrorism: Theory and Practice,* ed. Yonah Alexander, David Carlton, and Paul Wilkinson (Boulder, Colo.: Westview, 1979), p. 126.
6. Richard Deutsch and Vivien Magowan, *Northern Ireland: 1968-73: A Chronology of Events* (Belfast: Blackstaff Press, 1973), 1: 10.
7. Cameron Commission, p. 25.
8. Ibid., p. 28.
9. Ibid., p. 93.
10. Ibid., p. 92.
11. Deutsch and Magowan, *Northern Ireland*, p. 11.
12. *Keesing's Contemporary Archives*, November 23-30, 1968, p. 23046.
13. George Devlin, "Ivan Cooper: Derry Civil Rights Leader," Dublin *Irish Independent,* 6 December 1968.
14. *Keesing's Contemporary Archives*, p. 23047.
15. Ibid.
16. Government of Northern Ireland, *A Commentary ... to Accompany the Cameron Report* (Belfast: HMSO, Cmd. 534, September 1969), pp. 3-4. Italics eliminated.
17. Ibid., pp. 5, 9-11; Cameron Commission, p. 115.
18. Cameron Commission, p. 115.
19. Northern Ireland Civil Rights Association, *"We Shall Overcome": The History of the Struggle for Civil Rights in Northern Ireland 1968-1978* (Belfast: NICRA, 1978), p. 17.
20. Bowes Egan and Vincent McCormack, *Burntollet* (London: L.R.S. Publishers, 1969), p. 56.
21. Michael Farrell, *Northern Ireland: The Orange State*, rev. 2nd ed. (London: Pluto Press, 1980), p. 251.
22. Cameron Commission, p. 93.

23. Leslie Scarman, chair, Tribunal of Inquiry, *Violence and Civil Disturbances in Northern Ireland in 1969* (Belfast: HMSO, Cmd. 566, April 1972), 1:6. Hereinafter referred to as Scarman Tribunal.
24. Ibid., p. 7.
25. Ibid., p. 8.
26. Ibid., pp. 9-10.
27. Ibid., 2:36.
28. Ibid., p. 43.
29. Ibid., 1:10-11.
30. Ibid., pp. 241-42, 245.
31. W. D. Flackes, *Northern Ireland: A Political Directory 1968-79* (New York: St. Martin's, 1980), pp. 210-11.
32. Scarman Tribunal, p. 248.
33. Michael Poole, "Riot Displacement in 1969," *Fortnight* (Belfast), no. 22 (August 1971): 9-11.
34. D. R. Campion, statement, p. 35 in House of Representatives, Committee on Foreign Affairs, Subcommittee on Europe, *Northern Ireland* (Washington, D.C.: Government Printing Office, 1972).
35. Jimmy Breslin, statement, pp. 79-82 in ibid., p. 80 quoted.
36. Presbyterian Church in Ireland, "A Presbyterian View of the Northern Ireland Situation," pp. 357-58 in ibid., p. 357 quoted. Memorandum submitted to British Home Secretary, 29 August 1969.
37. "The Presbyterian Attitude to Violence," pp. 109-16 in C. B. Daly and R. D. E. Gallagher, joint chairmen, *Violence in Ireland: A Report to the Churches,* rev. ed. (Belfast: Christian Journals, 1977), p. 109 quoted.
38. Joint statement by J. T. Carson, Moderator of the Presbyterian Church in Ireland, William Cardinal Conway, Primate of All Ireland of the Roman Catholic Church, George E. Good, President of the Irish Methodist Church, and Archbishop G. O. Simms, Primate of All Ireland of the Church of Ireland, p. 359 in House of Representatives, *Northern Ireland, op. cit.*
39. Lord Diplock, chairman, *Report of the Commission to Consider Legal Procedures to Deal with Terrorist Activities in Northern Ireland* (London: HMSO, Cmnd. 5185, 1972), p. 7.
40. I. R. K. Paisley, speech quotations by A. J. Menendez, *The Bitter Harvest: Church and State in Northern Ireland* (Washington, D.C.: Robert B. Luce, 1973), pp. 60-61.
41. W. Van E. Casey, "Ulster: The Anglo-Irish Ulcer," *Holy Cross Quarterly* (Worcester, Mass.) 6 (1974): 2-5, p. 5 quoted.
42. Daly and Gallagher, *Violence in Ireland,* pp. 71-72.
43. N. J. Gibson, "The Irish Problem," *Holy Cross Quarterly* 6 (1974): 6-19, p. 18 quoted.

CHAPTER 5

Learning to Be Violent

"At this point in Belfast [1971] the kids play at riots. They use tomato sauce for blood Monday, then see real blood on Tuesday. Fantasy and reality exist side by side. Some of these kids can't tell the difference any more."[1]

"Few sights can be more harrowing than the daily spectacle of files of youngsters flanked with soldiers going to and from school—Catholics on one side of the street, Protestants on the other."[2]

The Belfast child psychiatrist spoke his deep concern. The quotations give an intimate glance behind mass media reports. They suggest a little of the tensions with which children now live in a Northern Ireland Orange or Green ghetto.

When other recourses are at least theoretically available, why waste lives and substance in actual and feared violence? Especially, why should children have to grow up in such a distorting environment? Some light on these questions can come from studying patterns of personal socialization within the ethnic and class groups involved in such a situation as the current civil war in Northern Ireland.

As we saw in the previous chapter, even though the fuel for conflict existed in Northern Ireland and had burst into flames many times before, none of the participating groups was prepared to cope with violence on the scale into which it began to escalate. They organized from event to event. Among police and military, as well as among vigilantes, terror begot terror. In this chapter, let us look briefly at how social contexts of various class and ethnic groups condition people to make violent reactions to interpersonal irritants and opportunities and at how certain typical socializing experiences of childhood and youth are shaped by those social contexts.

Are British and Irish cultures and subcultures violence-prone? It is evident that they have potentialities for both violence and nonviolence. A student of violence in Irish society, Conor O'Neill, agrees with many other social scientists when he concludes, "Physical violence is a cultural trait ... which has evolved within a particular sub-culture. It is transmitted from generation to generation in the same manner as other cultural traits, i.e. the young are constantly being socialized to behave in this manner."[3]

Conditions of current industrial and imperialist society brutalize most obviously those who are persistently excluded from the so-called social system. These are people sometimes called "roughs" or "ne'er-do-wells" but who require a less value-charged term, perhaps lower-lower class or underclass. These include groups notably violence-prone whether they are Orange, Green, West English, Scottish, Welsh, Cockney, or plain English. At the same time, this brutalization has its significant and often alarming ramifications throughout the other classes of society.

Many organized efforts that we have mentioned and will discuss in more detail later illustrate commitments to nonviolent reaction patterns on many social levels and among the various ethnic segments. They demonstrate how even the violence-prone can be led as individuals and sometimes as groups to support nonviolent alternatives.

At first glance, the middle- and upper-class districts of Northern Ireland might appear to be less involved in the current struggle, but this is a delusion. Admittedly, these neighborhoods still tend to be unsegregated, even though they are—as they always have been—disproportionately Protestant. Such districts have been visited by only an occasional shooting or bombing, chiefly of political leaders, but their residents' preoccupation with the struggle is very deep—albeit less obvious than among working-class people. Their ethnocentrism appears to be just as great, but their ways of participating in the province's internecine conflict are less direct, more conspiratorial, as befits their traditional roles in this society as small-time entrepreneurs, resident managers for British or multinational corporations, professionals, and skilled technicians. These are prejudiced roles for which their families, schools, and play groups equip them.

Symptomatic of the reactions of both Roman Catholics and Protestants among the more privileged are their high rates of emigration; their absenteeism in the Republic, Great Britain, and elsewhere; their increased tendency to send their children to boarding schools in Great Britain or in the Republic; and the great difficulty with which competent managers and professional or technical personnel are recruited. Their families and the "playing fields" frequented by these people as they grow up teach them to reject Christian moral ideals in interethnic and interclass relations and to engage in group-centric conspiratorial acts in terms of a discreet and gentlepersonly etiquette. Members of these classes who serve as provincial and local administrative, legislative, and judicial officials have to confront the open conflict more directly. They are often confused and frustrated by their lack of credibility among the lower classes.

In one sense the involvement of business people in the conflict is more complicated than that of public officials, but in another sense, it is relatively more simple! It is more complicated because of the necessary relations of Northern Ireland's business elites with networks of control and with struggles for power centering in London, New York City, and other world capitalist centers. It is simpler to the extent that decisions can be made by an elite group *in camera* on the basis of stereotypical assumptions. They may give little heed to a possible public accounting, and therefore decision making may concentrate solely on benefits to the controllers of a corporation, too often with little reference to their publics and even less to society more generally. They trust subservient governmental officials to "clean up any mess," as it were, that their decisions might create. One cannot help but think of the same people in childhood or youth plotting a neighborhood feat of derring-do in their favorite hangout. They were not sissies or "momma's boys" or "momma's girls." They knew how to "play the game"! The spirit in which they carry out their exploits has changed in little but complexity and suavity between the hangout and the board room.

As far as violence is concerned, female socializing experiences tend to resemble more those of men as they join the movement toward "women's lib." Anthropologist Margaret Mead asserts: "The boys' gang ... is a desperate defensive measure against being sissies ... but the girls are also busy not being sissies."[4] To judge from the Northern Ireland experiences, this development—slower to arrive there than in Great Britain—is helping to assimilate women into violent activities and thus to spread the social base of those available for vigilante combat, as well as for aggressive nonviolent efforts.[5]

Decision-makers' relations with violence are largely abstract. They make plans as to policy and strategy, order their implementation, but the blood seldom flows in their conference rooms and command posts. When they are aware at all of what their decisions cost in human degradation and even in lives, they take recourse to the "higher strategy" or "basic cost benefit" rationales of entrepreneurs, politicians, generals, and gangsters: There was *nothing personal* in the decision. They just had to be "objective." They demonstrate again "that men [and women] of power and the criminals in our society are distinguished only in their situation, not their morality."[6]

The thought that violence pervades one's own society at all times and not just during current "troubles" is more than most people can frankly face.

It requires people to perceive the extent to which violence is permitted and used or stimulated by both informal family and public exploitative practices. Who wants to ponder how greatly business, politics, police, and military work is dominated by morals-rejecting, conspiratorial thinking? Who wants to perceive what these patterns owe to unhappy family life and to juvenile groups mockingly imitative of their elders' delinquencies? This is one reason we do not seriously seek to reflect in social policy an understanding of violence and its causes, to cope constructively with more than just its symptoms, perhaps to find dependable alternatives for it—either in Ireland or anywhere else.

The two social strata most obviously involved in the current conflict are the upper-lowers and the underclass. The upper-lowers are the families of wage earners who have achieved a sense of occupational and community identity. In defense of their tenuous positions, they have a strong attachment to being "respectable." They do what they can to maintain appearances. They flatter themselves on their "independence." They look down on those who have to accept charity. On the other hand, the underclass gives the appearance of defeat. Their men and women are at best marginally employed. They include casual laborers, the chronically unemployed, and criminals.

The underclass lives with, gains prestige from, and treasures memories of violent events. Even though there may be neutralizing devices available and sometimes used, underclass men in particular feel they have to face up violently to an interpersonal challenge or challenging situation. Those who fail to meet such a problem bravely in a pub or on the street characterize themselves as weak and available for abuse. Certain families, blocks of flats, and employments thus become reputed for toughness.

As viewed from the perspectives of these classes, the Northern Ireland struggle arises from the efforts by the Orange segment to monopolize upper-lower-class statuses, to keep as many of the Green in the underclass as possible. At the outset of the current overt conflict, two of the largest employers (Harland and Wolff, Mackies) were said to have numbered only 620 Roman Catholic manual workers among 17,500 employees.[7] The coincidence of class level and ethno-religious label was then especially marked in the province's second city, Derry. There "no-one familiar with the place will confuse the genuine confidence of constant success with the superficial cockiness of constant failure" between the "Prod" upper-lower class and the "Papish" underclass. They even called them "doers and dossers."[8]

Parallels between the Green middle class and their American black equivalent are striking. On the one hand, "Prods have a blitheness that won't acknowledge the existence of workies and allows them to carry on with their Puritanism or wife swapping, whichever takes their fancy." On the other, the Roman Catholic middle-class members have an awareness of their proximity to the lower class and especially the underclass that haunts them, "an awareness that forces them into a desperate emulation of the Prods to try to hold their slender advantage."[9]

The identities of cultural characteristics of the Green and Orange lowers confuse both foreign journalists and British soldiers. "A Protestant Orange Order march, with its drumming and its chanting and its rowdy King Billy patriotism, is as much a piece of Irish bravura as an I.R.A. funeral, with its company of scrubbed and uniformed virgins presenting rifles over a hero's grave."[10] In spite of such confusing similarities that can be detailed and that permeate modal personality types, the groups called Orange and Green are separate, self-segregating, polarized, contending segments of the population with carefully nurtured ethnic differences. Members of each can quickly identify members of the other group by observing one or several of these indicators: accent, life style, given name if not surname, school attended, athletic interests, other pastimes, home location, or names of friends or references. Their church label is not needed, as the reports of the provincial Fair Employment Agency point out.

Conflict can take place in any interpersonal situation—between parents, neighbors, or strangers, between a parent and a child, among siblings, among unrelated youngsters who are associates or strangers. As children grow, their reactions of antagonism or compromise or ignoring to irritating situations become more and more conditioned by the roles they learn in the various groups in which they become habitual participants. These early groups, because of their indelible influence on children's patterns of thought and behavior, serve as prototypes for participation in later groups throughout life, subject to whatever adjustments experiences dictate. Of special concern in such developments as the Northern Ireland struggles are the participant roles of children and youth in family, sibling, controlled peer, and autonomous peer groups.

Let us look at the general character of such groups and then at how they vary among social class and ethnic groups in Northern Ireland. In order to do so, it is first necessary to define several terms to be employed in the discussion. Reference is to culture, subculture, multivalence, and monovalence, as well as to the types of group just mentioned.[11]

The term, culture, is commonly used in social science both in a general and in more specific or limited senses. Comprehensively, it refers to "patterns, explicit and implicit, of and for behavior acquired and transmitted by symbols, constituting the distinctive achievements of human groups, including their embodiments in artifacts." The symbols referred to embrace non-verbal ones such as gestures and role modeling as well as spoken and written communications. On the society-wide level, the "core of culture consists of traditional (i.e., historically derived and selected) ideas and especially their attached values."[12] These societal patterns are usefully labeled conventions and morals. Morals are conventions or customary patterns to which greater societal sanction or sense of value is attached.

As the foregoing implies, there are levels of culture in any society that are more or less related and more or less in contrast or even in conflict. In other words, cultures are multivalent. They include not only conventions and morals typical of the society in general. They also number the compulsive patterns—folkways and mores[13]—that are typical of a society's various class and ethnic segments and of socialization groups within those segments. Morals are parts of societal ideologies and rituals related to economic, political, family, and religious activities and beliefs. Among class and ethnic segments, there tends to be more agreement on moral symbols than on their meaning. Mores are group mandates for behavior with which people live more intimately in their various group contexts. In their own habits and covert sentiments, they adapt societal and group patterns to more individual considerations to the extent that they appear expedient. Group cultures are often called *subcultures*.

Table 1 provides a résumé of the relations among the terms mentioned above. The definitions used for the terms are those to be found in most dictionaries, sharpened for our purposes here. The terms are tabulated thus in order to indicate a little more clearly the ways in which they are associated. These relationships are not often made at all clear. For example, the omnipresent fact of multivalence in society's structure and of individual multivalence as an habitual adaptation to societal multivalence requires emphasis in this discussion of how people learn to be violent because societal morals glorify compromise and other nonviolent recourses. The following offers further definitions and illustrations.

Such early groupings in one's experiences of social life as those of mother and self, of the family, of siblings alone, of controlled peers outside the family, and of relatively autonomous peers furnish experiences that lead to differing collections of attitudes, values, and patterns for action that become multivalent facets of a "mature" personality. Is this to say that a "mature" person is schizoid, has a split personality? To a degree this is typically the case, but for the "mature" it is not to a pathological degree. In contrast, the schizoid individual caricatures the "normal" by being awkward,

Table 1.
Résumé: How People Relate to Multivalent Society

Level of Social Organization	Patterns or Traits	Central Patterns	Internalized in Self as:	Verbal Applications	Role Types	Institutional Function	Largely Derived from:
Societal	Conventions (a culture)	Morals	Nuclear superego or conscience	Opinions of *the* public	People-as-they-should-be (cultural cloaks); societal personalities	Institution-as-it-should-be (cultural façade)	Traditional and customary societal stereotypes that idealize selected folkways and mores
Group	Folkways (a subculture)	Mores	A configuration of attitudes	Opinions of *a* public	People-as-they-have-to-be (operating traits); social personalities	Association-as-it-has-to-be (operating traits)	Customary group generalizations of selected practices and habits
Personal (overt and multivalent)	Practices	Habits	Colorations of superego, other attitudes	Typical personal opinions	A person as he or she appears to be; individual stances	Creature, carrier, creator, and manipulator	Societal and group patterns, participation in social process, maturational social experiences
Self (covert and multivalent)	Attitudes	Sentiments	Thoughts		A person as he or she is	Adaptations to self's needs, desires, understandings, aspirations	Societal and group patterns, participation in social process, maturational social experiences

Source: Adapted from A. McC. Lee, *Multivalent Man* (New York: George Braziller, 1966), p. 75.

inadequate or inappropriate in responses, and hence more or less neurotic in reactions to the various aspects of society's multivalent complexities. The "normal" individual can be relatively stable and integrated in the sense of functioning customarily and hence "maturely" in a variety of social environments. This means being inconsistent in order to deal appropriately with society's inconsistencies. Stated otherwise, the "mature" are habitually compliant with different group expectations and with other situational opportunities and pressures for which custom prepares them.

A student of propaganda, Edward S. Herman, relates personal and social multivalence to social manipulations thus:

> People have a lot to hide, from themselves as well as from their neighbors. Countries also have a lot to hide, more from their own people than from outsiders. In each country a web of myths evolves that allows the loyal citizenry to feel good about their nation, that depicts it and its people as generous, progressive, decent to a fault in its institutional behavior. People who question these myths, whether myths about a beneficent past, or the myths currently employed to put today's actions and policies in a favorable light, are thus highly offensive to good taste and basic feelings of right and wrong. These doubters of myths may even pose a threat to communal integration and policy, which rest on the foundation of myths, and societies therefore usually have methods for containing or squelching critics who raise such questions.[14]

In this quotation, the "web of myths" refers to societal morals as they are symbolized and taught. Fear of doubters and critics make it difficult for most people to understand multivalence, the powerful roles of hypocrisy in human relations. It is so much easier to be a manipulable "normal" believer than to try to be an autonomous perceiver. Society would have much less promise than it does without those autonomous perceivers—artists, social scientists, and social actionists—that we have.

Socialization groups and their folkways and mores provide prototypes we use in the processes of living that remain influential upon our thoughts and behavior throughout life. They shape future anticipations about family life and about relations with parent substitutes, peers in controlled and in autonomous groups, and strangers. They provide patterns for thought and action we try to use not only as we grow up but also later. For example, fellow employees sometimes fit into our conceptions of fellow members of controlled groups and sometimes of autonomous groups; it depends upon how we view them and relate them to the parent-substitute management and to ourselves. The autonomous peer relationship is usually clearer in pub roistering and group-centered conspiratorial efforts. An insiders' strategy conference in the higher circles of the Royal Ulster Constabulary, the Provisional Irish Republican Army, or the House of Commons at Westminster has much in common in spirit and action with one in teen-age autonomous peer groups, modified among them chiefly by class and ethnic differences.

Controlled and autonomous peer groups have typically one significant difference. *Controlled* peer groups are supervised play and school groups and their successors. They have about them something of the air of a sibling-substitute group in that a person resembling a parent substitute is present or felt to be involved. The teacher, playground director, adult sponsor of an organization, or employer functions as a surrogate of societal or class or ethnic controls and values, an authority figure unmixed with the more intimate ties of love and frustration/rejection of an actual parent. On the other hand, relatively *autonomous* peer groups are the more or less egalitarian and at least self-structuring play and identity groups (clubs, gangs, cliques) of children and youth of both sexes and their succeeding and similar groups in adult life. They tend to be conspiratorial, critical of the values idealized by their parents, or, in the case of adult versions of such groups, critical of societal values inconvenient for or opposed to their own group or individual aspirations and procedures.

It is instructive to try to observe another person in a day's activities to the extent that this is possible, especially in such a place as Belfast. Even though people there tend to be indelibly labeled as to their position in the ongoing current struggle, a given individual "seems to be a different person" with his or her children, with a spouse, with a political or business associate, with a stranger. It makes one wonder at the ease with which such a "well-adjusted" person makes words and actions fit different situations without hesitation, embarrassment, or consistency. For that matter, as much can be said about people in any society. The cleavages in a conflict-ridden society may sometimes only appear to make such inconsistencies more obvious.

This splitting of the self in terms of the social personalities we develop, the roles we perform, starts in our early childhood. The individual learns very young, as the sociologist C. H. Cooley notes, "to be different things to different people, showing that he begins to apprehend personality and to foresee its operation." Among his illustrations of this Cooley points to how "children often behave worse with their mother than with other and less sympathetic people."[15] An Irish journalist tells of girls and boys going to separate but neighboring schools with separate playgrounds "for little girls must grow up with different manners from little boys. But after school they'll all be on the road home together, satchel on back, exchanging the tales which belong to the great freemasonry of children."[16] They do not share the school controlled environment, but after school they participate together in sibling and autonomous peer groups. As the writer hints, the values and habit patterns of the members of these groups are different.

It is interesting to observe a child discovering that parents have a different community of interests between themselves and a different kind of identification with other adults than with their child. Children find that they can discuss some things more readily and freely with other children, with other members of a play group, than with a parent or sibling. A mother or father shows surprise at how different a son or daughter acts among peers away from the presence of parents or parent substitutes. Much of this ease in slipping from one role, from one set of valences, one social personality, into another comes from our long habituation in the etiquette of group identifications, in thought and behavior keyed to group referents. This "division of the man into several selves," as the psychologist William James discerned, "may be a discordant splitting, as where one is afraid to let one set of his acquaintances know him as he is elsewhere; or it may be a perfectly harmonious division of labor, as where one tender to his children is stern to the soldiers or prisoners under his commond."[17]

Social scientific literature contains a wealth of studies of childhood and youth peer groups, but such studies are typically from the outside and often carry in them an assumption that personality develops monovalently rather than multivalently. They tend to gloss over the significance of contrasting social personality portrayals in different group contexts. Sibling and autonomous peer groups are especially difficult for an outside observer to penetrate. Intimacies of the family repel invaders, and so do the defensive alliances of nonsibling peers. Since the would-be observers of such groups are often intellectuals whose own childhood and youth were untypical of those to be studied, the confusion of the characteristics of the various kinds of socialization groups has been extensive and distorting.[18]

Before returning more specifically to the discussion of socialization groups, let us look first at some more background information: According to the Department of Health and Social Services, 38 percent of Northern Ireland households in 1976 were deemed "poor."[19] In this connection is cited the large portion of housing deemed "unfit," 20 percent of all housing in the province and 50 percent in Belfast. The current "troubles" are exacer-

Learning to Be Violent   109

bating this situation. In 1969–73, some 50,000 people in Belfast were relocated. Most notably Roman Catholic families "became concentrated in a few parts of the city (mainly in the west), whilst Protestant families moved out of fewer areas to many parts of Belfast." West Belfast became especially overcrowded. These movements were further complicated by "the rent and rates strike which began in response to internment [of suspects without trial], squatting on an extensive scale [in empty houses] and, in some areas, control over housing allocation being exercised by paramilitary organisations."[20]

Couple these findings with the following official figures: Unemployment is typically the highest of any area in the United Kingdom. In 1971–80, the wholly unemployed rose from 8.3 to 13.7 percent of the "economically active" population, and then to 21.5 in August 1982, with percentages of 15.9 in Belfast, 34.3 in Cookstown, 28.1 in Derry, 34.4 in Dungannon, and 31.2 in Newry. Roman Catholic West Belfast—with a rate above 55 percent—has a disproportionate part of that city's unemployed, and the other towns mentioned are heavily Roman Catholic. In addition to this picture are those reduced to or continued on part-time employment and those "economically inactive."[21] This is all coupled with low average wages and with electricity costs about 40 percent higher than in Great Britain, and gas, twice the British price. As one consequence of these and related conditions, in 1977 the perinatal (21.1), infant mortality (17.2), and stillbirth (12.0) rates per thousand were as usual the highest for any part of the United Kingdom. For that matter, "on all available indicators the health of the population is poor."[22]

In view of the foregoing information, the educationist Joan I. Harbison observes that it is not surprising that "in areas of concentrated social malaise within urban Belfast and other towns ... are ... the highest incidence of violence and conflict." As she points out, "The number of children held for grave offenses in Northern Ireland is 13 times the rate of England and Wales."[23]

With that brief and dismal background, let us now turn again to the roles socialization groups play in learning to be violent. Special reference is to be given to the lower classes.

What is it like to grow up in an overcrowded home with inadequate amenities in Northern Ireland? My wife and I have visited many such homes and have talked at length with many social workers and other observers who have had much more extensive experience with them than we have, but in the space available only general suggestions as to their nature can be furnished. Certain systematic reports and some impressionistic accounts provide additional information. A few of these are cited.

This is a society in which people's activities are rather precisely divided by sex as well as by class and ethnic distinctions. In consequence, family conditions still bear some resemblance to those found by the famous labor leader James Connolly and reported by him in 1915. He expressed deep concern about the status of women in Dublin's and Belfast's families and industries. As he wrote: "The daughters of the Irish peasantry have been the cheapest slaves in existence—slaves of their own family, who were, in turn, slaves to all social parasites of a landlord and gombeen-ridden community."[24] (A "gombeen" is, in the Irish language, an usurious moneylender.) Between the welfare state's aid to the poor and the opposition of vigilante groups to gombeen operations, by the 1970s "those parasites who were still thriving on the hardship of the poor" were far less numerous. "It is one of the few socially beneficial actions to their [the paramilitary groups'] credit."[25]

Particularly in lower-class homes, such a "slave of slaves" functions as a wife and mother dedicated to husband, children, and church whether Roman Catholic or Protestant. Her parents raised her to believe that her security would depend upon a husband and children in this heavily man-centered society. She does much to help set the nature of mother-child, father-child, and intersibling relational patterns in the traditional molds. In Belfast and Derry, this is more and more accompanied by a role reversal in which the wife becomes the breadwinner, a blow to the tradition-sustained male psyche. For all the wife's frustrations, employment complications, difficulties with a frustrated husband, and discouraging facilities, she focuses on the problems she sees as those of childrearing and salvation in a community torn by conflict. Little wonder that this is associated with the outlet she finds in her "corrective" physical violence to her children.

In this environment, the husband has only "male" duties in his home: no cooking, no changing of nappies (diapers), no dishwashing. He might do some needed carpentry work or take some older boys to a football match, but problems with younger children including the wheeling of a baby in a pram are for his wife to do. Whether employed or unemployed, he often flees to the male comforts of a bar, club, or street corner. Such outlets for extreme frustration as gambling, drunkenness, communal violence, wifebeating, and divorce "Irish style" (through emigration and disappearance) are not uncommon. For his children, he provides not only a model of ineffectuality in dealing with a society controlled by others but also of masculine bravura. This aspect of the father model may be that of a veteran, a vigilante, a part- or full-time policeman, a part- or full-time soldier, or some combination of these. As one observer puts it, "Day begins in a violent home where guns are casually displayed on the kitchen table."[26]

A father or older brother who becomes a Prod or Provo vigilante ceases to be a pathetic loafer or ineffectual part-time worker: he is a hero, one to be emulated. A mother who defies a police raid and search of the home gives a daughter a different dimension of the female model.

These lower-class homes thus "provide a child-rearing atmosphere of conformity values, a submissive 'uncritical' attitude toward idealized authorities of the in group, a tendency to condemn, reject, and punish people who violate [their] conventional values." As the social psychologist Rona M. Fields, on the basis of her extensive and intensive field studies in Northern Ireland, continues: "Add to this the experience of belonging to a minority group that is the target of strong prejudice—a situation common to both the Protestant and Catholic populations—and the self-influence of that pressure becomes a determinant in developing self-protective schemata and expectations of violence and disaster."[27] The pervasion of all Northern Irish classes with this conformism, prejudice, and fear of prejudice underlies the whole continuing social tragedy.

High points for which families make great financial sacrifices are marriages, funerals, and preparations for participation in parades and confrontations. Such efforts and attending athletic events or participating in security clashes lift them temporarily out of the grinding routine of trying to find enough resources to get by from day to day.

The child psychiatrist and community worker Morris Fraser sums up the situation thus: "The standards of behaviour in a Belfast working-class area, Catholic or Protestant, are in fact as rigid as those of the Royal Enclosure at Ascot. The growing boy, picking his way painfully through the maze of selective reinforcement, slowly learns the hard lessons of life—the right language, the right clothes, the right degree of male asser tiveness—that men are men, and boys are men."[28] This obsessive need for boys and men to assert their masculinity leads to vandalism, an inclination to attack authority, upon which the underground vigilante organizations are able to build.

In discussing the moral absolutism—the bigotry—of Northern Irish society, a psychologist, Ken Heskin, concludes that there is nothing strange "about the attitudes of ... youngsters under the circumstances." The problem, as he sees it, is that "such attitudes so frequently appear to persist into adulthood."[29] Our studies in Northern Ireland and elsewhere and those of some others conclude that such persistance of role models and other group patterns into adulthood anywhere is not unusual.[30] The efforts of middle-class teachers and clergy to offset the influence of brutalizing lower-class conditions on the attitudes of youngsters are to be discussed in the following.

Developmental psychologists, novelists, journalists, and participant-observing social scientists help us to sense how childhood groups function among boys and girls and how those groups and their roles and subcultures serve as prototypes in adult minds and actions for some significant subsequent group patterns of participation. For our purposes here, sibling, controlled, and autonomous peer groups are especially significant.

In a sense, participations in sibling and controlled peer groups are steps toward activity in autonomous peer groups and the adult world. Especially in large families, the conspiracies, competitions, and conflicts within groups of siblings under some parental mediation, stimulation, and control are preparations for the ways in which the offspring will view the outside world. Such controlled peer groups as those in a classroom represent a shift from the intimate juggling of opportunities and favors and penalities in the home to a more formal, even ritualized set of relationships. For lower-class children, the middle-class teacher attempts to resocialize them in terms of moral and especially moral-actionist preachments acceptable to the status quo.

For both boys and girls, but especially for boys, autonomous peer groups are opportunities for more effective revolt against the compulsions of the mother-dominated home and the establishment-dominated classroom. Speculations or gossip about activities in adult peer groups provide children of both sexes with attractive ideas and justifications for what they try to do in their relatively autonomous play and activity groups. When fathers and older brothers are fighting the Prods, the Provos, or the Brits, when a relative is a heroic prisoner, it is all the more legitimate—they think—to form stone-throwing gangs.

For both boys and men, autonomous peer groups are vehicles for the expression of an uneasy and conspiratorial sexism, machoism, recourses to "masculine" brutality and violence, contempt for "feminine" moral contentions, and extreme clannishness. Members of such autonomous peer groups are typically ready to make "hard decisions" that apparently serve the group members' self-interests, at least in the anticipated short run. Such decisions frequently dehumanize others and even subject outsiders to inconsiderate or violent measures. References to longer-term disasters that might arise in part as a consequence of such "hard decisions" tend to be rejected as "speculative" or irrelevant, whether in a boys' gang, a vigilante meeting, or a corporate board session.

An observer points to the pervasive manner in which television and gossip carry the examples of revolting autonomous peer gang members to growing children: "I heard Belfast's eight- and ten-year-old Catholic children asking mothers and fathers if they might begin a sympathetic fast" during the Maze Prison hunger strike of Bobby Sands and others in 1981. In documenting the province's strife, television has even pictured "a boy throwing a rock or a gasoline-filled bottle, a girl facing down (with features twisted in anger) one of her majesty's clean-cut Tommies—himself tired, annoyed, and just perceptibly humiliated."[31]

Both Protestant and Roman Catholic unemployed males from twelve to twenty years of age form gangs and are called hoods. As John Conroy, an observer, puts it, they engage in "petty theft, usually burglary or shoplifting in city center shops." They even at night take cars, "not as a money making venture, but just to relieve their boredom." This has resulted in the army killing a few of them. "For some of these joyriders, the shootings are a deterrent; for others, they are an attraction."[32]

Parts of an autobiographical document written by a leader in a Loyalist paramilitary organization with the pen name of Sam Sloan take us more deeply into the behavior of some lower-class socialization groups in Belfast's Shankill area: He recalls his primary school's "enforcer," its headmaster, who "was extremely vicious in his use of the cane. We hated him. We did our best to make his life a misery." This alienating experience stimulated conspiratorial gang formation that spilled over into the community. Gangs of four or five turned to "a well organised spree of pilfering." They also liked the illegal gambling game of the streets, pitch-and-toss, a game that got Sloan "some cigarette money watching out for the law." Great occasions for the boys were the election-time street carnivals and the annual Twelfth of July Orange parades. Those parades inspired the autonomous gang members: "When I was a child I watched with awe the colorful spectacle of tens of thousands of Orangemen, marching four abreast, carrying pikes, swords and banners."[33]

When one wanders through the slum streets of Belfast or Derry, as others have remarked, one gets a sense of foreboding, even terror, in spite of the fact that nothing might be happening. It is not horror at people; it is a sense of horror that society should come to subjecting people to this.

Formal educational efforts to make lower-class children conform to middle-class idealizations of social behavior provide significant insights into the whole problem of how such children persist in their brutalized ways. In such educational efforts, the Protestant and Roman Catholic clergy perform crucial roles. Ecclesiastics utilize religious rhetoric both in churches and in church-controlled or church-operated schools in order to explain and justify the existing sex, class, and ethnic divisions. A critical Roman Catholic priest, Desmond Wilson of Belfast, looks upon this pervasive ideological effort as the way in which the churches maintain dependency.

As he states,

> ... the problem is not that Catholics and Protestants don't know how to live together, they're never allowed to. They weren't allowed to integrate education, to declericalise society, to change mixed marriage laws. There wasn't a single department of life into which some institution did not come in order to prevent people coming together naturally and forming alliances. At every turn, in sport, politics, education, marriage, even burial, power-groups interfered to prevent people coming together.[34]

Even though few clerics explicitly sanction vigilante activities, not only politicians and governmental officials but also leaders of underground paramilitary bodies exploit the results of clerical—backed by family—indoctrination.

The churches on the whole support the politico-economic status quo and assert that they have the personal answers to people's insecurity, answers embraced in religious salvation. Their clergy talk generally about social ills, but leave social actions to politicians and the state. Only extremist clerics give any explicit sanction to the Prod and Provo vigilantes who regard themselves as front-line defenders of the two minority communities.

The report of an official Advisory Council for Education in Northern Ireland in 1973 gives a clear impression of the manner in which church representatives succeed in blocking efforts to weaken their control of schools: The report accepts the fact that "basically our system is divided into schools attended by children of Protestant background and schools attended by children of Roman Catholic background." Since many in the province have "affirmed their regret at this situation," the Council "invited representatives of different churches to discuss the question with us." These church people stressed as principal obstacles to integration the problems of busing among segregated communities, of what to do with teaching members of religious orders, of the possibility of encouraging mixed marriages, and of the weakening of identities and social ties. The latter quite political point is stated thus: "Emphasis is laid less on the time spent specifically in the teaching of religious doctrine in schools than on the atmosphere which should permeate the whole of school life. Where it is held that this atmosphere must be clearly characteristic of the teaching of one church integration is not possible." Like many another body advising educational policies for the province, this one agreed that "it would be unrealistic to expect the introduction of integrated schools in the near future."[35]

Stimulated by an organization in Northern Ireland known as All Children Together, the Westminster parliament enacted the Education (Northern Ireland) Act of 1978. It was "to enable integrated education to develop in Northern Ireland where the majority of the parents desired it." It was to add a third to the "two main categories of schools, Controlled and Maintained. The former are entirely State run under the Department of Education ... and for the most part attended by Protestant children, taught by Protestant teachers, under Protestant managers. The latter are supported by public funds but teaching and management lie almost entirely in the hands of the Roman Catholic Church to which the pupils belong." The leaders of All Children Together were "disappointed that more use has not been made of its [the act's] enabling provisions, even though several public opinion surveys have revealed that a majority of parents would favour integrated education." In 1981, therefore, the same group founded Lagan College, "the first deliberately integrated Christian, all-ability, post-primary school for the education of boys and girls to be opened in Northern Ireland in this century." When it has operated on private funds for two or three years, it will be eligible for grant-aid status similar to that provided to Roman Catholic maintained schools. With this status, tax funds are available to cover 85 percent of capital costs and all running expenses. Lay Roman Catholics are sharing fully with Protestants in the college's funding and personnel.

This enabling act was "given repeated assurances of support from the Protestant Churches," but these "sentiments were not shared by the Catholic Hierarchy, which re-affirmed its insistence that *all* Catholic children should be educated in Catholic schools."[36]

All too often, intentions expressed about some vague future development fail to be transformed into practical social efforts. "Despite their synod resolutions, etc.," representatives of the Church of Ireland "would not push or take any initiatives: parents would have to do this—particularly the R.C. parents—but they would support experiments." Presbyterians similarly "recognised the past resolutions of their Assembly in favour of integration," but they "felt that pilot schemes should come first, and that the initiative should come from parents." Methodists "wanted to support pilot schemes," but they "were thinly represented on school management committees." All the Protestants in effect put the ostensible blame on the Roman Catholics; they did not want to "Countenance anything that might jeopardise ecumenical relations with the Catholic Hierarchy."[36] A. E. C. W. Spencer, a Roman Catholic leader of the ecumenical education organization All Children Together, concludes: "The Churches have *not* promoted pilot schemes, and school principals feel so exposed to ecclesiastical censure that only the boldest of them will even consider pilot schemes of interschool cooperation. ... Church representatives put power first and values second."[36]

An interim report in June 1980 by another official advisory panel, called the Chilver Review Body, urged the amalgamation of St. Mary's and St. Joseph's, the two voluntary Roman Catholic teachers' training colleges, and their relocation together with the provincially controlled teachers' education facilities in a Belfast Centre for Teacher Education. This was "not to replace the existing institutions ... but to permit them to continue to make academically strong and distinctive contributions to teacher education."[37] This proposal for constructive affiliation rather than consolidation met with the same resistance as other cooperative projects.

Even though Roman Catholics constitute only one-third of this ghetto-splotched province, 47.3 percent of the more than 360,000 pupils are in grant-aided (also called maintained) Roman Catholic controlled schools. They constitute 47.4 percent of the primary and 47.1 percent of the secondary pupils. The figures reflect the fact that the crude annual birthrate for Roman Catholics as of the 1971 census was 25.5 per 1,000, more than two-fifths higher than that (17.9) for Protestants. A survey report by the Ulster Pregnancy Advisory Association, however, stresses "the rapidity with which Roman Catholic attitudes to family planning are changing."[38]

A basic issue in this struggle for control of children's minds and loyalties is the possible encroachment of a general secular faith placed either in the state or in humanity, or somehow in both, at the expense of exclusively "religious" faiths. The manner in which such a secular faith in government has succeeded in minimizing intersectarian conflict in the United States impresses many intellectuals, and to judge by opinion polls, it has a rising number of popular supporters in Northern Ireland. As we have seen, however, it is a possible relinquishment of power that church leaders do not wish to make.

Unfortunately, lessons available on educational policies since 1973 in the integrated Lisnevin School for young offenders are not widely enough known, appreciated, and accepted. In that establishment, "young offenders from both sides of the Irish religious divide were brought together in the close living conditions of a residential setting." Community violence had reached new heights, and the inmates came "from areas which had known much trouble," especially from the bitterly sectarian Belfast ghettos. These children, "usually, within two or three days, adapted to the prevailing ethos in the school and made friends regardless of religion. Sectarian hostility was minimal and it was a common observation that quite deep friendships were formed."³⁹

The possibility of classroom socialization effectively offsetting the ethnic and class antagonisms of the homes and street gangs is thus reduced by the conflicting aims served by the schools. Instead of being dedicated single-mindedly to the preparation of children for practical roles in the politico-economic world, the schools are preoccupied with maintaining church constituencies and inculcating middle-class respect for established authority.

In order to get a better impression of the relations among the socialization groups, let us look at some experiences of children in the Ardoyne section of north Belfast. Serious rioting in this largely Roman Catholic area in August 1969 included explosions and the burning of more than 100 homes and many public houses. On 15 and 16 August, 26 civilians (15 Roman Catholics and 11 Protestants) were wounded by gunshot, and one man was killed.⁴⁰ The army finally moved in on the 16th and continued in the district to provide among other services "the 'lollipop patrols' which escort the rival groups home from school." On the secondary level in that area, Protestants attend Everton (girls) and Somerdale (boys) schools; Roman Catholics go to St. Gemma's (girls) and St. Gabriel's (boys). As two teachers in those schools, one Roman Catholic and the other Protestant, assert: "there are very few areas of cooperation between the schools and even less common ground between the two communities. The physical evidence of the division is everywhere."⁴¹

In describing the impact of community violence on pupils at St. Gabriel's Secondary School in 1969–72, teacher Alphonsus M. Thornton reported no dramatic incidents but "an inexorable progression downhill" in the "effects of civil unrest, on the pupils individually, and on the school." Here are some details, as Thornton describes them:

> 1969–70. Our area had suffered ... massive population shifts. When classes resumed in September there were about one hundred pupils missing. However, as time went on many showed up, some of them travelling quite a distance from their new homes. There did not seem to be any significant effect on pupils. This I would attribute partly to the quieter situation then obtaining, and partly to the resilience of youth. There was a deep, solid hatred for the police and "B" specials [part-time citizen police] who were, rightly or wrongly, blamed for what had happened. Very little reference was made to "Prods" [Protestants] as such—a significant point to which I will return later.

1970–71. Trouble had re-started. There was continual heavy army raiding (I have personally confirmed numerous instances of brutality) and the people retaliated often and as viciously as they could. The media made great play at the time of children out stoning troops. Horrifying it certainly was, and also quite inevitable in the circumstances. In school, latecomers were more numerous; we began to notice changes in pupil's attitudes: it seemed as though to them there was a certain unreality about the normality of school, as if school was somehow not relevant to the real, exciting outside world. But we had no disciplinary problems of any consequence, and examination classes were still achieving reasonable standards. In reply to the hordes of inquirers from all the news media we could say that the pupils did not seem to be greatly affected by the troubles, but how could they fail to be? The conclusion was quite sinister and inescapable: violence, insecurity, raids, stonings and shootings had become a normal way of life. ...

Naturally, the object of their hatred (an ugly word, but unfortunately the only valid one in the circumstances) was now the army, who were unfairly discriminating between them and "the Orangemen"—not the "Prods," be it noted.

1971–72. Internment [of suspects without trial beginning 9 August 1971] brought in its train more population shifts and the burning of two hundred houses, not to mention the horrific outbreak of violence. ... Back at school, we found about a hundred pupils missing, of whom some twenty or thirty have drifted back since. Many fathers and brothers have been seized, brutalised and interned; very many more were on the run. I need scarcely comment upon the effect of broken homes on young people. As the year went on the raids and internments continued, never was a community so gathered in upon itself—down to the last child. Although, miraculously, no pupils lost their lives, several recent past pupils were killed and we had funerals and Requiem Masses to underline the tragic situation around us.

The effects are now clear. There is a high rate of absenteeism and latecoming; it is more and more difficult to interest boys in class-work; there is an upsurge of buffoonery, noisiness, excitability. Class-work is suffering and teachers are feeling the strain. Teachers' authority is not being *directly* challenged—thankfully we had developed over the years fairly easy relationships with the boys—but a new and very significant factor is showing, one which bodes ill for the school in the long term: first year pupils, usually overawed and very amenable in their first term, are rowdy and not over receptive to rebukes.

There is one ray of hope at the end of this third year's survey. The minor clashes and incidents on the roads at half past three do not on the whole occur with "Somerdale" or "Prods," but with "Orangemen." I am optimistic enough to think that the terminology is significant. I hope and believe that hostility against "Orangemen" is being directed more against some kind of abstraction than against the concrete idea of real, live "Prods," who, after all, are to be met at all hours every day of the week!

The most serious overall effect on these young people is the fact that the police, never exactly popular, are now totally unacceptable in the area. Respect for due process of law has vanished. How on earth the area is to be policed (as it must be), and the law administered, when peace returns, is a problem of truly mind-boggling proportions.[42]

Further testimony would be valuable, but this statement suggests the applicability here of the preceding discussion in this chapter. The parent-substitute teacher, a surrogate of societal and Roman Catholic ethnic morality, an assimilated representative of middle-class mores of accommodation, at the outset of community violence was able to maintain his customary relationship with his teen-age pupils. Training in hatred, based on custom, experience, gossip, and media reports, took place in other group contexts: the home and play areas. In the second year, the example of father or brother involved in violence outside the home encouraged autonomous-peer-group participation beyond the usual horseplay and mild delinquencies common among youth; an important game became stoning soldiers. With such an increasingly preoccupying outside environment, gang life of the streets disrupted the controlled-peer-group role demands of the school. The teacher continued to maintain as much of the customary classroom atmosphere as possible, but he admits that in a paternal manner he hid the disturbing behavior of his pupils from the media. Finally, in the third year, he has to grant that classwork has suffered. Upsurges in autonomous as well as more intimate sibling-type "buffoonery, noisiness, excitability" have become problems. He can only hold on to the hope that his pupils are not directing their hatred against rank-and-file Prods, including students in the Protestant Somerdale school.

In describing the impact in 1969–72 of violence upon the Protestant Everton Secondary School for Girls, teacher Erskine Holmes points out that "the two communities in Ardoyne have not been equally battered by events." Less than 20 percent of the homes burned were those of Protestants. The Protestant Shankill area "has confronted the army and been gassed for its pains but it has not been under constant siege; there has been wholesale resettlement and yet it has been the relatively ordered movement of re-development as the old Shankill disappeared under high rise concrete." Most significantly, Holmes asserts that the "policy of internment has not been a two edged sword and the Protestant community has only suffered the rough justice of 'rule of thumb' sentences in the Magistrates' Courts."

Other than some decline in attendance, Holmes does not report behavior problems arising from the community troubles. Only rarely have girls experienced involvement in a skirmish in the streets. Opinions expressed in classrooms did concern him, "although it is possible to suppress all discussion of the situation in school and ignore the reality of polarised Protestant opinion." In the Government and Citizenship course, he used "Schools' Community Relations material on topics like 'integrated Education' but I have to put it on record that not a single girl appeared to change her mind as a result of any of the material we worked with." He concluded that such a modification will come only through experience "and there is absolutely nothing in their experience at this moment to give them any reasons to question their own attitudes."

Holmes discovered that "the range of opinion starts at 'Tartan' [a Protestant youth organization that cooperates with adult vigilantes] and rarely goes beyond Official Unionist [the old-line long-time-ruling Protestant political party]." After 1969, Holmes found that "few girls continued to attend the [religiously] mixed youth club." He "sadly ... noticed them drop out one by one." Especially among lower-class girls—"the lower streams"—were "the extremist opinions." They were often expressed in "political poems of the ghetto poets—too extreme even to find their way into the variety of 'loyalist' news-sheets which also circulate." These Protestants thus have "attitudes and slogans to correspond to those of the Catholic community in moments of crisis."

Among other efforts, Holmes tried to get the girls to speak of Catholics or Roman Catholics rather than of "Fenians." To Protestants, "Fenians" are terrorists even though to Roman Catholics they recall the revered nineteenth-century Fenian Brotherhood of insurgent fame. This labeling effort failed. "Indeed it is almost counterproductive to try."

Holmes speaks of some of his girls being "female camp followers of the Tartan army." These girls were critical of the Royal Ulster Constabulary and used "soldier-lover" ("when the British Army was fighting a running battle on the Shankill") to belittle some of those who would not join in their efforts. He was surprised that his pupils opposed a ban on Republican parades, but then he realized later that they did this so that they might be able to enjoy their own "traditional parades."[43]

Thus these Protestant girls, in a more discreet fashion than the Roman Catholic boys, also found themselves pushed to be less distinctly multivalent. Family and autonomous-peer-group bitterness invaded the classrooms, even though the teachers could "suppress all discussion of the situation." Holmes, like Thornton, persisted in his faith in the terms and rituals of his controlled-peer-group classroom and in the need for helping his pupils—symbolically at least—to know people across sectarian borders. At the same time, he realized that their community experiences would somehow have to change before he and they could contribute much in an effective manner to a calmer social order.

This Roman Catholic and this Protestant teacher look forward to the creation of a joint Ardoyne campus for the four secondary schools that "would really institutionalise co-operation." They say they "foresee an evolution towards the acceptance" of such a development "in the minds of the pupils, teachers and public." It would "accept that the religious divisions of the schools will remain because this is not integration in its commonly accepted meaning. ... The avenues of co-operation are endless." They admit these are "only halting suggestions, coming from teachers who do not pretend to have the answer but we know that we must have something to offer these children and we cannot sit around waiting for 'peace' before we make a start."[44]

With autonomous peer groups among juveniles given new recognition and freedom, even encouragement, by their elders, with sympathetic teachers in the uniformly sectarian schools taking an understanding attitude toward their pupils' involvement in street violence, and for that matter with many of the teachers nostalgic war veterans, both Irish ethnic groups are developing ever more combative and brutalized fighters both male and female. In a war that almost literally has no civilians, boys aged six to twelve bother little with peacetime street games. Their play has become "important." They serve as messengers, decoys, spies, carriers, placers of gelignite bombs that are not too heavy, and throwers of stones and petrol and nail bombs. With their "limited death-concepts, unable through immaturity to anticipate all the risks of their actions," these children become disastrously effective in combat roles.[45] This is especially the situation among the three-fourths of the population classifiable as lower class and in which juvenile and adult play-and-identity peer groups have long had traditions of recourse to individual and group conflict.

A psychiatrist asks: "What drives young children to violent, almost nightly confrontations with a fully-equipped army at very great risk of death and injury, and why is nothing being done to prevent them?" He is especially concerned about the increasing number of those children who in consequence exhibit "severe and lasting emotional damage."[46]

In the foregoing discussion, the impression has possibly been given that autonomous peer groups are all necessarily violence-prone and that they might well be replaced with controlled peer groups. The fun and games of the latter would presumably result in less disastrous personality developments. On the contrary, the character of learning processes within autonomous peer groups depends upon the character of the social class and society within which they operate, upon the role models available for emulation. They can be quite constructive experiences. In any society, relatively autonomous peer groups can provide useful steps toward maturity, toward broader and more effective social participation. Controlled peer groups, such as one finds in schools and voluntary organizations, help prepare the young for adult society, but in autonomous peer groups, the young can have what amounts to "clinical experiences" of an experimental sort in the less structured "real world."

Other approaches to the learning of violence might well be used, especially the more psychological and educational, but perhaps this sociological perspective is helpful. In this chapter, an effort is made to suggest the influence of various levels of culture on behavior and the role of prototypical socialization groups in personality formation. The subcultures of such prototypical groups, especially the sibling and autonomous peer groups, need to be better understood and taken into consideration in any program to make formal educational efforts more effective in allaying internecine bitterness and strife.

Notes

1. Morris Fraser, quoted by Bernard Weinraub, "Psychiatrist in Belfast Finds Children Are Deeply Disturbed by the Violence," *New York Times,* 14 March 1971.

2. Morris Fraser, *Children in Conflict* (London: Secker & Warburg, 1973), pp. 70–71.

3. Conor O'Neill, "The Social Function of Physical Violence in an Irish Urban Area," *Economic and Social Review* (Dublin) 2 (1970–71): 481–96, p. 493 quoted.

4. Margaret Mead, *Male and Female* (New York: William Morrow, 1949), p. 270.
5. Lil Conlon, *Cumann na mBan and the Women of Ireland* (Kilkenny, Ireland: Kilkenny People, 1969); and Bernadette Devlin, *The Price of My Soul* (London: Andree Deutsch, 1969).
6. P. D. Zimmerman, "Sly Sleeper," *Newsweek,* 5 June 1972, pp. 98–99.
7. Kathleen Boehringer, "Discrimination: Jobs," *Fortnight* (Belfast), 14 May 1971, pp. 5–7, at p. 5.
8. Michael Foley, "Can You Spot Them?" *Fortnight* (Belfast), 20 November 1970, p. 11; cf. D. P. Barritt and Arthur Booth, eds., *Orange and Green,* 2nd ed. (Brigflats, Yorks., England: Northern Friends Peace Board, 1972).
9. Foley, "Can You Spot Them?"; cf. D. P. Barritt and C. F. Carter, *The Northern Ireland Problem,* 2nd ed. (London: Oxford University Press, 1972), chap. 6.
10. Jane Kramer, "Letter from Ireland," *New Yorker,* 12 February 1972, pp. 46–50, 52, 54–56, 61–64, 66–68, 70–79; p. 46 quoted.
11. A. McC. Lee, *Multivalent Man* (New York: George Braziller, 1966), esp. chaps. 5–10. The following summarizes briefly certain theories set forth and discussed at length in that book.
12. A. L. Kroeber and Clyde Kluckhohn with Wayne Untereiner, *Culture: A Critical Review of Concepts and Definitions* (Cambridge, Mass.: Peabody Museum of American Archeology and Ethnology, Harvard University, 1952), p. 181.
13. W. G. Sumner, *Folkways* (Boston: Ginn, 1907), esp. chap. 2.
14. E. S. Herman, *The Real Terror Network* (Boston: South End Press, 1982), p. 1.
15. C. H. Cooley, *Human Nature and the Social Order,* rev. ed. (Glencoe, Ill.: Free Press, 1956), p. 197; cf. William James, *The Principles of Psychology* (New York: Henry Holt, 1890), 1:121, 292–96, 401; and Willard Waller, *The Family: A Dynamic Interpretation* (New York: Cordon, 1938), p. 163.
16. Monica Sheridan, "Irish Children," *Ireland of the Welcomes* (Dublin), 12, no. 2 (July/August 1964): 6–10, p. 8 quoted.
17. James, *Principles of Psychology,* p. 294.
18. C. J. Friedrich, *The New Image of the Common Man* (Boston: Beacon Press, 1950), p. 246.
19. Department of Health and Social Services, *Report of the Supplementary Benefits Commission for the Year Ended 31/3/1976* (Belfast: HMSO, 1976), p. 9.
20. Eileen Evason, *Ends That Won't Meet: A Study of Poverty in Belfast* (London: Child Poverty Action Group, June 1980), pp. 15–16.
21. Northern Ireland Information Service, *Northern Ireland Facts and Figures* (Belfast, December 1981), p. 8; *Fortnight,* no. 186 (May–June 1982): 15.
22. Evason, *Ends That Won't Meet,* pp. 11, 16–17; cf. Evason, *Poverty: The Facts in Northern Ireland* (London: Child Poverty Action Group, 1976).
23. J. I. Harbison, "The Children of Northern Ireland," *New Society* (London), 17 April 1980, pp. 100–101.
24. James Connolly, *Labour in Ireland* (Dublin: Sign of the Three Candles, 1922), p. 223.
25. Jack Holland, *Too Long a Sacrifice: Life and Death in Northern Ireland Since 1969* (New York: Dodd Mead, 1981), p. 174.
26. T. J. O'Hanlon, *The Irish* (New York: Harper & Row, 1975), p. 206.
27. R. M. Fields, *Northern Ireland: Society Under Siege* (New Brunswick, N.J.: Transaction Books, 1980), pp. 54–55.
28. Morris Fraser, *Children in Conflict,* p. 23.

29. Ken Heskin, "Children and Young People in Northern Ireland: A Research Review," in Jeremy and Joan Harbison, *A Society Under Stress: Children and Young People in Northern Ireland* (Somerset, England: Open Books, 1980), pp. 8–21; p. 15 quoted.

30. A. McC. Lee, *Fraternities Without Brotherhood* (Boston: Beacon Press, 1955), pp. 106–20; idem, *Multivalent Man* (New York: George Braziller, 1966), esp. chaps. 11–12; and A. McC. and E. B. Lee, *Marriage and the Family* (New York: Barnes & Noble, 1961), chap. 8, esp. pp. 102–12.

31. Robert Coles, "Belfast's Children," *New Republic* (Washington, D.C.), 14 October 1981, pp. 16–18, p. 16 quoted.

32. John Conroy, "Crazy Joe's School," *APF Reporter* 4, no. 1 (February 1981): 6–9, p. 8 quoted.

33. Sam Sloan, "A Hard Youth in the Hammer," *Fortnight* (Belfast), no. 185 (March/April 1982): 18–19. See also "Who'd Be a Hood in Belfast?" in Workers' Research Unit, *Belfast Bulletin*, no. 10 (Spring 1982): 75–76.

34. Desmond Wilson, interviewed by Barré Fitzpatrick, "The Role of the Churches in Northern Ireland," *The Crane Bag* (Holmsdale, Co. Wicklow, Ireland) 4, no. 2 (1980): 79–84, at p. 84.

35. Advisory Council for Education in Northern Ireland, *Reorganisation of Secondary Education in Northern Ireland* (Belfast: HMSO, Cmd. 574, February 1973), pp. 20–21.

36. Lord Charles Dunleath, "That They May Be One," proposal for Lagan College Belfast, 1982 (leaflet); A. E. C. W. Spencer, "All Children Apart," *Fortnight* (Belfast), no. 176 (May 1980): 9–10.

37. A. E. C. W. Spencer, "Chilver: A Catholic Defence," *Fortnight* (Belfast), no. 185 (March/April 1982): 10.

38. P. A. Compton, *Northern Ireland: A Census Atlas* (Dublin: Gill and Macmillan, 1978), pp. 24, 29. See Also A. E. C. W. Spencer, "Alienation in English Catholicism, 1958–1972," *Proceedings of the Sociological Association of Ireland*, Second Annual Conference (Belfast: Queen's University, 1976), pp. 115–34.

39. W. H. Lockhart and Ruth Elliott, "Changes in the Attitudes of Young Offenders in an Integrated Assessment Centre," Chap. 11 in Jeremy and Joan Harbison, *A Society Under Stress*, (Somerset, England: Open Books, 1980), p. 100.

40. Leslie Scarman, chairman, Tribunal of Inquiry, *Violence and Civil Disturbances in Northern Ireland in 1969* (Belfast: HMSO, Cmd. 566, April 1972), 1:209–21.

41. Erskine Holmes and A. M. Thornton, "Children in Distress," *The Northern Teacher* (Belfast) 10, no. 4 (Summer 1972): 29–33, p. 29 quoted.

42. Thornton, pp. 29–31, in ibid.

43. Holmes, pp. 31–33, in ibid.

44. Holmes and Thornton, ibid., p. 33.

45. Fraser, *Children in Conflict*, p. 41.

46. Ibid., pp. 12–13.

CHAPTER 6

Terror in Upper-Class Strategy

Terrorism in this Northern Ireland conflict engages or confronts people in many different ways, all interrelated. It can be (1) strategic procedure, (2) theater, (3) direct personal involvement, and/or (4) indirect entanglement. More broadly, it can be seen as symptomatic of (5) social change.

Persons and groups sympathetic to or participant in *(a)* official, law-enforcement, "peacekeeping" terrorism act or react rather differently in each of these perspectives from those in *(b)* subversive, agitational, "guerrilla" terrorism. Official law-enforcing terrorists have a sense of having an established and secure claim on the legitimacy of their behavior. This is of a different order from the faith of the subversive or agitational and their friends in an ideological legitimacy-on-trial. On all sides in Northern Ireland, there are true believers in one or the other kind of legitimation for their disparate courses of action.

In this chapter and the next, we look at aspects of strategic procedure with special reference to its class stratification. What social groups figure most significantly in terrorizing strategies? This discussion suggests the degrees of direct personal involvement and indirect entanglement that have been enmeshing the people of Northern Ireland in this struggle.

In the Northern Ireland conflict since 1968, as I have been able to perceive it through observation, interviews, and documents, terrorist acts and threats of such acts reflect a definite class orientation in their patterning. In this perspective, terrorization has included (1) decisions and indecisiveness by upper-class Loyalists; (2) "law and order" procedures of *(a)* middle-class and *(b)* lower-class governmental functionaries guided by their own interpretations of official policies; (3) threats and actions by other middle-class "respectables" on the three principal sides of the conflict; and (4) actions by the predominantly lower-class insurgents. These acts and threats have been directed against (i) symbolic prestige persons; (ii) symbolic groups; (iii) rank-and-file members of the three sides' organized efforts; (iv) random members of the three quasi-ethnic populations, often "innocent bystanders"; and (v) property, chiefly symbolic structures, business buildings and public utilities, and lower-class ghetto dwellings.

The present chapter and the next deal with all four types of class involvement. In them, we focus on terrorization through the maintenance of unequal social services and opportunities and the organization of techniques and procedures for such maintenance.

Upper-Class Decisions and Indecisiveness

Successive Northern Ireland and from 1972 United Kingdom governments authorized ever more wide-ranging and repressive "emergency" powers and procedures. The emphasis of these measures was persistently on attacking unsettling symptoms, on stifling the dissent of the deprived, rather than on dealing with causes. The changing perceptions of political opportunism gave these policies a reputation of inconsistency and to a degree of indecisiveness.

When nonviolent civil rights agitation became prevalent in the late 1960s, as we saw in chapter 4, administrative policy permitted Loyalist paramilitary harassment of demonstrators. These interferences were notoriously carried out and exacerbated by part-time and regular police. This terrorizing encouraged the violent among Nationalist dissenters. Thus, rather than attempt to mitigate bitterness and build consensus positively, official policies permitted and even encouraged violence. It was met by retaliatory violence.

The legislation as interpreted or enacted at Stormont became so permissive to the Northern Ireland authorities that it precipitated a decision by the province's highest court in February 1972 questioning the legality of a part of the Special Powers Acts. The court contended that Stormont's parliament had gone beyond the authorizations contained in the province's basic constitutional document, the British Government of Ireland Act of 1920. Under that act, only Westminster could control Crown armed forces in the six counties; with the Special Powers Acts of Northern Ireland, the provincial government had assumed control. Faced with this embarrassing ruling, the Westminster Parliament rushed to enact a nullification of the court's decision.[1] Shortly thereafter, on 24 March, the British government in effect lost its patience with the "law and order" procedures of the provincial government—with its lack of recognized legitimacy—and took over its control. No wonder that the ethnic minority and organized labor have little faith in recourse to establishment politicians or to the courts to defend their rights!

In 1976, the British court of final appeal—the House of Lords—went so far as to grant to security people the benefit of any possible doubt in judicial reviews of homicide cases. The incident involved a British soldier who had shot and killed an unarmed civilian he suspected inaccurately of being an IRA member. Granting that the soldier had had good intentions, the court called the homicide "justifiable." Thus the control of crowds with lethal weapons was further legitimized.

Terrorization through Interrogation. In an "enquiry into allegations against the security forces of physical brutality," the U.K. Compton committee in 1971 admitted that the following "methods have been used in support of the interrogation of a small number of persons in Northern Ireland who were believed to possess information of a kind which it was operationally necessary to obtain as rapidly as possible in the interest of saving lives, while at the same time providing the detainees with the necessary security for their own persons and identities." The committee listed:

> Standing detainees with their arms against a wall, presumably "not in a position of stress."
>
> Hooding in transit or with other detainees to "increase their sense of isolation."
>
> Continuous noise to prevent overhearing or communication and thus to "enhance the detainee's sense of isolation."
>
> Bread and water at six-hour intervals as a form of "discipline."

Detainees complained to the committee that wall standing was often enforced "with batons to maintain posture." They were "so kept till collapsed, when lifted up again; treatment continued for 2 or 3 days, or up to 4 days." They also objected to "loud and deafening noise," to food deprivation "for 2 or 3 days," and to lack of sleep or very little for a similar period.

The Compton committee concluded "that the following actions constitute physical ill-treatment: posture on the wall, hooding, noise, deprivation of sleep, diet of bread and water," but it rejected allegations of physical brutality "as we understand the term." They took brutality to be "an inhuman or savage form of cruelty, and that cruelty implies a disposition to inflict suffering, coupled with indifference to, or pleasure in, the victim's pain."[2] Mere damage was not enough! It had to be for fun!

Even at that, the Compton committee apparently went too far. In 1972, the U.K. Parker committee reported on an investigation of "authorised procedures for the interrogation of persons suspected of terrorism." It concluded that the techniques listed above should be used by skilled interrogators and in the presence of "a doctor with some psychiatric training" who would observe "the course of oral interrogation." It contended "that a person suspected of ordinary crime, who may thereafter be found not guilty, can be subjected to some measure of discomfort, hardship and mental anxiety."[3] One member of the Parker committee, Lord Gardiner, disagreed both with it and with the Compton report. He pointed out that with the Compton definition of brutality, "which some of our witnesses thought came from the Inquisition, if an interrogator believed, to his great regret, that it was necessary for him to cut off the fingers of a detainee one by one to get the required information out of him for the sole purpose of saving life, this would not be cruel and, because not cruel, not brutal." With regard to the Parker committee's justification of the listed techniques, Gardiner asserted that the "army never considered whether the procedures were legal or illegal" and that the Royal Ulster Constabulary merely followed the army precedent. He adds: "The blame for this sorry story, if blame there be, must lie with those who, many years ago, decided that in emergency conditions in Colonial-type situations we should abandon our legal, well-tried and highly successful wartime interrogation methods and replace them by procedures which were secret, illegal, not morally justifiable."[4]

Upper-class decision making with regard to interrogation methods continued to fluctuate. Lord Diplock's 1972 commission report "would not condone practices such as those which are described in the Compton Report ... and the Parker Report. ... The use of any methods of this kind have been prohibited for many months past." They are "now regarded as counter-productive."[5]

In spite of these assurances, the government of the Irish Republic submitted to the European Commission of Human Rights written evidence concerning 228 cases of the ill-treatment of prisoners in 1971–74 in Northern Ireland, 154 of which had to do with interrogation abuses. The commission dealt with eleven of the latter in detail and unanimously labeled as "torture" the interrogation practices to which the prisoners had been subjected.[6] Upon appeal, the European Court of Human Rights refused to go that far, but it did decide with only one negative vote that the interrogation techniques complained of "constituted a practice of inhuman and degrading treatment."[7]

Amnesty International made an investigation of Northern Ireland interrogations for eliciting "confessions" in 1977. As part of this, it expressed concern at trial of "terrorists" charged under "emergency" legislation by nonjury courts sitting with single judges. It concluded "that the maltreatment of suspected terrorists by the RUC has taken place with sufficient frequency to warrant the establishment of a public inquiry to investigate it." It also pointed out "that the machinery for investigating complaints against the police of assault during interview is not adequate."[8] According to a study prepared by legal experts advisory to Amnesty International, the percentage of cases in Diplock nonjury courts resulting in convictions rose from 83 in 1973 to 96 in 1979. The percentage of cases with guilty pleas and thus based on self-incriminating confessions rose from 56 in 1973 to 79 in 1979. Cases against the security forces resulted in "one plea of guilty and a very high acquittal rate."[9]

In response to the Amnesty International report, the Secretary of State for Northern Ireland appointed still another committee to investigate "police interrogation procedures." Headed by Judge H. G. Bennett, its 1979 recommendations suggest the persistence of interrogation abuses. It claimed that the "prohibition against the unlawful use of force against a prisoner is already sufficiently specific," but it sought to forbid "degrading physical or mental ill-treatment" by barring these practices:

> (i) any order or action requiring a prisoner to strip or expose himself or herself;
> (ii) any order or action requiring a prisoner to adopt or maintain any unnatural or humiliating posture;
> (iii) any order or action requiring a prisoner to carry out unnecessarily any physically exhausting or demanding action or to adopt or maintain any such stance;
> (iv) the use of obscenities, insults or insulting language about the prisoner, his family, friends or associates, his political beliefs, religion or race;
> (v) the use of threats of physical force or of such things as being abandoned in a hostile area; and
> (vi) the use of threats of sexual assault or misbehaviour.

The committee also concerned itself with "the number and length of interviews which prisoners have undergone," and it recommended:

> (i) no single interview should go on longer than the period between normal meal-times, and interviews should not continue during meal-times;
> (ii) an interview should not commence or continue after midnight, except where operational requirements (for example,

an urgent need to find out where an explosive device has been placed) demand that it should;

(iii) not more than two officers should be present at the interview of one prisoner at any time; and

(iv) not more than three teams of two officers should be concerned with interviewing one prisoner.[10]

The Bennett committee admitted that "examination of medical evidence reveals cases in which injuries, whatever their precise cause, were not self-inflicted and were sustained in police custody." It also called attention to the fact that for "a number of civil claims against the R.U.C., damages have been awarded or settlements made out of court," but that in criminal cases against police officers, "no final conviction has resulted."[11]

Three students of the current legal situation in the province, Kevin Boyle, Tom Hadden, and Paddy Hillyard, feel that the Bennett committee recommendations do not go far enough. They would like to see the enactment of "a statutory code of practice for the conduct of interrogations" that would include such provisions as the following:

i. the medical examination of suspects before, during and after interrogation;

ii. the limitation of interrogation sessions to four hours per day in sessions of not more than one hour each without a break for refreshment;

iii. a limited daily right of access for the suspect's relatives while the suspect is not undergoing interrogation, an unconditional right of access for his own doctor or a doctor nominated by him, and an unconditional right of access for his legal adviser after the first twenty-four hours of detention;

iv. a requirement that all juveniles and persons with subnormal intelligence should be interrogated in the presence of a parent or guardian;

v. the maintenance of a detailed formal record of arrest, medical examination, medication, interrogation sessions, meals, visits and complaints in respect of each suspect; a copy of this record should be available as of right to any person with a legitimate interest;

vi. a clear statement of the applicability of the general principle that confessions must not be obtained by force, threats or inducements.[12]

These authors clearly demonstrate in their analyses of Northern Ireland legal controls the need for such a code of practice further to limit interrogation abuses.

Amnesty International welcomed the Bennett committee's confirmation of its "concerns about the ill-treatment of suspects, the inadequacy of legal safeguards, incommunicado detention and the complaints procedure," but it pointed out that the "committee's numerous recommendations are aimed mainly at strengthening internal control by uniformed officers over plainclothes detectives." It remained concerned "that, as internal discipline had not prevented ill-treatment in the past, the absence of a reliable record of interrogation was likely to continue to raise controversy." It asked consideration of "the whole framework of the criminal process—in particular the rules of admissibility of statements in court."[13]

Amnesty International pointed to an example of such continuing abuse through the use of confessions in its 1981 report: In December 1979, Stephen Paul McCaul, an illiterate aged fifteen with a mental age of seven, was sentenced for hijacking buses, burning a bus, burglaries, and associated firearms offenses. The police knew about his mental retardation, but "he was held incommunicado and questioned without his parents or a lawyer or other third party present, in breach of regulations." A psychiatrist testified that McCaul "could not have dictated the statement alleged to have been made by him." After Amnesty International "expressed serious concern about what it regarded as a highly unsafe conviction," the authorities released McCaul early in 1981.[14]

Here and, as we shall see, elsewhere, upper-class decision makers try to make defensive policy statements that will appear constructive in terms of their presumptions concerning societal morality. Middle-class functionaries provide rationalizations. Lower-class police operatives, depending upon their own mores and upon the mores of accommodation traditional to their relations with the upper classes, rely upon those mores and upon pleas of expedient efficiency to protect them when they ignore official detainee safeguards.

Terrorization through Imprisonment. The English social science weekly *New Society* illustrated in 1970 the differential treatment of citizen and police offenders. It cited the six-month sentence of Bernadette Devlin, a Northern Irish member of the British Parliament, "for helping raise barricades in Derry so that the Royal Ulster Constabulary could not terrorise again the Catholic inhabitants there." In contrast, the "police involved in the initial invasions of the Bogside [a Catholic ghetto in Derry] have been given amnesty." Thus nonviolent civil rights efforts were again "proved inadequate to secure Catholics what they demand: justice and freedom from fear."[15]

At roughly 4:30 a.m. on 9 August 1971, on the basis of a compilation prepared by the RUC, soldiers "lifted" from their homes and arrested 342 men. The Prime Minister of Northern Ireland, Brian Faulkner, had decided that "the terrorist campaign continues at an unacceptable level, and I have had to conclude that the ordinary law cannot deal comprehensively or quickly enough with such ruthless viciousness." He therefore announced he was exercising "where necessary the powers of detention and internment vested in me" and ordered the sweep. He placed 4,000 members of the largely Protestant Ulster Defense Regiment in full-time service for the emergency.

The RUC and army had planned to arrest some 450 to 500, but the "IRA had known it for some time and as a result virtually every senior IRA man was billeted away from home." The lists, too, were defective. Thus those "lifted" many times represented poor guesses; 116 had to be released within 48 hours. By 10 November, some 980 had been arrested, and 508, released. The rest were either interned or held for disposition.[16]

This sweep reinstituted internment without trial. Of those interned, many were "political opponents of the Unionists—like the PD [People's Democracy] and NICRA [Northern Ireland Civil Rights Association] members, old retired IRA ex-internees, militant trade unionists, public speakers, and, in some cases, people held on mistaken identity."[17] It escalated protest, violence, and the destruction of property. Rioting broke out throughout the province. The first day alone ten people died (two security men and eight civilians). Some one hundred houses were set afire. The Nationalist, Republican Labour, and Social Democratic and Labour parties all asked their constituents to protest such summary arrests and internment by refusing to pay rents and rates. The Northern Ireland Civil Rights Association called for "all people to engage in a united massive campaign of resistance to internment through demonstrations and civil disobedience."[18] A spokesman for the Irish army revealed that 4,338 refugees from the north were now camping in the twenty-six counties. As Chapter 3 outlines, the power to intern without trial had existed for some time and had been used off and on.

All this is scarcely the outcome for which Faulkner had hoped. Senior soldiers assumed that the "surge of violence and a further estrangement of the Catholic community from the governing authorities ... could be contained and would soon fall back. ... They had foreseen rioting, but not warfare." In April–July 1971, 4 soldiers and 4 civilians had been killed, but in

August–November, 30 soldiers plus 11 RUC and UDR members and 73 civilians died. In five months, 1,576 suspects were "lifted" as the drive continued, but by mid-December, 934 of them had been interrogated and released without a charge. The men "seldom came back as tolerant of the regime as they had gone in." It drove even "moderate Catholics away from the middle ground."[19]

As a bulletin of the British Information Services candidly admits, British and provincial legislation and actions sanctioned "detention; the power to search, arrest and question suspects on suspicion of being involved in terrorism; the proscription of organisations; the abolition of trial by jury for terrorist offenses (because of the intimidation of jurymen and witnesses); and the making of exclusion orders [of people from a given area or from the province]."[20] In 1971–75, about 2,000 Nationalist and Loyalist suspects were detained for more than a few days. On 5 December 1975, the last detainees were released, but the holding of charged prisoners on remand presumably awaiting trial for long periods continues.[21]

A prison hunger strike and the growing volume of prisoners led the British administrator in June 1972 to try to cope with terrorist symptoms in the limited available facilities by according vigilante prisoners "special category" status. This was granted to those sentenced to nine months or more for an offense related to the civil conflict. Such prisoners did not have to do prison work, might wear their own clothes, and could have food parcels and extra visits. They lived in compounds that housed as many as ninety each and were granted a degree of self-government under one of the paramilitary organizations.

The British called this arrangement a matter of administrative expediency and not a granting of "political status," but it was taken by the vigilantes to be in effect a recognition of such a status. It helped the British to justify their use from 1973 of the arbitrary "Diplock" nonjury courts to which reference is made above.[22]

By 31 December 1974, prisoners on special category numbered 1,065 men and 51 women. They came from both Loyalist and Nationalist paramilitary bodies. The total prison population had mounted from 712 on 1 January 1969 to 2,848 on 30 November 1974.[23] In consequence of these figures and the conditions they suggest, an investigative commission headed by Lord Gardiner came to these conclusions in January 1975:

> The housing of male special category prisoners in compounds means that they are not closely controlled as they would be in a normal cellular prison, discipline within compounds is in

practice exercised by compound leaders, and they are more likely to emerge with an increased commitment to terrorism than as reformed citizens. The special category prisoners regard themselves in much the same light as detainees, expecting that an amnesty will result in their not having to serve in full the sentences imposed on them by the courts, and the para-military organisations find it easy to encourage this misunderstanding in the public mind for propaganda purposes. The result of this is that the sentences passed in the courts for murder and other serious crimes have lost much of their deterrent effect.

The Commission therefore decided "that the introduction of special category status was a serious mistake; we even have some doubt as to whether its introduction administratively by a surprisingly liberal interpretation of Prison Rules was legal."[24]

Prompted by this recommendation, the British quit granting this special status to prisoners convicted of an offense committed from 1 March 1976. Loyalist and Nationalist participants in the struggle both called this a "criminalisation program" because it placed their convicts in the same classification as the nonpolitical, as "common criminals." It ceased to give new prisoners any possible implication of "political" status. Those who had been in this status, to the extent that they could not readily be "phased out," continued in it. In November 1975, they numbered 1,465 (about three-fifths Nationalist, two-fifths Loyalist); by mid–1978, 800; and by September 1981, 309.[25]

In response to "criminalisation," vigilante prisoners took recourse to noncooperation in order to try to obtain again the status that carried special privileges. This effort took the form of the "on the blanket" or "dirty" protest in the H-Blocks of the Maze (Long Kesh) Prison and later among the women in the Armagh jail. Those "on the blanket" refused to accept "criminal status," with its requirement of prison garb and prison work. They wore nothing but a blanket.

In retaliation, especially in the H-Blocks, the wardens—among other actions—confined the men to their cells and refused to let them empty their slop containers. When prisoners broke windows in order to have an outlet for their urine and feces, wardens boarded up the windows and often upset slop containers in the cells. The prisoners were placed on half rations, and evidence has been produced of the extent to which prisoners were abused by the wardens.[26]

Cardinal Tomás O'Fiaich, after visits with the Maze prisoners, contended, "One would hardly allow an animal to remain in such conditions, let alone a human being." He added: "The authorities refuse to admit that these prisoners are in a different category from the ordinary, yet everything in their trials and family background indicates that they are different."[27] On the contrary, the British Northern Ireland Office asserted that the prisoners "foul their cells" in order "to establish that their murders, their bombings are in some way special and that they should be treated more favorably." To offset "the propaganda campaign ... that the Government is responsible for the conditions in which these prisoners live," the Office claimed that "the prisoners have imposed the conditions upon themselves."[28]

This 1980 statement contains no reference to the continuing existence of "special category" prisoners. The differences between the prisoners "on the blanket" and those in "special category" led to the hunger strikes of 1980–81.

On-again off-again indecisiveness by upper-class policy makers is well further illustrated by the hunger strike of late 1980. To end that strike, the government's representatives agreed to more tolerable prison conditions, and then they reneged. In consequence, the hunger strike tactic was resumed in 1981 and led to the deaths of IRA and British parliamentary member Bobby Sands and a series of nine others, as discussed below.

Even a former Royal Green Jackets commander, Colonel Robin Evelegh, expressed considerable frustration with the "unpredictability" of British law enforcement: "Flexible law has many synonyms. It is variously called 'showing political sensitivity,' or 'restraint,' or 'winning hearts and minds,' or 'low profile.' But whatever it is called, it always has the characteristic that the extent to which the published law will be enforced is uncertain to both the law breakers and the law enforcers." He found that "One illegal procession would be permitted and another, apparently similar to it, would be stopped." Even vigilantes "would be allowed" one week, "and the next week firmly suppressed."[29]

The suspension of ordinary civil rights and a protective definition of terms make it quite easy for the British to claim that "there are no political prisoners in Northern Ireland."[30] Many other countries, including the Soviet Union, take a similar position. Except in political terms, however, it is difficult to explain the jump in prison population from about 500 to as many as 3,000 during this period.[31]

The picture that emerges from these and other data is one of stumbling efforts by upper-class groups in the province and in England to shore up their control through the use of short-range terrorizing procedures. Rather than face and adapt to the changing social scene through negotiating nonviolently with deprived dissidents, they attempt to erase symptoms without examining and then dealing with causes. They rigidify their stance and the social structure more and more by sweeping aside many of the libertarian provisions that presumably gave plausibility to their claims to benign and legitimate control. It is part of a gradual stripping away of the pretentions of liberal democracy by an increasingly authoritarian and inflexible regime. Let us look at another example:

Terrorization through Maintaining Inequality. Beginning with the Government of Ireland Act of 1920, the province's "constitution," Northern Ireland presumably has a "body of law designed to combat all forms of discrimination and to protect human rights generally."[32] In response to the current disorders, representatives of the United Kingdom and Northern Ireland governments met at 10 Downing Street and issued a statement on 19 August 1969 to reaffirm "that in all legislation and executive decisions of Government every citizen of Northern Ireland is entitled to the same equality of treatment and freedom from discrimination as obtains in the rest of the United Kingdom, irrespective of political views or religion."[33]

What did all this mean to people, especially to those less privileged, in the province? Laws aimed at preventing discrimination in employment include the following:

- Two Northern Ireland acts in 1969 provide as "ombudsmen" a Parliamentary Commissioner for Administration and a Commissioner of Complaints. The former investigates complaints by parliament members and the latter by the public of governmental maladministration. The two channels have led to a trivial number of findings of religious discrimination.[34]
- The Local Government Act (NI) 1972 sets up a commission "to prevent possible abuses (including discrimination on religious or political grounds) in the recruitment, training, and terms and conditions of employment of local government staff."
- The Northern Ireland Constitution Act 1973 includes "provisions of fundamental importance in outlawing discrimination on grounds of political opinion or religious belief in the public sector." It established a Standing Advisory Commission on Human Rights to make redress available for persons aggrieved by discrimination.

- The Fair Employment (NI) Act 1976 broadened the ban against discrimination in employment to include the private sector, but it continued to except the schools. It established the Fair Employment Agency as "an independent body."
- The Sex Discrimination (NI) Order 1976 apparently became necessary to supplement and implement the Equal Pay (NI) Act 1970. It set up still another body, the Equal Opportunities Commission.[35]

As a characterization of these efforts, the detailed annual reports of the Fair Employment Agency are significant. Some 2,400 employers and vocational organizations, public and private, have agreed to the agency's Declaration of Principle and Intent. This voluntary action covers 80 percent of the province's work force. In the period from September 1976 until the end of 1981, the agency "registered 249 individual complaints of unlawful discrimination." After investigating 144 of those cases, 13 were found to involve "unlawful discrimination." The other 131 were dismissed as containing "no discrimination." Only 42 cases remained under investigation because 57 others had either been withdrawn or (6 cases) dropped for security or safety reasons.[36]

As the Oxford law Professor Christopher McCrudden concludes in a 1981 report, the British have failed to enforce laws against discrimination. With regard to their Fair Employment Agency, he states: "If one way of assessing the success of the agency is its ability to have findings of discrimination supported in the courts, it has clearly failed." Another legal specialist, Professor David R. Lowry, adds: "Most Catholics are discouraged from complaining as there seems to be little point to it, given the fact that the FEA lacks proper prosecutorial power, personnel, financial support, and legislative enforcement machinery."

Lacking what McCrudden calls "full-blooded affirmative action," these proceedings focus on the key word, "intent." The attack is only indirectly and not at all effectively on de facto discrimination. The Agency admitted in its 1980 report that Roman Catholic school leavers were not served by the informal networks through which more than half of available jobs are filled. For discrimination to be illegal, it must be "intentional"! As the sociologist Liam O'Dowd puts it, "The problem ... is to establish motivation in the first place and secondly to show that there were no extenuating circumstances. Instances of discrimination have proven exceedingly difficult to establish."[37] No wonder that Kevin Boyle and his legal associates found that "the pace and manner of implementation [of these measures] was certainly not sufficient to gain their [the Roman Catholic community's] confidence or meet their expectations."[38]

The explicit ban on interfering with segregated school employment practices is a significant one. No such ban was apparently needed on investigating discrimination in security force employment. As Liam O'Dowd notes, "it would be impossible to insist that the local security forces should be balanced," and he adds, "it was precisely the Protestant Unionist control of the security forces which underpinned the sectarian state from 1920 onwards."[39]

After an investigation of the Fair Employment Agency in 1980, the London-based National Council for Civil Liberties spoke of its "failure to protect people from discrimination" and attributed this to "the environment within which it operates." The council pointed to the agency's "painstakingly slow progress without any sense of urgency or strategy; consistent underfunding and shortage of staff; vitriolic opposition from the Unionist and Democratic Unionist Parties and luke-warm support from the Government and Opposition front benches." Even research reports sponsored by the Fair Employment Agency, done by outside investigators, "highlight the way in which the higher unemployment rate among Catholics is perpetuated by employers' informal recruiting practices (hiring on the recommendation of existing employees, etc.) and equally informal methods of finding jobs (being told of vacancies by one's family or friends)."[40]

That these efforts to abate discrimination among the sectarian factions result in only token changes could easily have been predicted by their planners. Loyalists criticize these steps, but they have lost little control of jobs through them. When it is so easily possible to base the choice on an employee, a house renter, a trainee, or whomever on one or more criteria other than the religious or the ethnic, insistence on proof of an unlawful *motive* destroys most of the thrust of such efforts to offset de facto discrimination. The governmental moves listed make a promising façade, but they serve chiefly to make sectarian conflict more subtle without destroying its usefulness as a diversion from class conflict.

Entrepreneurial Gains from Upper-Class Manipulations. What do entrepreneurs gain from such situations as that in Northern Ireland? What opportunities exist against such a background of terror? One recent development illustrates vividly the nature of such possibilities:

John Z. DeLorean, a former $500,000-a-year General Motors vice president, decided in 1973 to go into business manufacturing "on his own" smart and expensive sports automobiles. He shopped around in several countries for a spot for his factory and finally selected Dunmurry in Northern Ireland. *Newsweek* of 1 January 1979, clearly states the basis of this choice:

> In Northern Ireland, DeLorean says, workers have a better attendance record than those in either England or the U.S., and he will only have to pay $3 to $3.50 an hour for labor—approximately one-third what Detroit automakers earn. What's more, because Ulster [i.e., Northern Ireland] is eager to attract foreign investment and reduce Dunmurry's 30 percent unemployment rate, government agencies have agreed to put up almost $122 million of the $190 million DeLorean needs, in the form of equity investment, building loans and employee-training grants.

The venture did not work out. The British government had to declare DeLorean Motor Cars, Ltd., bankrupt in 1982, but the pattern is a revealing one.[41]

In addition to low absenteeism and low wages assured by the Orange-Green division of the labor supply, such entrepreneurs as DeLorean can place themselves in a position in such a depressed area as Dunmurry to take full advantage of the routinization and further segmentation of the labor force. To illustrate, egalitarian mandates of the Sex Discrimination Act of 1975 can be sidestepped and sex discrimination maintained through such devices as steering women rather than men into training for technical tasks such as typing. In Northern Ireland, women hold 54 to 70 percent (depending upon definition) of the clerical positions and 99 to 100 percent of the typing jobs.[42] These are, with few exceptions, dead-end fields of employment.[43]

More broadly, such routinization or de-skilling in the sense of placing people in relatively simple and specific tasks rather than providing them with broader and more adaptable skills and knowledge "not only increases production, but also lowers wages for lower skilled workers." This creates a divisive hierarchy in which "a series of levels of work" wipes out promotion ladders.[44] With such a high level of unemployment as that common in Northern Ireland and with governmental subsidies available to employers for employee training, entrepreneurs can utilize the implications of de-skilling and routinization to the fullest measure.

As background for this sort of exploitation of taxpayers and workers, it is to be noted that the Northern Ireland provincial government publicizes that "the package of industrial incentives which it can offer is much more generous than those available in any of the Assisted Areas in G.B. [Great

Britain] and also more competitive than those on offer elsewhere in the European Community." Grants are made "towards the cost of buildings, machinery and equipment, help with research and development costs and the provision of complete factories." These assistances are "available to the local businessman as to the new foreign investor." This has attracted 37 American firms, such as General Motors and DeLorean, that have "an employment potential of 25,000 people."[45] Data on the relationship between the "potential" and the actual are not available. Socialism this is not; an adjustment to plutocratic imperialism of a clear sort it surely is.

In addition to all this, the British and multinational corporations that influence British policies apparently hope to continue to control Northern Ireland as a useful military outpost as well as a profitable colony.[46]

Notes

1. H. Kelly, "High Court Holds N.I. Role of Army Unconstitutional," Dublin *Irish Times,* 24 February 1972, pp. 1, 6; James Downey, "Troops Get Legal Footing in North, " Dublin *Irish Times,* 24 February 1972, pp. 1, 6.

2. Edmund Compton, chairman, *Report of the Enquiry Into Allegations Against the Security Forces of Physical Brutality in Northern Ireland Arising Out of Events on the 9th August, 1971* (London: HMSO, Cmnd. 4823, November 1971), pp. 13, 15, 23, 71. Hereinafter referred to as Compton Report.

3. Lord Parker, chairman, *Report of the Committee of Privy Counselors Appointed to Consider Authorised Procedures for the Interrogation of Persons Suspected of Terrorism* (London: HMSO, Cmnd. 4901, March 1972), pp. 7, 9.

4. Ibid., pp. 13, 22.

5. Lord Diplock, chairman, *Report of the Commission to Consider Legal Procedures to Deal With Terrorist Activities in Northern Ireland* (London: HMSO, Cmnd. 5185, December 1972), p. 31. Hereinafter referred to as Diplock Report.

6. European Commission of Human Rights, *Ireland Against the United Kingdom of Great Britain and Northern Ireland: Report of the Commission* and *Annexes* I and II (Strasbourg, France, Application No. 5310/71, 25 January 1976); and *Decisions and Reports* 4 (October 1976): 4–176.

7. European Court of Human Rights, *Case of Ireland Against the United Kingdom: Judgment* (Strasbourg, 18 January 1978), p. 82.

8. *Report of an Amnesty International Mission to Northern Ireland (28 November–6 December 1977)* (London: Amnesty International, AI Index: EUR 45/01/78, June 1978), p. 70.

9. Kevin Boyle, Tom Hadden, and Paddy Hillyard, *Ten Years on in Northern Ireland* (London: Cobden Trust, 1980), pp. 62–63.

10. H. G. Bennett, chairman, *Report of the Committee of Inquiry Into Police Interrogation Procedures in Northern Ireland* (London: HMSO, Cmnd. 7497, March 1979), pp. 63–64.

11. Ibid., p. 136.

12. Boyle et. al., *Ten Years on in Northern Ireland,* p. 51.

13. *Amnesty International Report 1979* (London: Amnesty International Publications, 1979), pp. 143–44.
14. *Amnesty International Report 1981* (London: Amnesty International Publications, 1981), p. 339.
15. Editorial, "No Place for Sentiment," *New Society* (London), 2 July 1970, p. 3.
16. Compton Report, p. iv.
17. John McGuffin, *Internment* (Tralee, Co. Kerry, Ireland: Anvil Books, 1973), p. 87.
18. *Keesing's Contemporary Archives*, 6–13 November 1971, p. 24913.
19. London *Sunday Times* Insight Team, *Northern Ireland: A Report on the Conflict* (New York: Vintage, 1972), pp. 269–70.
20. British Information Services, *Northern Ireland* (New York, 1978), p. 11.
21. British Information Services, *Policy Statements*, no. 77/75, 5 December 1975.
22. Boyle et. al., *Ten Years on in Northern Ireland*, p. 62; see also Diplock Report.
23. Lord Gardiner, chairman, *Report of a Committee to Consider...Measures to Deal With Terrorism in Northern Ireland* (London: HMSO, Cmnd. 5847, January 1975), p. 66.
24. Ibid., p. 34.
25. British Information Services, *Policy Statements*, no. 67/75, 5 November 1975, p. 5; Northern Ireland Information Service, *Northern Ireland: Facts and Figures* (Belfast, December 1981), p. 23.
26. Denis Faul and Raymond Murray, *H Blocks: British Jail for Irish Political Prisoners* (Dungannon, Co. Tyrone, Northern Ireland, 1979).
27. Tomás O'Fiaich, "Statement on Long Kesh," pp. 93–94 in U. S. Committee on the Judiciary, *Northern Ireland: A Role for the United States?* (Washington, D.C.: Government Printing Office, 1979).
28. Northern Ireland Office, *H-Blocks: The Reality* (Belfast, November 1980).
29. Robin Evelegh, *Peace-Keeping in a Democratic Society* (Montreal: McGill-Queen's University Press, 1978), p. 21.
30. British Information Services, *Northern Ireland*, rev. ed. (New York, 1981), p. 7.
31. Faul & Murray, *H-Blocks*, p. 4; O'Fiaich, *"Statement on Long Kesh."*
32. British Information Services, *Policy Background*, no. 2/82 (19 March 1982): 1.
33. "Joint Declaration of August 1969," pp. 11–12 in *A Commentary by the Government of Northern Ireland to Accompany the Cameron Report* (Belfast: HMSO, Cmd. 534, September 1969), p. 12.
34. Parliamentary Commissioner for Administration and Commissioner of Complaints, *Annual Reports* of each (Belfast: HMSO, 1970–).
35. British Information Services, *Policy Background*, pp. 1–3.
36. D. R. Lowry, "Keeping Catholics in Their Place," *Commonweal* (New York), 16 July 1982, pp. 400–01.
37. Parliamentary Commissioner for Complaints, *Annual Reports*; Liam O'Dowd, p. 24 in O'Dowd, Bill Rolston, and Mike Tomlinson, *Northern Ireland: Between Civil Rights and Civil War* (London: CSE Books, 1980) p. 24.
38. Kevin Boyle, Tom Hadden, and Paddy Hillyard, *Law and State: The Case of Northern Ireland* (Amherst: University of Massachusetts Press, 1975), p. 16.
39. O'Dowd, *Northern Ireland*, p. 25.
40. National Council for Civil Liberties, "The Fair Employment Agency: Northern Ireland's Damp Squib," *Rights!* (London) 5, no. 2 (November/December 1980): 6–7.
41. "DeLorean's Dream Runs Out of Gas," *Newsweek* 1 March 1982, p. 62.
42. Joy Rudd, "The Economic Dependence of Women in Ireland," *Proceedings of the*

Fifth Annual Conference, Sociological Association of Ireland (Belfast: Queen's University, 1979), pp. 96–104.

    43. Harry Braverman, *Labor and Monopoly Capital* (New York: Monthly Review Press, 1974), chap. 15.

    44. Ann Wickham, "Women and White Collar Work," *Sociological Association of Ireland Bulletin,* Autumn 1978, pp. 11–15, pp. 13–14 cited.

    45. Northern Ireland Information Service, *Northern Ireland,* pp. 5–6.

    46. Kennedy Lindsay, *The British Intelligence Services in Action* (Newtownabbey, Co. Antrim: Dunrod Press, 1980), chap. 20; Dublin *Sunday Tribune,* "British Want Irish Bases," 22 February 1981, pp. 1–2, 18–19; "Why NATO Wants an Irish Foothold," 1 March 1981, pp. 8–9; "British Have 50 Agents in Ireland," 5 April 1981, pp. 1–2, 8–9.

CHAPTER 7

Terror in Middle- and Lower-Class Strategies

The terrorizing policies pursued by the upper class in Northern Ireland are short-sighted enough. As we have seen, their interpretation and implementation by their rank-and-file functionaries alerted social concern organizations internationally to the gravity of what was happening there. In addition, these policies and activities proved counterproductive insofar as promoting a viable consensus among the population's segments is concerned.

Middle-Class Official Terrorizing

A statement by a Northern Ireland police surgeon broadcast from London Sunday, 11 March 1979, dramatizes the class-stratified patterning of roles in the implementation of official interrogation procedures. Dr. Robert Irwin broke the middle-class functionaries' code of silence when he reported that 150 to 160 suspected IRA vigilantes whom he had examined in the Castlereagh Interrogation Centre during the preceding three years had been beaten and otherwise "physically illtreated" by Royal Ulster Constabulary personnel.[1] The official response was "to orchestrate a campaign against him [Irwin]". Various anonymous informants within the government used "the facts that his wife had been raped [by an RUC member] to try to belittle his witness." The brutal smear gained circulation, but Irwin's revelations had weight. In addition, the chief medical officer at the Armagh interrogation center, Dr. Denis Elliot, resigned with a statement that he could not continue there under the prevailing conditions. Irwin's action helped bring enough pressure on the British government to have it publish on 16 March 1979 the long-delayed Bennett report on *Police Interrogation Procedures*.[2]

Middle-class functionaries in that tense society, whether they be physicians, judges, or administrators, are habitually expected to ignore violations of rules protective of the rights of alleged subversives in cases where the putative ends of "security" appear to be served by such "practical expedients." As a theorist of repressive measures for the British asserts, "From the start [of a struggle] insurgents, their supporters, and sympathizers, constantly try to limit the soldier's [and he might have added, the policeman's] ability to carry out his functions and to force him bit by bit into a state of uselessness." Thus this middle-class rationalist for social rigidification contends that physicians, judges, and administrators are in effect justified and even required to cover lower-class operatives' excesses that assure the latter's "usefulness."[3]

Among other middle-class complications in terrorizing are problems associated with the recruitment of professional people for secret service jobs that "could hardly be advertised." They are employed "via the ramifications of personal introduction." In consequence also of their lack of "either civilian or military self-discipline, it was easy for the upper echelons of the secret departments to become havens of mediocrity or vapid eccentricity."[4] Reference is especially to leaders in the British Defence Intelligence 5 (DI5) and DI6 secret services, both of which have operations in Northern Ireland.[5] Such individuals provide guidance and permissive assistance to the largely lower-class counterguerrilla guerrillas, "dirty trick" operatives, and *agents provocateurs* entrusted with fighting and infiltrating insurgent groups.[6]

To try to humanize the RUC's public image, its middle-class leaders organized what has been called "soft" policing. This takes the form of a large community relations branch that offers teen-age rambles with police, four- to seven-day and weekend adventure camps, Blue Lamp discos, Blue Lamp Football games, school events, seminars for "key people," cadet training for eighteen-year-olds, and involvements for pensioners and others.[7] At the same time, the use of "hard" policing, sometimes of a reckless sort, continues. The use of plastic bullets, presumably as a harmless but scary crowd-control device, has resulted in at least eleven deaths since their introduction in 1973, and the deliberate driving of armored cars into groups of people has had murderous consequences.[8] The RUC has become an important "testing ground for the latest police riot control technology" in one of the most closely monitored areas in the world.[9]

Lower-Class Official Terrorizing

The chief governmental instruments in intersectarian strife are made up predominantly of lower-class Loyalists plus similar people recruited in Great Britain, especially in the more depressed areas. They serve in the Royal Ulster Constabulary (RUC), the RUC Reserve (RUCR), until 1970 the Ulster Special Constabulary (USC, or "B" Specials), since 1970 the Ulster Defence Regiment (UDR) of local people under army control, and the British army.

Unofficially, the RUC actually succeeded the private army organized in 1912 to oppose home rule for Ireland, the Protestant Ulster Volunteer Force (UVF). Many UVF members joined the RUC, and others came over from the disbanded Royal Irish Constabulary (RIC). These groups gave the RUC a strong Loyalist, anti-Nationalist, anti-Green character from its establishment in 1922.

The RUC is a centrally controlled body that in 1982 includes 7,467, of whom one-tenth are women; the RUCR has 4,900, mostly part-time members, of whom about one-sixth are women. The UDR numbers some 7,500 army troops, of whom two-thirds serve part time; about 9 percent of these troops are female "greenfinches." The British army in the province in 1981–82 totaled 12,100 troops. Thus the control of 1.5 million people requires 31,967 security personnel, almost three times the force of 1969.[10] Annual prison costs expanded from £596,000 in 1968 to £30,773,773 in 1976. Expenses since then, with totals not available, include considerable new construction as well as staffing. In 1969–78, total prison officers rose from 292 to 2,339.

Estimates of the percentage of Roman Catholics in the RUC and RUCR range from 4 to 10 and in the UDR, as low as 2 percent even though that ethnic group constitutes one-third of the province's population.[11] As the writer Jack Holland recalls from his own Belfast youth: "The state of which we were citizens ... was set up to ensure privileges would be accorded to 'loyalists.' And loyalists were Protestants. By definition, a Catholic was a rebel."[12]

The total number of complaints recorded against RUC members rose from 1,366 in 1975 to 2,331 in 1978 and 2,183 in 1979, but the complaints procedure is notoriously ineffective. Only 13 of the 1979 complaints were "substantiated"; 813 were not; 42, withdrawn; 17, not proceeded with; 561, under investigation; 747 await decisions. On the one hand, the Bennett Committee of Inquiry claimed there to be "a concerted campaign intended to discredit the R.U.C." and also an effort "of the terrorist organisations simply to swamp the force with complaints and so reduce its operational efficiency." On the other hand, the committee admitted "that, although criminal proceedings have been brought against a number of police officers in respect of alleged offences in the course of interrogation, no final conviction has resulted." The committee added: "We record here that, at least since 1974, no disciplinary proceedings have been brought in respect of the interrogation of persons in custody."[13]

The old USC, of "B" Specials, including 8,000 mostly part-time members in 1969, were characterized by a governmental commission at that time as follows:

> The recruitment of this force, for traditional and historical reasons, is in practice limited to members of the Protestant faith. ... Until very recent years, for drill and training purposes, the Ulster Special Constabulary made large use of Orange Lodges and this ... tended to accentuate in the eyes of the Catholic minority the assumed partisan and sectarian character of the force. ... There were ... a number of complaints that among the groups of "loyalists" who from time to time were involved in clashes and conflict with Civil Rights demonstrators there were identified members of the "B" Specials. ...
>
> This catalogue of grievance deserves, in our judgment, to be seriously regarded in any analysis of the immediate causes of the disturbances.[14]

Protests forced the disbanding of the "B" Specials and their replacement in 1970 with what was promised to be a smaller Ulster Defence Regiment. The latter was to be mixed religiously, only lightly armed, and under British army rather than local RUC control. Early on, it is said to have enrolled some 18 percent Roman Catholics, but by January 1974, above 97 percent of its 8,000 and more members were Protestants, and its soldiers were heavily armed with rifles and machine guns. Protestant vigilantes had again infiltrated and also discouraged Roman Catholic participation. They were thus able to operate both inside and outside of the governmental establishment.[15]

The lower-class rank-and-file soldiers whom the British send to Northern Ireland are a mixed lot. As a British journalist reports: "By the middle of 1973 there were virtually no British Army infantry units who had not seen service in Northern Ireland during the previous four years." Prior to his arrival there, "the ordinary soldier knew little of Northern Ireland and its developing problems."[16] They were "briefed," as it were, for the duties they would have there chiefly by the anti-Irish accounts in the sensational popular media of Great Britain and by the typically anti-Irish gossip of their social circles.[17] Thus, to them, all Irish, regardless of religious label, are "paddies" and problems! This is shocking to Loyalists who also look upon

Nationalists in rejection as "paddies"![18] The province thus is useful as a place in which to train soldiers and experiment with new weapons and techniques, such as CS gas and rubber or plastic "crowd-control" bullets.

Macro-events that we describe in the next chapter help characterize the roles of the lower-class "security forces" in terrorism, but the people of the province are more constantly and intimately touched by frequent groups of soldiers and police on patrol, armed and armored cars, body searches before being admitted to public buildings, barriers to be passed at key street points, the harassment of not-at-all-gentle house searches, and the brutalizing involvement of children and teen-agers in the spirit of the struggle. For example, in 1971-80, there were 315,124 house searches, with peaks of 74,556 in 1973 and 74,914 in 1974.[19] Few lower-class families do not have a friend or relative who has been "lifted" for interrogation. The so-called Ulsterisation of security forces through the use of less soldiers from Great Britain and more members of the RUC, RUCR, and UDR has done little to change this ambience; the ethnocentrism of those functionaries is well known.

What do security people gain from working under such conditions? This differs somewhat between the police and the army. With increasing unemployment, "defence" work is an attractive recourse, especially for Protestant males. "Public administration and defence" account for 10.5 percent of the work force. An investigative group summed up the contrast of the lots of the locals versus those of the Brit soldiers thus: " 'Defence' has replaced ship-building as the backbone of male protestant working class employment. ... In short, there is money in the 'troubles' for everyone but the Brits. Their wages are low, with no chance of overtime money and little by way of danger money."[20]

Some of the thoughts expressed by Brit soldiers about their participation are instructive, but unfortunately, under the British Official Secrets Acts, only ex-military personnel in exile or in defiance of prosecution can reveal their socially significant experiences. Brian Moran, a Royal Marine Commando who deserted to Sweden, writes: "We were supposed to be there to keep the peace, but I found a lot of prejudice in the Marines against ordinary Catholics. They gave a lot of public abuse in the streets. It was always covert—when there weren't any newspaper reporters about."[21] Ian Phillips, another Marine Commando, reports: "The amount of desertion is incredible, the numbers applying for discharges is increasing and this is very much connected with Northern Ireland as well as with pay and conditions."[22]

Meurig Parri, ten years in the army, five of them (1967–72) as a commissioned officer in an infantry regiment, makes these points:

> The troops ... discovered that the people they were fighting against ... spoke the same language as themselves, they lived in streets in Belfast or Derry which were identical in all respects to the streets of Cardiff or Sheffield or wherever the troops came from. The troops actually started to identify with the enemy. ... The effect of this on Army morale was absolutely catastrophic. ... The number of desertions from the Army, the number of people who wanted to buy themselves out, the general sort of depression that sets in, was really hard to cope with. ...
>
> [To] its own Army, the government is saying you are fighting a war in Northern Ireland, so get at it and sort these people out. But the British government is obviously saying to the Americans and people all over the world that this is not a war at all. What they are saying is that the British Army is doing a wonderful job sorting out a few criminals, a few terrorists, who are sort of making life terrible for the vast majority of peaceful, law-abiding citizens. ... But that is a total travesty of the truth ... there is a war situation by any sensible definition of the term. ...
>
> It is probably true to say that the British Army in Northern Ireland has failed to win this war in some measure because of the lack of cooperation between themselves and the police. One of the reasons for that lack of cooperation is that the ordinary soldiers are really quite disgusted at the blatant religious sectarianism of the police. The RUC ... makes no bones about the fact that they hate Catholics. They show great discrimination in favor of Protestants.[23]

Curiously enough, the British General Sir John Hackett in 1979 agreed with a significant part of Parri's statement when he wrote: "Whatever minor modifications may from time to time emerge, there will continue to be no alternative to persistent and effective military containment of this explosive mixture, and no one who should or can provide this but the British. The UK can go on doing this for a very long time yet."[24]

What dismal notions these statements give of the present and future of this ancient colony of the British police state! The only optimism that the empire police strategist Evelegh can offer is that "to counter terrorism successfully, the Government must conduct a coordinated campaign bringing into harmony its economic, political, social, legal, military, police and public relations efforts against terrorism and insurrection so that each reinforces the others."[25] He did not offer one wholly successful example of such a campaign under United Kingdom auspices.

Terrorizing Threats by Middle-Class "Respectables"

Terrorizing threats sometimes involve direct efforts to coerce and sometimes indirect ones through raising the possibility of lower-class violence as an alternative to compliance. They reflect the deep middle-class embedment in the three Northern Ireland ethnic conspiracies. They find expression in policy statements, actions, and agreements relating to employment, housing, and social services including public safety. They contribute to segregation and efforts to aid members of the in-group at the expense of, or at least in preference to, members of other groups.

Middle-class dedication to compromise, a dedication that more often serves upper-class establishment interests than those of society more generally, finds many sophisticated forms of expression. For example, middle-class people devote themselves to so-called peace organizations connected with religious denominations and to voluntary social work, demonstration, and protest societies of a "respectable" or discreet sort. Effective, actionist efforts by small groups of Dissenters, Protestants, Roman Catholics, and Quakers get grudging support, if any, from the bulk of the middle class. The net effect of "respectable" efforts is largely either cosmetic or the promotion of a kind of social anesthesia that looks to the restoration of the preexisting exploitative social order with no appreciable modification. These allegedly benign efforts terrorize the lower class because of the hopeless realization they give that lower-class needs may be obscured by rhetoric. Chapter 9 deals with these problems in more detail.[26]

The Roman Catholic section of the middle class expanded after World War II under the stimulation of an education act of 1947, as well as other changes. That act "threw open the door for Grammar school education for all those who by 'age, aptitude and ability' were suited for it." It also called for the provision of "scholarships to institutions of Further Education, which of course included Universities."[27]

Some examples of middle-class leadership in organizations and events that appear to substantial opposing publics as terrorizing take place in (1) ethnic socializing bodies, (2) the Reverend Ian R.K. Paisley's crusade, (3) the civil rights movement, (4) political parties, (5) the litigation situation, and (6) social scientific investigations.

Ethnic Socializing Bodies. The Loyal Orange Institution (LOI), or Orange Order, and the Ancient Order of Hibernians (AOH) are often referred to as "opposite numbers," but this is scarcely an accurate characterization. Both have strong religious orientations. Both have initiation rites. Both offer social halls and annual celebrations in the form of spectacular parades. What the Reverend S. E. Long says about the LOI could also be asserted about the AOH: "Its encouragement of innocent party pleasures, its big family holidays and its sympathetic and practical concern for community needs is obvious to all but the blindly prejudiced."[28]

The size and influence of the two organizations is, however, vastly different. The reason that Northern Ireland has been called "The Orange State" is that at least one-third of the province's Protestant males belong to the LOI. Membership estimates range from 90,000 to 130,000. In contrast, the AOH is said to have only 5,000 to 10,000 members. On 19 October 1981, the Reverend Martin Smyth, Grand Master of the LOI, claimed that he could offer a vigilante force of 10,000 which would work without pay under direction of the security forces if the government would agree. Apparently this was to resurrect the discredited "B" Specials and offset Paisley's "third force."[29]

According to community relations specialist John Darby, the AOH "attempted to function as a Catholic equivalent of the Orange Order" and to benefit from strong links with the American AOH, but its support is chiefly in country areas "and the Catholic church itself provides a social cohesion similar to that encouraged by the Orange Institution."[30] Many Protestants, especially in the middle class, regard the LOI as a necessary evil, and it is also stronger in rural than urban districts. Particularly since the 1880s, however, politically ambitious middle-class leaders have exploited the LOI as a power base through inflaming its overwhelmingly lower-class membership against lower-class Roman Catholics.

Paisley's Crusade. Early after his ordination as a reformed Presbyterian clergyman in 1945 at the age of nineteen, Paisley reacted against what he denounced as the liberalism of his domination. In consequence, he founded in 1951 a separate denomination, the National Union of Protestants, now called Free Presbyterian. By the onset of the "troubles" in 1968, his sect had expanded from about 1,000 to 15,000 members in 12 churches in the province. The next year, he dedicated his large Martyrs' Memorial Church in Belfast.

As that ecclesiastical base developed, Paisley discovered the utility of spectacular events to magnify his fundamentalist, anti-Roman-Catholic drive into something of a politico-religious crusade. An early event was a parade to protest the lowering of the United Kingdom flag in 1963 on the occasion of the death of Pope John XXIII. The march was banned under the Special Powers Act, and he was fined £10. He refused to pay the fine, preferring to go to prison, but someone anonymously paid it for him. He accused the government of paying the fine to avoid its own embarrassment. His and Major Ronald Bunting's massive demonstration in Armagh on 30 November 1968 blocked a civil rights campaign march. For this the two were imprisoned six weeks for unlawful assembly, a "persecution" that Paisley fully exploited. His participation in such events has continued.

After investigating Paisley's 1969 agitations, the Northern Ireland Scarman Tribunal of Inquiry decided that "his speeches and writings [published in the *Protestant Telegraph*, his newspaper, and elsewhere] must have been one of the many factors increasing tension in 1969," but it concluded that "he neither plotted nor organised the disorders." They also found "no evidence that he was a party to any of the acts of violence investigated by us."[31]

That is a convenient characteristic of many middle-class roles related to terror. They stimulate others, usually of the lower class and the "security forces," to do the dirty work—or at least to threaten it. Paisley even chaired from 1966 the Ulster Constitution Defence Committee, which counter-demonstrated against many Republican Easter parades and civil rights marches. This body had associated with it in 1968–71 the paramilitary Ulster Protestant Volunteers, a body shortly proscribed by the government and then disclaimed by Paisley. In 1981, however, he again admitted to have enlisted a body called a "third force," the purpose of which, he told a Glasgow Loyalist rally on 28 November 1981, is to "kill the terrorists."

Paisley's power has continued to grow. He became a member of the Stormont Parliament in 1970, the Westminster Parliament in 1971, and the Strasbourg European Parliament in 1979. His actions in those bodies have scarcely been diplomatic. For example, on 16 November 1981, he and two of his Democratic Unionist Party colleagues were suspended from the Westminster House of Commons in response to their disruptive behavior. His general propaganda line thus continues to feature these points:

> The usual bunch of ecumenicists ... state that the troubles are based on political and social issues with deep historical roots and they deplore the fact that the situation has been described as religious in character. ...

> The fact is the troubles stem from the interference of Popes and Popery in Irish affairs. ... This is a religious war—a battle between Truth and Error, Light and Darkness, Bible Protestantism and Popery.[32]

Civil Rights Movement. The civil rights movement is described elsewhere, but its middle-class leadership is to be emphasized here. Like the middle class generally, the Roman Catholic middle class are responsible for terrorizing threats that are not necessarily so intended. In the civil rights movement, into which they attempted to attract Protestant professional people, they mostly wanted "to reassure Protestants that Catholics were prepared to work within Northern Ireland to achieve a more democratic state." Few of those who took part in the Northern Ireland Civil Rights Association protest march in August 1968 appeared to realize that they would terrify Loyalists, that Loyalists would oppose them violently, and that that opposition would "set off a sectarian chain reaction." These Roman Catholics "were mostly moderate, middle-class people, with a sprinkling of earnest radical young students and some republicans who were eager to get away from the failed politics of violence."[33] That NICRA included some members of the Irish Republican Army and later of its Official offshoot has been used to denigrate its program, but NICRA's effective dedication to nonviolent confrontations can scarcely be doubted.[34] NICRA still terrifies the Loyalists.

Political Parties. Even though there were minority political parties, the Official or Ulster Unionist Party (OUP) controlled the government of the province from 1921 to 1972, but factions of a divisive nature began to grow within it from the 1960s. The intimate relationship of the OUP with the semisecret LOI "makes it difficult to discover exactly how its [LOI's] influence in the Party is exercised, and this, in turn, causes the frustration and antagonism of the very considerable non-Orange section of the population."[35]

While the OUP tried to appear at least to represent a broad spectrum of left-to-right Protestant groups, Terence O'Neill's reformist policies as Prime Minister in 1963–69 led to some splintering of the OUP. Among other things, he tried to make the party religiously nonsectarian, but few people inside or outside the OUP held with that view. The redevelopment of political parties organized tension rather than abated it.

From 1970, the Social Democratic and Labour Party (SDLP) absorbed smaller groups and came to represent the majority of the Roman Catholics.

At the same time, pro-O'Neill and other concerned citizens started the reformist Alliance Party in an effort to attract support from both sides of the community. Paisley, in the late 1960s, had been involved in the Protestant Unionist Party and won a Stormont seat with its label in 1970. In 1971, however, he founded the Democratic Unionist Party, "The Unionist Party You Can Trust," and it gave him a growing political instrument.

Election returns in 1975 and 1979 give a notion of the changing and threatening political situation. The 1975 election of constitutional convention delegates had these first-choice votes: 62.5 percent for all Unionists, including 14.8 for DUP; 23.7 for SDLP; 9.8 for Alliance; and 4.0 scattered. In the 1979 election of three members to the European parliament, winners and their percentages of first choices were Paisley (DUP), 29.8; John Hume (SDLP), 24.6; and John Taylor (OUP), 11.9. The other third of the vote was scattered among ten other candidates. These results worried both the Orange and the Green: the Orange about Paisley and Hume, the Green about Paisley and Taylor.[36]

Litigation. Like other aspects of the "security industry," the legal profession has expanded substantially since 1968, a tripling of the number of barristers and almost a doubling of the solicitors. It has been called "the most secretive and exclusive private club in the North." Since partition, the law faculty at Queen's University, Belfast, has been the chief training school for the province's lawyers, " a key role in reproducing 'proper' professionals and servicing them." Like many schools, its "relationship to the repressive state has been supportive, even if indirect," but at the same time, its students do include individuals who think and eventually act to the contrary, " 'rebels' despite the Law Faculty."[37]

Relatively effective nonviolent actionist work in behalf of civil rights has taken the form of data gathering for litigation and then of the litigation itself. NICRA, such social investigators as the Reverend Denis Faul and the Reverend Raymond Murray,[38] and the lawyers belonging to the Association for Legal Justice, the Irish Association of Democratic Lawyers, and the Northern Ireland Association of Socialist Lawyers have been outstanding in this work. These groups carry on their projects not only through the United Kingdom courts but also through those of the twenty-six counties and the European Commission and Court of Human Rights. Whether these efforts are looked upon as supporting or mitigating terrorization depends upon the vested interests of the commentator.

Social Scientific Investigations. Reference is made to reports of such work at various points in this book. Only the typically middle-class-oriented nature of much of its activity—for better or for worse—is to be mentioned here. The nearest one can come to seeing lower-class-oriented research reports is in the pieces of in-depth investigative reporting that appear in the more radical periodicals.

In the welter of social scientific studies dealing with the small statelet's woes, many investigators attempt to serve upper- or middle- or lower-class interests. These efforts can be clarifying even though biased. Some reports demonstrate the potential utility of a freewheeling style of objectivity such as is idealized in social scientific theorizing. Notable among the latter have been certain sample interview surveys, participant observation and clinical reports, and sociolegal analyses.

All studies of any consequence have been attacked, and the discussions of their merits in various forums have been useful.

Terrorizing by Predominantly Lower-Class Insurgents

Orange, Loyalist, or Unionist terrorists are organized principally into the Ulster Volunteer Force (UVF) as reconstituted in 1966, the Ulster Defence Association (UDA) set up in 1971, and the Ulster Freedom Fighters (UFF) formed in 1973 apparently as a splinter from the UDA. There are other splinters or names-of-convenience under which gangs operate, but these three have attempted to bring together a variety of local defense bodies that had sprung up throughout the province in response to the renewal of the struggle.

Green, Nationalist, or Republican ranks are divided principally among the old Official Irish Republican Army (OIRA); the Provisional Irish Republican Army (PIRA), dating from the split within the IRA in 1969–70; and the Irish National Liberation Army (INLA), a product of an OIRA division in 1972.

The third principal collection of rank-and-file combatants consists, as we have seen, of largely lower-class security people, police and military, who include undercover and plainclothes operatives to a degree infiltrated into the above organizations.

The most active insurgent groups militarily have been the UVF, UDA, and UFF and the PIRA and INLA, of which all but the UDA have been formally proscribed for most of the period. At the same time, all have close ties with legal and open political parties!

Loyalist Vigilantes. The UVF claims a long history of Loyalist military efforts. Upon its revival in 1966, it asserted its descent from the organization of the same name formed in 1912 to fight for Unionist Protestants against the Irish home rule then being sought. The old organization had even furnished most of the members of the 36th (Ulster) Division of the British army in 1914, a unit that lost many in the Battle of the Somme in July 1916.

Amid a rash of petrol bombings of premises owned by Roman Catholics in the spring of 1966, coincident with the IRA's celebration of the fiftieth anniversary of the Easter Rising, the UVF again burst upon the Ulster scene. On 21 May, Belfast newspapers carried a statement by a man said to be "Captain William Johnston, Adjutant, First Batallion, Belfast UVF," in part as follows: "From this day on we declare war against the IRA and its splinter groups. Known IRA men will be executed mercilessly and without hesitation. Less extreme measures will be taken against anyone sheltering or helping them. ... [We] solemnly warn the authorities to make no more speeches of appeasement. We are heavily armed Protestants dedicated to this cause."[39] In response, Prime Minister Terence O'Neill at first announced that he would not invoke the Special Powers Act to proscribe any Protestant outfit, but after further atrocities, he stated on 28 June 1966: "This organisation [the UVF] now takes its proper place alongside the IRA in the schedule of illegal bodies."[40]

In May 1974 to November 1975, the proscription was removed in order to try to turn the UVF from violence to political activity, but that recourse failed. Its paramilitary campaign continues.

By 1981, the UVF was taking a slightly more judicious view, one that suggested some compromise. In its periodical, *Combat: The Journal of the Ulster Volunteers,* it came out for "an all-party conference and attempt to break the deadlock." It linked this with "the granting of Special or Emergency Status for persons convicted for politically motivated offences." In other words, "Special Category must be linked with a political settlement which in turn must be linked to discussions on a phased Amnesty." It thus wanted to "use our influence to bring a stable democratic administration to Northern Ireland."[41]

The UVF's support for special category status arose from the fact that some of its own prisoners had been so recognized. It even brought together an Ulster Loyalist Co-ordinating Committee "determined to ensure that the British Government cannot and will not be permitted to ignore the legitimate aspirations of ALL Loyalist prisoners of war."[42] The UVF had found itself in part in much the same position as the PIRA: Many of its "political" prisoners were being treated as "criminals." It was still a proscribed organization. It, too, would like to look forward to a settlement in which its objectives might be gained and its prisoners amnestied. Thus *Combat* rejected "the spurious cries of 'criminal' from the unthinking lips of those who should know better." It reminded UVF prisoners: "Ulster has always, from the time of the Shutting of the Gates of Londonderry [1689] to the raising of Carson's Volunteer Army [1912], resorted to independent and illegal armed resistance in times of great peril."[43]

Not at all hopeful of a British-sponsored compromise of an agreeable sort, the UVF joined in 1981 in the reforming of both the Ulster Army Council (UAC) and the Ulster Workers' Council (UWC). The UAC had originally been established in 1973 to be a united front of the UVF, UDA, Ulster Special Constabulary Association, Loyalist Defence Volunteers, Orange Volunteers, and Red Hand Commandos. It had been instrumental in supporting the Loyalist strike organized in May 1974 by the UWC that led to the collapse of a power-sharing administration set up on 1 January that year at Stormont by the British government. When the UWC organized another strike in 1977, a more limited one, it had the backing of the United Unionist Action Council but not of the Official Unionist and Vanguard political parties. It thus failed to gain sufficient support to succeed.

In announcing the reforming of the Ulster Army Council in 1981, the UVF spoke of "the gravity of the situation" and said the UAC "has been formed for the defence of Loyalist areas in Ulster." It added: "If the need arises, it will have no hesitation in retaliation, even to the extent of taking the offensive."[44] In making a similar announcement for the UWC, the UVF reminded that the UWC "destroyed the [N.I. political] structure in 1974," and promised: "If need be, we will destroy [it] once more."[45]

Even though it is associated in the Ulster Army Council with illegal organizations and is understood to be related to the Ulster Freedom Fighters, the UDA maintains its legal status. Its uniformed members constitute the largest voluntary paramilitary organization. Advocating "Law before Violence," its membership reached a high point of 40,000 in 1972, but it claims to have limited itself to 10,000 to 12,000 members by 1978 in order to have a more controllable, more disciplined body. All along, the UDA, like the UVF, has sought to restore the "Orange State" of 1921–72 or some dependent or independent approximation of that one-party Protestant setup.[46]

In 1981, UDA's chairperson since 1973, Andy Tyrie, still sticks to this presumably "legal" stance: "We are a counter-terrorist organisation. The only way we'll get peace here is to terrorise the terrorists." From 1977, the UDA also worked through a political wing, the New Ulster Political Research Group, more practically renamed in June 1981 the Ulster Loyalist Democratic Party. The responsibility of UDA members for the killing of four prominent Republicans and for the wounding of Bernadette Devlin McAliskey (former British M.P.) brought on agitation again early in 1981 for the organization's proscription. As the London *Economist* noted on 7 February, however, "The British government's opinion ... is still that a ban [on the UDA] would not only be unenforceable, but also unhelpful to the security forces. It would tend to wipe out whatever influence the more moderate and more politically-minded elements in the UDA might have." UDA's legal status, the *Economist* realizes, "makes a mockery of the law" to many people.

Green Vigilantes. Loyalist reactions against the civil rights marches and confrontations of 1968–69 found the IRA following a changed policy. The IRA's campaign of 1956–62 had been a violent one, and it had failed. This had led to a decision to infiltrate nonviolent organizations that might forward its efforts to undermine the current provincial government. Thus, when the Cameron Commission reported to the Stormont parliament in September 1969 on *Disturbances in Northern Ireland,* it spoke especially of the roles on the Green side of the Northern Ireland Civil Rights Association (NICRA), the People's Democracy (PD), and the Derry Citizens Action Committee (DCAC), but the IRA was there. As the commission concluded: "Because the Civil Rights movement and its published objects were (at the time) wholly rejected by the Government it was to be expected that the I.R.A. or members of it in Northern Ireland would seek to turn that situation to their advantage." At that stage, the commission found "no evidence ... that such members either incited to riot or took part themselves in acts of violence." IRA members served especially as marchers or stewards in demonstrations and as organizers of street-by-street "defence committees" in the Green ghettos.[47]

NICRA, organized in 1967 as an affiliate of the English National Council for Civil Liberties, and related civil rights bodies shortly ceased to be the principal concerns of either the government or the Loyalists. Militants in the IRA had become restive with their organization's political, Marxist-Leninist leanings. The PIRA break occurred in December 1969 when the IRA Army Council decided to give token recognition to the Westminster, Dublin, and Stormont parliaments, a decided change from its traditional absententionism and reliance on violence. Sinn Féin, the political party affiliated with the IRA, similarly split at its January 1970 convention. After the division, the Caretaker Executive for Provisional Sinn Féin asserted that the break occurred because of:

> the failure to provide adequate protection for Nationalist areas in the North in August [1969]; the adoption of an extreme Socialist policy leading to totalitarian dictatorship; favouring the retention of the Stormont Parliament as opposed to a takeover by Westminster; and the changes within the Movement since 1964, which saw the departure of many genuine Republicans and their replacement with people interested *in a more radical form of movement*.[48]

As a close observer notes, "Both I.R.A.s, the Officials and the Provisionals, had the basis of an organisation in Northern Ireland when the British troops invaded the Falls [area of Belfast] in July 1970, but neither had the capability nor the backing necessary to be a credible fighting force. The British action changed all that, with the strength of the Provisionals, in particular, increasing rapidly." PIRA amalgamated many local defense groups that were springing up and that also would not accept OIRA's Marxist-Leninist orientation.[49]

PIRA's ideology is not well defined. It has had financial support at times from well-placed politicians and businessmen in the twenty-six counties.[50] But it says it aims at establishing an island-wide democratic and socialized state such as was envisioned by leaders of the Easter Rising of 1916.[51] An admirer nevertheless contends: "The Provos, despite all their imperfections and the heavy historical impedimenta they carry into political battle, are the vanguard of the anti-imperialist struggle in Ireland—this partly because of the failures of the left."[52]

In May 1979, PIRA captured a copy of a memorandum on "Northern Ireland: Future Terrorist Trends" that had been prepared by Brigadier J. M. Glover for the Ministry of Defence. It gives a fascinating assessment of PIRA's operations. Here is a summary of the chief conclusions reached by Glover:

In 1979–83, he predicts the continuance of the PIRA "while the British remain in Northern Ireland." He foresees no recruitment problems, and popular support will continue. In order to purchase arms, PIRA "will probably have to rely increasingly on armed robbery" because of declining support from overseas and from other sources. He adds: "We believe that the Republic will continue to act as a haven for terrorists and that they will continue to receive arms through Eire, particularly from the USA and through contacts with overseas terrorists groups. We believe however that there is little risk of any foreign government giving active support to PIRA." He expects PIRA to focus violence against the security forces, their bases, and the public utilities. PIRA is not likely to employ "chemical, biological or nuclear methods of attack during the next 5 years."[53]

The Glover report checks well with other sources. It clearly indicates that PIRA has not been developed and controlled—as some allege[54]—as part of a Soviet Union international terrorist network.

PIRA's £1.5 million a year, or thereabouts, comes from bank and postal robberies and also from their control of pubs, from collections, and from the levying of "protection" assessments. For example, in West Belfast, "no builder could operate there without Provisional consent." In East Belfast, the UDA "holds similar sway." Allegations of PIRA involvement in drug trafficking are brushed aside by the investigative journalist Tim Pat Coogan who insists, "Drugs, or rather drug traffickers, have at times been the subject of very severe I.R.A. punishments." After all, as Coogan points out, the PIRA depends upon quite "conservative supporters both in Ireland and America."[55]

In the mid-1970s it became clear to the PIRA leadership that the traditional army type of organization into brigades, battalions, and companies was too easily investigated or even infiltrated in an effective manner by security forces. As a PIRA "Staff Report," captured in 1977, notes, "The three-day and seven-day detention orders [under the Special Powers Act] are breaking volunteers and it is the Republican Army's fault for not indoctrinating volunteers with the psychological strength to resist interrogation." The old structure was therefore being dissolved and replaced with one based on cells that placed "unknown men and new recruits into a new structure." Each cell of four members was to have such a specialty as sniping, execution, bombing, or robbery.

> Cells should operate as often as possible outside of their own areas; both to confuse Brit Intelligence ... and to expand our operational areas. ...
>
> All present volunteers under old structure must be re-educated and given up-dated lectures in combating new interrogation techniques.
>
> Women and girls have greater roles to play as military activists and as leaders in sections of civil administration in propaganda and publicity. ...

CLUBS: Clubs are bases of support, places of cultural activity and fund-raising venues. Clubs should now be expanded into Community services (e.g. for the youth, mothers, pensioners, etc.)

Sinn Fein ... should come under Army organisers at all levels. ... Sinn Fein should be radicalised (under Army direction) and should agitate around social and economic issues which attack the welfare of the people. S.F. should be directed to infiltrate other organisations to win support for, and sympathy to, the Movement. S.F. should be re-educated and have a big role to play in publicity and propaganda departments.[56]

The Irish National Liberation Army (INLA) is much smaller than PIRA, but it "has been blamed by the British security forces for many murders and acts of violence in NI between 1976 and 1979."[57] Its activities are publicized in the periodical of its affiliate, the Irish Republican Socialist Party, called *An Camchéachta: The Starry Plough.*

INLA did not split from OIRA because of the latter's then Marxist-Leninist ideology but because of OIRA's willingness to work from within the Dublin and Belfast establishments. As the IRSP notes, "As early as 1972 the leadership of the Officials abandoned the struggle by declaring a cease fire at a time of escalating British repression." INLA is both Marxist-Leninist and terrorist. Its IRSP is amused that by 1979 the "existence of the Official I.R.A., despite public protestations that it is disbanded, is the most embarrassing contradiction that SF WP [OIRA's affiliated Sinn Féin the Workers' Party] had to contend with."[58] In Northern Ireland, the Republican Clubs are the OIRA's political affiliate.

Tomás MacGiolla, president of SF WP, asserts: "I have no reason to think that (the Official IRA) still exists. ... I am satisfied that it certainly doesn't exist in any association with us." Sean Garland, the party's general secretary, claims that "this party wanted nothing to do" with OIRA from 1972 on. In response to these statements, the investigative reporter Vincent Browne points out "that almost all the 100 or so members of the Official IRA are members of SF WP." The party has about 1,000 dues-paying members, but it is "probably the wealthiest party in the entire country" with its office buildings in Dublin and Trevor Hill, Newry, its five social clubs in Belfast, and other facilities. For the Workers' Party, the OIRA "became primarily merely a fund-raising organisation but it served other purposes too."[59]

OIRA's "other purposes" include policing the Northern Ireland and Dublin drinking clubs; the maintenance of organizational discipline "through intimidation and beatings"; the feudings with PIRA and INLA, mostly in 1974, 1975, and 1977, and the management of rackets, especially in Belfast. These activities have involved murders, knee-cappings, evictions, and bombings. As to the actual relationship existing between OIRA and SF WP, OIRA "was always used to control Sinn Féin and this did not end certainly until well after 1978, if even then,"[60] as Browne sees it.

Just how leftish the party is now is difficult to judge. It has been known as Sinn Féin, Official Sinn Féin, Sinn Féin (Gardiner Place), Sinn Féin the Workers' Party, and now The Workers' Party in the twenty-six counties and Republican Clubs in the six. A recent editorial in the party's monthly magazine, *Workers Life,* sums up its position: "Absolute and total resistance to terrorism combined with a commitment to building the unity of working people is the only answer." It calls for combining this with "disarmament and the ending of people's fears of nuclear annihilation."[61] The party plus the OIRA constitute a strange complex.

Statements by spokespeople for the OIRA and the PIRA give their currently contrasting views on terror as strategy. OIRA's Chief of Staff Cathal Goulding sums up his organization's position on terrorism from 1973 thus: "Nothing could be more contrary to the revolutionary strategy of the Republican Movement than the indiscriminate bombing and burning campaigns. ... To the militarist, sustaining a struggle becomes more important than achieving victory and it is apparent now that there are sinister elements at work who are leading some sincere people by the military nose to utter defeat."[62] The OIRA of the 1970s was not pacifist. It just did not at the time of that statement look upon anti-British violence as its best strategy.

In contrast, the 1979 Christmas message from the PIRA Publicity Bureau in Dublin contained these sentences:

> 1979 has seen us perfect some of our attacks against the enemy and we have dealt them several deadly blows—not just at Narrow Water [scene of the slaughter of 16 paratroopers and two other British soldiers with three-quarters of a ton of explosives] and in the execution [on the same day, 27 August] of Lord Mountbatten but in the determined way we militarily roared back at them in contradiction to their propaganda. ... The Republican Army cannot be stopped![63]

The Provo party newspaper contended at the end of 1979: "Since the first civil rights march eleven years ago, up to IRA bombings this week, British control over Ireland has been slowly slipping out of their grasp." It claimed that their "armed struggle and the incredible resistance of the people and the prisoners will eventually take its toll in the despairing will of the British to continue."[64]

All sorts of estimates are made of how many Loyalist and Green insurgents there might be in Northern Ireland and of their support. The Northern Ireland Attitude Survey revealed that in 1978 70.7 percent of the Protestants rejected the establishment of a united Ireland even "by peaceful means." On the contrary, 82.8 percent of the Roman Catholics wished that solution. The Reverend Ian Paisley's extreme Protestant Democratic Unionist Party then claimed 11.8 percent backing, and the OIRA-affiliated Republican Clubs, 2.3 percent.[65] At the same time, it is well to consider the point made by a careful sociological investigator, Frank Burton, that "the particular ideology of Provisional Republicanism has been able to fuse the social consciousness of Catholicism into political practice ... a politics of civil rights through national liberation."[66] This strength does not necessarily show up in voting records.

Lower-class Goals. Loyalist terrorists of the UVF and UDA seek to destroy the leadership of the Green organizations; to discourage recruitment into them; and to make support for Green programs appear to be foolish, immoral, or futile gestures. As the American Central Intelligence Agency generalizes: "Unlike publicity-seeking left-wing terrorist groups who tend to select targets that provide the greatest political impact, right-wing groups tend to be motivated by desire to terrorize or destroy specific enemies. ...they most often conduct assassinations and bombings."[67] This is a reasonable summary of Loyalist objectives. Loyalist leaders regard their procedures as the only ways available to them for stimulating the British government to restore the "Orange state" as a protection for them from encroaching Green power from the south and from the more prolifically breeding Northern Roman Catholics.

From a Green standpoint, as viewed by PIRA and INLA, terrorism and the melodrama of the hunger strikes offer the only ways available with which to destabilize British imperial control of the province. They hope they will make the six counties too expensive to retain. As part of this, they hope to embarrass Westminster with terrorizing events in Great Britain and even in British military installations on the continent of Europe. As the American Central Intelligence Agency reports, "The PIRA has conducted more international terrorist attacks than any other single terrorist group. They routinely attack the British military in Europe."[68] As time has gone on and the paramilitary organizations have worked out tested procedures for financing themselves, for maintaining and protecting their members, and for assaulting their selected enemies, members have settled into terrorism and gangsterism as a way of life. It is an exciting alternative to the scant labor market with low wages.

It is curious to contrast the idealism and/or adventurism of the insurgent vigilantes with the typically routine, job-holding stance of the British military. The latter are assigned to deal principally with what are merely symptoms of discontent, a discontent that they do not understand. Their service is dedicated to the provision of official terror as a force for "law and order." A slogan in an Armagh army gym has it, "The strong shall live and the weak shall die!" What few soldiers' wives accompany them in Northern Ireland have problems: "Some of the wives have just given up and gone home. Some have had nervous breakdowns. A lot of them are very low." The chief entertainment for the men, other than watching the same TV newscasts that also preoccupy the insurgents, consists of strip-tease shows and pornographic materials. Life is very restricted, especially by the closely surrounding and not easily identifiable enemies.[69]

The Broader Picture

To what extent has terror become a way of life in Northern Ireland among all social classes? The perceptive reporter Coogan suggests its spread in speaking of how "groups of young men, uprooted by the troubles, roamed around the country pulling off robberies, either on behalf of some para-military organisation or for themselves—it was, and is, often very difficult to tell which—the skills and the guns required for such activities becoming all too easily available in the disorder of the times."[70] The robbing of banks and post offices north and south of the Irish border has become commonplace and has syphoned off millions of pounds. Both Loyalists and Green vigilantes have put together "protection" rackets that have become both extensive businesses and, for their staffs, ways of life.

In a hauntingly accurate sense, there are no nonparticipants in this current conflict. The American social psychologist Rona M. Fields concludes from her extensive and intensive field studies in the British Isles that all the people there share in being a composite of "villains, heroes, and victims" in the Northern Irish struggle.[71] As she and others—for example, the psychiatrist Morris Fraser[72]—have shown, the children are the most tragic victims, with so many of their lives distorted by violent experiences and an atmosphere of doom. And they grow into it as participants. Out of all this, as the Belfast psychiatrist H. A. Lyons observes, "The Troubles have engendered a very powerful feeling of belonging."[73] That "feeling of belonging" gets translated into the obsessive ethnic and class conspiracies for which middle-class people furnish so much in the way of leadership and rationalization in the service of upper-class desires and in exploitation of lower-class dissatisfactions.

Interethnic struggles are much too serious to be called games, but seasoned strategists often find it helpful to try to analyze the current phase of such a struggle in terms of competing game plans. This exercise has the merit of helping one perceive how competitors in an aspect of the social scene attempt to use as actual or potential playing pieces almost everything in sight. These items can include economic and political opportunities, ethnic myths and symbols, laws and public policies, popular sentiments, opinions, aspirations, and frustrations, religious and other organizations, neighborhoods, spokespeople, printed and electronic media, and dramatic events. In the foregoing, we have discussed how many of these items are being used in Northern Ireland. In the next chapter, special attention is given to dramatic events and their coverage in the popular media. With them, "Ulster was pitch-forked into the twentieth century by the men and women of broadcasting and the press. They came, they saw, and to the alarm of those in high places they reported what they came across."[74]

Notes

1. Leonard Downie, Jr., "Ulster Doctor Says IRA Maimed in Police Custody," London dateline, *Washington Post,* 11 March 1979.

2. Tim Pat Coogan, *The I.R.A.,* rev. ed. (Douglas, Isle of Man: Fontana Paperbacks, 1980), p. 548. The RUC made an investigation of how the "rape smear" originated and formally stated that "it was not established that any particular member of the RUC or of the press office had committed any offence." Reporters for such papers as the Manchester *Guardian,* Dublin *Irish Times,* and London *Observer* contradicted this statement's intent and pointed to the word "particular." Ed Moloney, "RUC Clears Itself of Irwin Smears," *Hibernia* (Dublin), 7 February 1980, p. 2; *Fortnight* (Belfast), no. 173 (October-November 1979): 11, 15; H. G. Bennett, chairman, Committee of Inquiry, *Police Interrogation Procedures in Northern Ireland* (London: HMSO, Cmnd. 7497, March 1979).

3. Frank Kitson, *Bunch of Five* (London: Faber & Faber, 1977), p. 301; cf. Robin Evelegh, *Peace-Keeping in a Democratic Society* (Montreal: McGill-Queen's University Press, 1978), pp. 6–90.

4. Bruce Page, David Leitch, and Philip Knightley, *Philby* (London: Sphere, 1977), pp. 137–38.

5. Special Correspondent, "Spy Chief Checks Out Nerve Centre," *Hibernia* (Dublin), 18 October 1979, pp. 6–7.

6. Frank Kitson, *Low Intensity Operations* (London: Faber & Faber, 1971), chaps. 6–7; Kennedy Lindsay, *The British Intelligence Services in Action* (Newtownabbey, Co. Antrim: Dunrod Press, 1980), pp. 274–88.
7. Workers' Research Unit, "The Law in Northern Ireland," *Belfast Bulletin*, no. 10 (Spring 1982): 14.
8. Lord Gifford, "Plastic Bullets—but the Deaths Are Real," *Rights!* (London) 6, no. 4 (March/April 1982): 3.
9. Martin Kettle, "Policing: Bringing It All Back Home?" *Rights!* (London) 5, no. 2 (November/December 1980): 8.
10. Northern Ireland Information Service, *Northern Ireland: Facts and Figures* (Belfast, July 1982), pp. 20–21; W. D. Flackes, *Northern Ireland* (New York: St. Martin's, 1980) pp. 197–204.
11. Workers' Research Unit, "Law in Northern Ireland," pp. 9, 11, 13; Kettle, "Policing"; Mairin de Burca, "Prison Business booming," *Hibernia* (Dublin) 14 August 1980, p. 3; Joe Costello, "Locking-Up—Looking Up," *Hibernia*, 21 August 1980, p. 6.
12. Jack Holland, *Too Long a Sacrifice* (New York: Dodd Mead, 1981), p. 3.
13. H. G. Bennett, chairman, Committee of Inquiry, *Police Interrogation Procedures in Northern Ireland*, pp. 112, 143; annual report of Chief Constable for 1979, *Fortnight*, no. 179 (December-January 1980–81): 10.
14. Lord Cameron, chairman, Commission Appointed by the Governor of Northern Ireland, *Disturbances in Northern Ireland* (Belfast: HMSO, Cmd. 532, September 1969), p. 63 (hereinafter, Cameron Commission); cf. John Hunt, chairman, *Report of the Advisory Committee on Police in Northern Ireland* (Belfast: HMSO, Cmd. 535, September 1969), chaps. 8–9.
15. Northern Ireland Information Service, *Northern Ireland*, p. 21; Mike Tomlinson, "Housing, the State and the Politics of Segregation," pp. 119–47, and Liam O'Dowd, Bill Rolston, and Tomlinson, "Reforming Repression," pp. 178–202 in their *Northern Ireland: Between Civil rights and Civil War* (London: CSE Books, 1980), esp. p. 185.
16. David Barzilay, *The British Army in Ulster* (Belfast: Century Services, 1973), intro.
17. L. P. Curtis, Jr., *Apes and Angels* (Washington, D.C.: Smithsonian, 1971); Ann Dummett, *A Portrait of English Racism* (Harmondsworth, England: Penguin, 1973); Steve Chibnall, *Law-and-Order News* (London: Tavistock, 1977), esp. pp. 17–18, 120–21.
18. London *Sunday Times* Insight Team, *Northern Ireland* (New York: Vintage, 1972), pp. 152–53; Edmund Leach, "The Official Irish Jokesters," *New Society* (London), 20/27 December 1979, pp. vii–ix; Evelegh, *Peace-Keeping*, p. 1.
19. Flackes, *Northern Ireland*, p. 212.
20. Workers' Research Unit, "Law in Northern Ireland," p. 13.
21. Manchester *Guardian*, 28 February 1978.
22. *Information on Ireland* (London), no. 1 (1979): 25.
23. Meurig Parri, television interview with Peter Farley, recorded by Patricia A. Gibbons, pp. 10–15 in Maurice Burke, *Decade of Terror* (New York: Irish Northern Aid, August 1981), pp. 10–14 quoted.
24. John Hackett, "Containing the Explosive Mixture," *Hibernia* (Dublin), 9 August 1979, pp. 6–7, p. 7 quoted.
25. Evelegh, *Peace-Keeping*, p. 3.
26. A. McC. Lee, "Nonviolent Agencies in the Northern Ireland Struggle: 1968–1979," *Sociology and Social Welfare* 7, no. 4 (July 1980): 601–23.

27. Norman McNeilly, *Exactly Fifty Years: The Belfast Education Authority and Its Work (1923-73)* (Belfast: Blackstaff Press, 1973), p. 112.

28. S. E. Long, "The Union: Pledge and Progress: 1886-1967," pt. 3 in M. W. Dewar, John Brown, and Long, *Orangeism: A New Historical Appreciation* (Belfast: Grand Orange Lodge of Ireland, 1967), p. 197.

29. Richard Rose, *Governing Without Consensus* (Boston: Beacon Press, 1971), pp. 257, 260; J. F. Harbinson, *The Ulster Unionist Party, 1882-1973* (Belfast: Blackstaff Press, 1973), p. 93; *Fortnight* (Belfast), no. 184 (December/January 1982): 16.

30. John Darby, *Conflict in Northern Ireland* (New York: Barnes & Noble, 1976), pp. 96, 155.

31. Leslie Scarman, chairman, Tribunal of Inquiry, *Violence and Civil Disturbances in Northern Ireland in 1969* (Belfast: HMSO, Cmd. 566, April 1972), p. 14.

32. I. R. K. Paisley, editorial, *Protestant Telegraph* (Belfast) 9 June 1973; Paisley's books include *Billy Graham and the Church of Rome* (Belfast: Martyrs' Memorial Church, 1970), *Northern Ireland: What Is the Real Situation?* (Greenville, S.C.: Bob Jones University Press, 1970), and *The Dagger of Treachery* (Belfast: Puritan Printing, 1972).

33. Holland, *Too Long a Sacrifice*, p. 31.

34. *"We Shall Overcome": The History of the Struggle for Civil Rights in Northern Ireland 1968-1978* (Belfast: Northern Ireland Civil Rights Association, 1978).

35. Harbinson, *Ulster Unionist Party*, p. 95.

36. Flackes, *Northern Ireland*, pp. 175, 181.

37. Workers' Research Unit, "Laws in Northern Ireland," pp. 30, 33.

38. Denis Faul and Raymond Murray, *H Blocks: British Jail for Irish Political Prisoners* (Dungannon, Co. Tyrone, Northern Ireland, 1979), *SAS Terrorism—The Assassin's Glove* (July 1976), and *Majella O'Hare: Shot Dead* (September 1979); Brian Brady, Faul, and Murray, *British Army Terror: West Belfast* (October 1976).

39. Martin Dillon and Denis Lehane, *Political Murders in Northern Ireland* (Harmondsworth, England: Penguin, 1973) p. 28; David Boulton, *The UVF: 1966-73* (Dublin: Torc Books, 1973) p. 40.

40. Dillon and Lehane, *Political Murders*, pp. 29, 34.

41. "Bobby Sands, M.P. and Francis Hughes," *Combat* (Belfast) 4, no. 41 (1981): 1.

42. "Loyalist Prisoners Will Not Be Ignored," *Combat* 4, no. 43, p. 1.

43. "Fellow Volunteers," *Combat* 4, no. 43, p. 7.

44. "Ulster Army Council," *Combat* 4, no. 41, p. 5.

45. "The Ressurection of the U.W.C.," *Combat* 4, no. 42, p. 5.

46. Boulton, UVF; Geoffrey Bell, *The Protestants of Ulster* (London: Pluto Press, 1976), chaps. 9-10.

47. Cameron Commission, p. 86.

48. James Kelly, *The Genesis of Revolution* (Dublin: Kelly Kane, 1976), p. 23.

49. Ibid.

50. Vincent Browne, "The Arms Crisis 1970," *Magill* (Dublin) 3, no. 8 (May 1980): 33-56; idem, "The Misconduct of the Arms Trial," *Magill* 3, no. 10 (July 1980): 17-25; Peter Berry, "The Peter Berry Papers," *Magill* 3, no. 9 (June 1980): 39-75; James Kelly, "We Were Framed," *Hibernia* (Dublin), 31 July 1980, p. 3; Sean Edmonds, *The Gun, the Law, and the Irish People* (Tralee, Co. Kerry: Anvil Books, 1971), p. 248.

51. Provisional Irish Republican Army, *Freedom Struggle* (1973), pp. 94-96.

52. Eamonn McCann, *War and an Irish Town*, rev. ed. (London: Pluto Press, 1980), p. 176.

53. J. M. Glover, "Northern Ireland: Future Terrorist Trends," Ms. Reference No. D/DINI/2003 (London: Ministry of Defence, 15 December 1978), pp.18–19.

54. Claire Sterling, *The Terror Network* (New York: Holt, Rinehart & Winston and Readers Digest Press, 1981), and "The Other Face of the IRA," *60 Minutes*, CBS Television Network, 4 October 1981, exemplify efforts to prove that PIRA is subject to a Soviet terrorist network; Conor Cruise O'Brien, no friend of the PIRA, asserts: "In short, so far as the Provisionals are concerned, Claire Sterling has got it all hopelessly wrong," in his "The Roots of Terrorism," *New Republic*, 25 July 1981. See also Maurice Burke, *A Decade of Deceit* (New York: Irish Northern Aid, April 1981).

55. Coogan, *The I.R.A.*, p. 536.

56. Ibid., pp. 579-81.

57. Flackes, *Northern Ireland*, p. 72.

58. "Officials Accept Partition," *Starry Plough* (Dublin), April 1979, p. 8.

59. Vincent Browne, "In the Shadow of a Gunman," *Magill* (Dublin) 5, no. 7 (April 1982): 6-16, pp. 9, 15 quoted; idem, "Political Lobotomy," *Magill* 5, no. 8 (May 1982): 4-6, 8-9, p. 9 quoted.

60. Browne, "Shadow of a Gunman," pp. 15-16.

61. Editorial, *Workers Life* (Dublin) 3, no. 1 (May 1982): 3; ibid., no. 2 (June 1982): 3.

62. Cathal Goulding, statement in *Eolas* (periodical of the International Affairs Bureau, Irish Republican Movement), no. 10 (October 1973).

63. P. O'Neill, "Christmas Message," *An Phoblacht* (Dublin), 23 December 1979, p. 1.

64. *An Phoblacht* (Dublin), 1 December 1979, p. 1.

65. E. Moxon-Browne, "The Northern Ireland Attitude Survey," Ms. report (Belfast: Queen's University, May 1979), pp. 11-12, 21, 26.

66. Frank Burton, *The Politics of Legitimacy* (London: Routledge and Kegan Paul, 1978), p. 128.

67. National Foreign Assessment Center, Central Intelligence Agency, *Patterns of International Terrorism: A Research Paper* (PA81-10163U, June 1981), p. 11.

68. Ibid., p. 13.

69. Ian Walker, "Barrackroom Ballads of Northern Ireland," *New Society* (London), 24 April 1980, pp. 148-52, pp. 148, 150 quoted.

70. Coogan, *The I.R.A.*, pp. 534-35; British Information Services, "Northern Ireland: Special Squad Formed to Fight Mafia-Type 'Godfathers' " (New York, PR-14, 24 September 1982), 4 pp.

71. R. M. Fields, *Northern Ireland: Society Under Siege*, new ed. (New Brunswick, N.J.: Transaction, 1980), p. xii.

72. Morris Fraser, *Children in Conflict* (London: Secker & Warburg, 1973).

73. H. A. Lyons, quoted by Dan van der Vat, "Social Focus: Ulster, a Legacy of Violence," London *Times*, 15 August 1978.

74. David Bleakley, *Peace in Ulster* (London: Mowbrays, 1972), p. 20.

CHAPTER 8

Terror as Theater

When a Detroit black man heard a detailed description of the Northern Ireland struggle, he commented, "I don't know the words, but I seem to recognise the tune."[1] For that matter, he might have heard the late Malcolm X[2] orate much as did Chief of Staff Cathal Goulding of the Official Irish Republican Army. Spirited into Northern Ireland in 1972 to speak at the illegal funeral of a slain OIRA officer in Belfast, Goulding defied the British army by shouting, "You have the weapons and the strength but with men like Joe McCann to carry on the struggle we will ... task your strength and break the heart of your empire."[3]

The theme of resistance by the deprived and the countertheme of maintaining the depriving status quo have points of similarity wherever they may be found, but they are acted out in terms of many different scenarios. Let us now look at some of the Northern Ireland scenarios, both those of the local insurgents and those introduced by the British from other parts of their empire.

Acts of political terrorization can well be perceived as a form of theater. They become dramas with possible and then sometimes actual consequences that are well or poorly calculated, predicted, assessed, and reassessed by the various participants. The purpose of a given terrorizing scenario is at the least to try to force a propaganda message into public awareness, discussion, and action. It may be to weaken or destabilize the opposing insurgent or governmental organization. Sometimes its peak is reached in the liquidation of a rebel initiative or in the actual seizure of the control of a state. It may take the form of brutalizing and even killing prisoners in interrogation sessions or secret trials. It may use ambush, explosion, assassination, insurgent or governmental trials of captured opponents, raiding, rioting, hunger striking, or some other form of spectacle.

Ideally, in an allegedly democratic society, nonviolent protest theatricals should be the dependable medium for effective dissident expression. As we have seen, such efforts are regarded by both Loyalists and Brits as threats to be met with force and even violence. At the same time, both

Loyalist and Green dissidents have learned that terrorizing scenarios require fewer operatives and involve fewer problems of maintaining organizational morale and confidentiality than do massive nonviolent procedures. As the British anti-insurgent strategist Frank Kitson contends, "It is fatally easy to underestimate the ability of a small number of armed men to exact support from exposed sections of the population by threats."[4] Such considerations unfortunately and all too often are used to brush aside the authenticated social wisdom that nonviolent efforts produce more durable results.

Political terrorizing goes a step beyond the dramatists' "guerrilla theatre," a type of " 'theatre which pretends not to be theatre'; i.e., a planned event which takes the spectators off-guard by acting as if certain things were true, and ideally never revealing their staged qualities."[5] In the case of the theater of terror, those "certain things" are believed to be quite real, and that constitutes the step beyond "guerrilla theatre" and is not left in doubt. The "certain things" may or may not actually take place. They may merely be threatened, but there is little doubt in opponents' minds that the threats are menacing.[6]

A synonym for "theater of terror" is "armed propaganda." In spite of death tolls, injuries, and physical costs, the chief purpose of official or insurgent terrorizing is not such effects as much as it is the stimulating of attention and the compelling of action. As former Royal Green Jackets commander Robin Evelegh points out, "It was the concept of 'armed propaganda' that lay behind the practice of the Provisional IRA giving warning of their bombs to avoid casualties, and in planting them in such dramatic places as cross-border trains and the Europa Hotel in Belfast, where most of the press stayed." He called the bombings "propaganda exercises rather than acts of physical offence in themselves." A similar conception of public relations or of armed propaganda also "frequently induced the British Army to stand inactively by while illegal uniformed marchers paraded the streets and while at funerals of extremists illegally armed parties fired volleys over the coffins of their dead comrades within a few yards of the troops."[7] Army officers apparently felt they had more to gain for their cause by not interrupting the insurgents than by battling them.

How effectively do terrorizing dramatics focus attention on official or insurgent grievances and compel some sought-for action? As we shall illustrate, such theatricals are often looked upon as things in themselves. They are symptoms of disorder that often distract attention from the causes giving rise to and maintaining disorder. This fits the strategies of officials bent on obscuring the government's contributions to insurgent oppression.

Insurgents themselves after a time get so caught up in their dramatic roles that they appear not to be able to move beyond them to more effective strategies.

Before turning to selected examples of terrorizing scenarios, let us first look at what such efforts have cost in a dozen years of turmoil.

Damages from Terror Theatricals

In 1970–81, micro- and macro-theatrical terrorizings claimed the lives of 1,534 civilians, 160 police, 119 Ulster Defence Regiment members, and 345 other soldiers, a total of 2,158 by official count. Some one-third of the civilians killed were said to be those of "terrorists" of an insurgent sort; the rest were intentional targets and "innocent bystanders." In the peak year, 1972, the 321 civilian murders represented a rate of 20.9 per 100,000 inhabitants, somewhat more than twice the mounting rate (8.3 in 1970, 9.2 in 1980) in the United States. When security people are also included, the total deaths in 1972 attributable to the "troubles," 467, raises the Northern Ireland rate to 30.4. The rate for the years 1970–81, based on an average of 180 troubles-related homicides a year, was 11.7, higher than the overall U.S. rate for "murder and non-negligent manslaughter" but well below these rates for certain metropolitan statistical areas in 1980: Fresno, California, 20.1; Mobile, Alabama, 20.5; Bakersfield, California, 20.9; New York City, 21.0; New Orleans, 22.3; Los Angeles and Long Beach, 23.3; Las Vegas, Nevada, 23.4; Houston, Texas, 27.6; and Miami, Florida, 32.7.[8]

In line with Evelegh's point about the felt importance of possible public reactions—to a degree at least—on all sides, it is significant to point out that in a different kind of armed conflict a German air raid on the night of 17–18 April 1941 killed about 750 people in Belfast. Evelegh also notes that the accidents, disasters, and other personal physiological problems of daily life bring far more people into Belfast's Royal Victoria Hospital than do civil disturbances. Since 1969, the latter have been including less than 3 percent, and even in the terrorist peak year 1972 they were just 5.39 percent of the total admissions there. The road accident death toll of the province in 1981 was 221, the lowest since 1968. These average a little higher than the political terror deaths, but it is difficult to separate the two.[9]

This is not intended to belittle the horrors of the internecine conflict in the province but to place it in perspective. On all sides, the major effort is to compel through creating a sense of terror rather than to slaughter or inflict personal injury.

As impossible as this situation appears to outsiders as one with which to live, it is also one to which people do adapt. For example, a Belfast saleswoman had this question put to her by the American investigative reporter Janet L. Barkas: "Have you thoughts of leaving Belfast?" When the woman learned that Barkas was from New York City, she shook her head and replied, "It's more dangerous there."[10] Statistically she is right, but is New York City constantly as terrifying to those who remain alive?

In 1970–81, 28,553 shooting and 10,528 bombing incidents were reported within the province. Civilians injured totaled 17,115, with the highest points at 3,813 in 1972 and at more than 2,000 in 1975 and 1976. In 1968–79, about 3,800 RUC and RUCR members were injured, with high levels of 711 in 1969 and 485 in 1972. In 1969–79, the total for the army and UDR came to some 3,600, with maximums of 620 in 1970, 578 in 1972, 548 in 1973, and 483 in 1974. For 1972–79, 147 tarrings and featherings were reported, and in 1974–79, 727 kneecappings. The RUC's estimate of "punishment shootings," including kneecappings, was 850 in 1973–81. Those arrested and "charged with serious security-type offences" included 10,063. The year-by-year breakdown of many of these figures is given in table 2. Compensation from public funds for damages to property in this period came to some £300 millions, to persons, £50 millions.[11]

Just how accurate these official statistics might be is, as usual, a matter of controversy. Whether a death is accidental, a suicide, or a homicide (a murder or non-negligent manslaughter) is not reviewed too objectively in the tumultuous and bitter atmosphere of Northern Ireland.

Another significant set of overall figures, especially for trends indicated, has to do with armed robberies, part of the loot from which went into coffers of the Loyalist and Green vigilante organizations. In Northern Ireland, the costs of these has varied from about £233,000 to £791,000 a year in 1971–81, with the peak in 1972. Even more to be noted is that such robberies in the twenty-six counties took less than £4,000 in 1967· but climbed yearly in 1970–75 from about £17,000 to £984,000. After 1975, the Eire police found the totals too alarming to publicize, but a secret British army report puts the take near the latter figure in 1976–78, "the greatest source of income for PIRA." The total for 1974, £434,000, does not include £5 million in recovered oil paintings.[12]

An indication of ethnic involvement in the disastrous human costs of the struggle comes from a careful study by Michael McKeown of the first 2,000 fatalities. Only 2 of the 182 Republican and all of the 43 Loyalist vigilantes killed were Protestants. Deaths among the locally recruited security forces—the Royal Ulster Constabulary, the Royal Ulster Constab-

Table 2.

Security Statistics, 1970–81

Year	1970	1971	1972	1973	1974	1975	1976	1977	1978	1979	1980	1981
Bombing Incidents	170	1515	1853	1520	1113	635	1192	535	633	564	400	398
Shooting Incidents	213	1756	10628	5018	3206	1803	1908	1081	755	728	642	815
Civilian Injuries	245	1838	3813	1812	1680	2044	2162	1027	548	555	513	878
Persons Charged with Terrorist Offences	N/A	N/A	531	1414	1362	1197	1276	1308	843	670	550	918
Civilian Deaths	23	115	321	171	166	216	245	69	50	51	50	57
RUC/RUCR Deaths	2	11	17	13	15	11	23	14	10	14	9	21
Army Deaths		43	103	58	28	14	14	15	14	38	8	10
UDR Deaths	5	26	8	7	6	15	14	7	10	8	13

(Northern Ireland Information Service, Belfast).

ulary Reserve, and the Ulster Defence Regiment—came to 215 Protestants and only 13 Roman Catholics, a suggestion of the extreme ethnic bias of those bodies. Of the 2,000 toll, 1,631 were Northern Ireland natives. Of these natives, even though one-third of the province's population is Green, 916 of the dead were local Roman Catholics and only 715 local Protestants. Because of misdirected efforts, the balance among the groups responsible for fatalities is different. The same study reports that of the first 2,000, security forces killed 220, or 11.0 percent; Republicans, 1,024, or 51.2 percent; and Loyalists, 574, or 28.7 percent; 182, or 9.1 percent, could not be classified. The distribution of the 2,000 victims was: 554, or 27.7 percent, security forces; 225, or 11.2 percent, "subversive groups"; 1,163, or 58.2 percent, civilians; and 58, or 2.9 percent, unclassified. As McKeown, the author, notes, "In a society where the militarists are in control, the civilians surely get the short and rough end of the stick."[13]

As these statistics suggest, there have been literally thousands of terrorist happenings. They have included riots, kidnappings, assassinations, ambushes, bombings, kneecappings, beatings, blackmailings, intense interrogatings, and property damage.

Another kind of damage from terrorizing theatricals needs to be summarized here: The Prevention of Terrorism Acts of 1974 and 1976 authorized detentions and long interrogations both in Great Britain and in Northern Ireland that led one journalist to assert: "You must have a record, you're Irish." In 1974–79, 4,350 people—all Irish—were detained on suspicion in Great Britain; only 46 were then charged, and of these only 24 were found guilty! One of the victims was an assistant editor of the Dublin *Hibernia* periodical, Paddy Prendiville. In December 1979, he was arrested, "held incommunicado for four days ... subjected to intense interrogation and mental stress." The paper's solicitor "was refused permission to visit him, and when a writ of Habeas Corpus was moved, ... the hearing, incredibly, was postponed for four days." Then he "was suddenly released."[14] The implementation of the same acts in Northern Ireland in 1975–81 appears to have been more productive: 1,191 detained, 987 extensions of detention granted, 60 charged under terrorism acts, but 504 charged under other acts (160 murder, 70 attempted murder, etc.).[15] Details of the struggle over civil rights under interrogation are discussed elsewhere. Calling such procedures antiterrorist does not keep them from being terrorizing efforts in the interests of a class and ethnic group.

Much is said about the terrorizing activities of vigilantes, but Amnesty International has described the "beatings, attempted strangulation, pressure to sensitive points of the body, bending of limbs, prolonged standing or squatting in awkward positions, prolonged physical exercises, and burning with cigarettes" that official interrogators have used. Their psychological pressures have included "prolonged oppressive questioning by teams, threats of death and of imprisonment, and threats to the family of the suspect, stripping, and verbal abuse and humiliation."[16] The U.K.'s Bennett Committee to a large extent confirmed those findings.[17]

In the chapter on how people learn to be violent, we mention the enticing game of joyriding in stolen automobiles. In 1980 the Royal Ulster Constabulary recovered 1,900 stolen cars in the Springfield Road, Andersontown, Lower Falls, and Divis areas of Belfast. They accused teen-age drivers of using seven- and eight-year-olds as "human sandbags" to protect themselves from shots at security checkpoints. The police had killed two teen-agers and wounded many others.[18]

Serious damage or destruction has visited thousands of homes as well as stores, manufacturing plants, roads, bridges, police stations, hotels, churches, and public utility installations. A government report concluded that by 1976, about 25,000 houses had been damaged.[19] The Europa, the principal hotel in Belfast and the one most frequented by media people, has been bombed repeatedly. In addition, coordinated "waves" of bombs have hit hotels and other structures in a range of places throughout the province from time to time.

So much for indications of overall human damages from terror theatricals. Let us now look at what might be called stage properties for such theatricals and then try to characterize with examples the scenarios attempted and used in this struggle.

Stage Properties for Terror

Literally anything and everything can be used by participants in such a struggle as that in Northern Ireland. Many items have been discussed or referred to in connection with arrest, interrogation, incarceration, and judicial procedures, as well as with insurgent activities. In addition to the usual firearms, security forces have been criticized for employing CS gas and rubber and plastic bullets to control crowds and military vehicles to terrify, ram, and even kill people.

The RUC began discharging CS gas during riots in Derry the night of 12 August 1969 that arose out of the annual Protestant Apprentice Boys' march. As a tribunal of inquiry later decided, police difficulties at that time "naturally led them, when the emergency arose, to have recourse to methods such as baton-charges, CS gas and gunfire, which were sure ultimately to stoke even higher the fire of resentment and hatred." On 12 to 14 August, the police utilized 1,091 cartridges and 161 grenades of CS gas "with some tactical success, but it caused deep resentment in Londonderry and elsewhere, and it could not, by its nature, end the disturbance." The tribunal reported that in July and August of that year, 562 people in Derry were treated for injuries, of whom 33 were sent to hospitals, but on 12 to 14 August, 373 of these had medical attention for CS gas exposure.[20] Stung by this as well as other aspects of public reaction to the well-media-covered "Battle of the Bogside," the U.K. government set up a Himsworth Committee to investigate consequences of CS gas exposure in Northern Ireland, but the use of the gas has continued. As an investigator of the Derry incident puts it, "It is a fact of military life that new munitions are rarely banned on any but tactical grounds."[21] The CS tear gas can apparently have disastrous effects on those who are at all susceptible.

Rubber and later plastic bullets have also been used by police and army to control crowds, called by the security people a "minimum force" defensive weapon. By the end of 1974, in about five years, 55,688 rubber bullets had been shot in Northern Ireland. After being introduced in August 1972, only 259 plastic bullets were fired by the end of 1974, but by November 1976, the plastic had replaced the rubber.

Rubber bullets are reported to have killed at least three people and to have caused skull fractures, brain damage, lung injuries, and complete or partial blinding of dozens more. In one study of 90 so injured and hospitalized in Belfast and Derry in 1970–72, four-fifths had head injuries, 17 were permanently disabled or deformed, and one was killed.

Plastic bullets were favored for their greater accuracy, due to greater velocity, but they were publicized as being less damaging—just terrifying. An army spokesperson claimed that both kinds of bullet "keep people out of danger." In April to August 1981, however, in Belfast and Derry, 7 people are said to have been killed by plastic bullets, and the total may be as many as twice that many civilians since 1973, half of them children aged fifteen and under. Injuries total some 200 of a serious nature, including blindness, brain damage, and paralysis.

On 13 May 1982, the European Parliament voted a ban on the use of such bullets, a vote opposed only by British Tories and one Northern Ireland Unionist, the Reverend Ian R.K. Paisley.[22]

Regular bullets admittedly kill more people, but then the rubber and plastic bullets are not supposed to kill any!

Army personnel carriers are also not supposed to be lethal projectiles but they have been so used to intimidate crowds. For example, on 19 April 1981, an army Land-Rover driven at high speed into a crowd in Derry killed two nineteen-year-olds. Dr. Edward Daly, Roman Catholic bishop of Derry, called this "a stupid and cruel deed" and characterized it as typical of too many other similar incidents. The Belfast Crown Court acquitted the two soldiers charged with the deaths on 20 January 1982. There were "angry scenes" in the courtroom.[23]

According to the Dublin *Irish Times* of 27 April 1978, the Northern Ireland struggle has been employed by the British for

> an accelerated development of materials and equipment during the '70s, geared specifically to urban disturbances, street surveillance, limited local response in riot control—the hardware and software of reaction, from nightsights to miniature, unmanned helicopters for street and area surveillance. Add computer storage of intelligence input and you are naming the kind of industrial expertise most countries of the world now have a use for.

It is expertise used to try to cope with symptoms in order to avoid, or at least delay, having to face the consequences of invidious exploitation.

An evolving aspect of the Belfast stage set is the so-called Peace or Orange-Green Line. British troops erected it in September 1969 as an expedient barrier between the Roman Catholic Falls area and the Protestant Shankill. It immediately became as much a way of maintaining the province's bitter siege mentality as is the segregation of children in ethnically distinct schools. In March 1981, the Ministry of Defence started to replace the makeshift barricade with a permanent brick wall. In August 1981, the Northern Ireland Housing Authority decided to erect a "peace wall" between Protestant and Roman Catholic areas farther east in Belfast.[24] And so the ghettos, made "purer" by the "troubles," are to be frozen ever tighter!

The stage properties of the insurgents depend upon what they can beg, borrow, and steal. Such problems were somewhat eased for Loyalist vigilantes through their close association until 1970 with the Ulster Special Constabulary ("B" Specials) and then with the succeeding Ulster Defence Regiment. Through these and other connections, in 1971 there were about 60,000 "firearms certificates" in private and largely Loyalist hands under a British act. In addition, under a provincial act, former members of the "B" Specials and their friends held about 22,000 "firearms permits." This led the police and army to call the Protestant Shankill "the most dangerous area" of Belfast. The total of licensed arms had grown in 1982 to 115,940.[25] With the addition of the unlicensed, largely in Green hands, the available arsenal is dismaying.

Stage properties employed by the Provisional IRA are mentioned in connection with illustrative scenarios, but several points made in the captured British assessment of the Provos are to be noted:

> The mature terrorists, including for instance the leading bomb makers, are ... continually learning from mistakes and developing their expertise. ...
> PIRA have shown great ingenuity in devising victim operated or booby trap devices. ... Items of electronic equipment operated by the Army such as search devices could themselves be exploited as triggers. ...
> The McGregor ... radio sold for control of model aircraft and boats has normally been used. ...
> Availability of long delay timers makes it feasible for bombs to be emplaced at a target before suspicion arises, even during the construction phase of a building or a site to be visited by a VIP.[26]

Theatricals of Terror

Five notable dramatic incidents have been discussed. In connection with the renewal of revolt, chapter 4 describes: (1) the June 1968 Caledon housing incident; (2) the 5 October 1968 civil rights march in Derry; (3) the January 1969 Belfast-to-Derry nonviolent march, harassed at many points and especially at Burntollet; and (4) the rioting on 12–14 August 1969, arising out of the annual Protestant Apprentice Boys' march in Derry, the "Battle of the Bogside," an event that brought the army actively into the struggle. In setting forth upper-class manipulations of social policies and practices, chapter 6 describes (5) the significant internment raids launched on 9 August 1971. Demonstrative marches, including funeral processions, have continued to be features of both Loyalist and Nationalist dramatics, and they are often subjected to interruptions and even violence by the "other side" and by security forces.

Ten other major incidents or events help develop further an impression of terror as theater in this conflict: (1) public house bombings in Northern

Ireland; (2) Bloody Sunday, 30 January 1972; (3) Bloody Friday, 21 July 1972; (4) Operation Motorman, 31 July 1972; (5) terrorizing in Great Britain; (6) terrorizing in the twenty-six counties; (7) Loyalist strikes; (8) the Miami Showband slaughter, 31 July 1975; (9) Mountbatten and Warrenpoint, 27 August 1979; and (10) hunger strikes.

Public House Bombings in Northern Ireland. Some of the most frightful terrorizing efforts have consisted of bombing public houses when they were full of people.

A 50-pound bomb demolished the McGurk public house in Belfast Saturday, 4 December 1971. It killed 15 people; 8 others were wounded. The Loyalist Belfast *Newsletter* on Monday carried the headline: *"Massacre Bomb Was Left Inside The Bar."* The pro-Nationalist Belfast *Irish News* the same day topped its account of the event: *"Empire Loyalists Take Blame for 15 Death Bar Blast."* Here is an excerpt from the *Newsletter* account: "The RUC is of the opinion that the bomb was brought into the bar earlier in the night and that a Provisional IRA man was to have set it off somewhere in the city later." The sharply contrasting *Irish News* write-up contains this sentence: "... an organisation calling itself 'Empire Loyalists' in telephone calls to newspaper offices claimed responsibility." The explosion in this pub frequented by Nationalists was a Loyalist event, but it was not until 1 August 1977, more than five and one-half years later, that a Loyalist was charged with it.[27]

On 17 February 1978, after an eight-week series of attacks on hotels, restaurants, and pubs without loss of life, the PIRA fire-bombed the La Mon restaurant in the Protestant Castlereagh section of Belfast, killed 12, and injured 30 of the more than 400 in the place at the time. Apparently the problem had been a breakdown in PIRA timing in this manner:

> The timing device in such bombs is almost invariably a cheap wristwatch. This limits the theoretical priming time to 60 minutes (the minute hand is used). A maximum of 55 minutes and, for practical reasons, a time of no more than 30 minutes is allowed. Thus the bombers had approximately half-an-hour to prime and plant the device, dump their hijacked car and get back to their base before giving ... a warning to the police. After La Mon the call was too late. ... And twelve innocent people having a Friday night out died horrible deaths.[28]

In the resurgence of violence following the Nationalist-protested 1982 Assembly election, the Irish National Liberation Army bombed the Droppin Well Pub in Ballykelly, County Derry, on 6 December. They killed 11 British soldiers and 5 civilians, 4 of them women, and wounded another 66. Some 150 were in the pub for its regular Monday night dance contest. As Jon Nordheimer reported in the 8 December *New York Times*, "Most of the casualties were young British soldiers from a nearby garrison and their dates."

Bloody Sunday, 30 January 1972. Despite a ban on marches by the provincial prime minister as of 9 August 1971, the first day of the internment sweep, the Northern Ireland Civil Rights Association held a protest march and rally on 30 January 1972 in Derry. As a governmental investigator later admitted, this march "placed the security forces in a dilemma. An attempt to stop by force a crowd of 5,000 or more, perhaps as many as 20 or 25,000, might result in heavy casualties or even in the overrunning of the troops by sheer weight of numbers." On the other hand, he contended, "To allow such a well publicized march to take place without opposition ... would bring the law into disrepute and make control of future marches impossible."[29]

The march took place on that January Sunday as a protest against such practices as internment without trial. Estimates of the size of the demonstration vary between the governmental guess of 3,000 to 5,000 and the journalistic and Nationalist estimate of 20,000. "The marchers did not move in any kind of military formation but walked as a crowd through the streets. ... [They] included many women and some children, were orderly and in the main good humoured."[30] When they came to a military barrier, some of the less disciplined marchers threw stones, and soldiers drenched the crowd with purple-colored water and fired cannisters of CS gas at them. "The Army had achieved its main purpose of containing the march and although some rioters were still active ... they could have been dispersed without difficulty." Nevertheless, the army leaders decided to carry out a massive arrest operation later called "debatable."[31]

In subsequent shooting by soldiers, at least 25 civilians were hit, and 13 of them died. "None of the many photographs shows a civilian holding an object that can with certainty be identified as a firearm or bomb. No casualties were suffered by the soldiers from firearms or gelignite bombs."[32]

In his report, the governmental investigator came to these significant conclusions:

> There would have been no deaths in Londonderry on 30 January if those who organised the illegal march had not thereby created a highly dangerous situation in which a clash between demonstrators and the security forces was almost inevitable. ...
>
> If the Army had persisted in its "low key" attitude and had not launched a large scale operation to arrest hooligans the day might have passed off without serious incident. ...
>
> None of the deceased or wounded is proved to have been shot whilst handling a firearm or bomb.[33]

An American jurist who studied the march evidence for the International League for the Rights of Man countered the first of these conclusions thus:

> The Northern Ireland Civil Rights Association (NICRA) which organized the march on January 30, planned, and took steps to insure, a non-violent march. ... Without any support from the record of testimony before him, Lord Widgery apportions a major share of the responsibility of the civilian deaths in Londonderry on January 30 to NICRA. ... But NICRA had informed the Chief Superintendent of Police of their plans to assure that the march would be non-violent. They had no way of learning about, or anticipating, the secret military strategy for the march, which involved substantial Army reinforcements, and they did not expect the special assignment of an aggressive combat paratroop regiment for arrest operations.[34]

What with extensive television coverage of the incident, reactions were substantial and immediate. The Irish Prime Minister (Taoiseach), Jack Lynch, demanded of the British government an investigation of the "unbelievably savage and inhuman" behavior of the British soldiers. He also announced that Wednesday, 2 February, would be a national day of mourning in Ireland.[35] Demonstrations and incidents of violence swept through Northern Ireland. The cause of the insurgents was greatly strengthened. The fall of Stormont, the resumption of the direct control of the province by the Westminster government on 24 March 1972, was substantially stimulated by this event.

Bloody Friday, 21 July 1972. Tensions mounted rapidly during the spring and summer. One form they took was the expansion of the "no-go area" movement that the Nationalists had started especially at the time of the "Battle of the Bogside" in 1969. In a number of such areas, Nationalist paramilitaries rather than police had taken control. In early May 1972, the Protestant Ulster Defence Association began a protest against Nationalist no-go areas by setting up their own in East Belfast, Derry, Ballymena, Bangor, and Coagh. Hooded and uniformed UDA members stopped and searched cars at their barricades but let army patrols pass. At first, these were 24-hour demonstrations on weekends. They they were expanded to 48-hour events on 11 June. On 1–2 July, the UDA even seized twenty-seven city buses in order to use them to block more streets, and the next day they would have started building twelve concrete barriers had not the army intervened. The army erected less permanent barricades and then let the UDA control the blocked streets. These no-go areas were for every day.[36]

In contrast with these events, the OIRA declared a truce on 29 May, and the PIRA, on 22 June. The PIRA's unilateral declaration was to take effect "provided that a public reciprocal response is forthcoming from the armed forces of the British Crown." The PIRA also offered "a peace plan designed to secure a just and lasting solution."

Apparently as a result of a riotous controversy over the occupation of sixteen houses vacated by Protestant families, the PIRA asserted that the army broke the truce, and it therefore on 9 July resumed "offensive operations." The fighting spread, and the PIRA rebuilt barricades surrounding Roman Catholic no-go areas that had been dismantled.

Part of the rising terror was the work of sectarian assassination squads. In five months to the middle of August, some fifty unsolved murders of civilians led the government to offer a reward of £50,000 for information leading to the arrest and conviction of anyone responsible for "the present apparently motiveless murders in Northern Ireland." As the London *Daily Telegraph* summarized this development on 17 August:

> These back-alley killings, which have happened at the rate of nearly one a day since the beginning of July, have spread as much fear as bomb explosions and gun battles. ... The police have little doubt that most of the victims were killed because they were either Protestants or Catholics. ...
>
> In about 30 cases the victims were tortured before being finished off with a bullet. ...
>
> The killers are said to pick their victims at random, selecting any Catholic caught alone in a Protestant area or a Protestant in a Catholic area. While some are shot dead on the spot, others are abducted to face perhaps days of torture before being shot.

A climax to these mounting brutalities came on 21 July 1972. In various parts of Belfast, 22 bombs exploded that day. They killed 2 soldiers and 9 other people. They injured 130; 44 men and boys and 52 women and girls were hospitalized. Twenty of the large bombs were detonated between 3:00 and 3:30 p.m. in bus stations, shopping centers, railway stations, and a river bridge. It was a time when those facilities were thronged with people. Belfast Brigade of the Provisional IRA that evening issued this statement: "We accept full responsibility for all explosions in the Belfast area today. In accepting responsibility we point out that the following organisations were informed of bomb positions at least 30 minutes to one hour before each explosion—the Samaritans, the Public Protective Agency, the Rumour Service and the press."[37] The PIRA thus tried to blame "the police and army for failing to act quickly enough to warn people, but it just would not wash. Many who had been prepared to give at least tacit support to the Provos were totally sickened."[38]

The next morning, the London *Times* gave grisly details of what it called "the most savage and ruthless bombing attack ever mounted in Belfast" to that time. Other mass media agreed. Where the PIRA had gained from Bloody Sunday, it lost heavily in popular confidence and support as a result of Bloody Friday.

An immediate consequence of Bloody Friday and its riotous aftermath was that the Secretary of State for Northern Ireland, William Whitelaw, announced in the Westminster Parliament on 24 July a further stepping up of the military campaign against the PIRA and UDA. This took the form of Operation Motorman.[39]

Operation Motorman, 31 July 1972. By 31 July, 21,000 regular troops together with 9,000 mobilized Ulster Defence Regiment and 6,000 Royal Ulster Constabulary members were available in the province. At 4 a.m. on that day, they were used to take control of no-go areas in Derry and Belfast. The army's 50-ton tanks equipped with bulldozer attachments and 100 other fighting vehicles entered Derry's Bogside and Creggan. Shots were exchanged, and two citizens were killed. In Belfast's Roman Catholic Andersontown and other no-go areas, the troops did not meet with PIRA resistance, and there were no casualties. PIRA claimed that they had been prepared for the operation and had withdrawn promptly in order to avoid a massive confrontation with the security forces. Orange leaders cooperated in the dismantling of their own no-go areas in Belfast, Derry, and Portadown and claimed the operation to be a victory—what they had sought. They celebrated it with the usual bonfires. Ulster Vanguard Party leaders wanted the British to take the further step of closing the many cross-border roads into the twenty-six counties, a step only partly taken.

In Derry in particular, the soldiers discovered quantities of ammunition, guns, radio equipment, explosives, and the largest "bomb factory" found so far in the province.

Paul Channon, British Minister of State for Northern Ireland, told the House of Commons the day of the operation, "Last night's military operation was by no means an end in itself. There can be no military solution to the complex problems of Northern Ireland; but political representatives cannot hope to discuss the future openly and without fear if the rule of law is defied by any section of the community." But the operation did not keep unidentified terrorists from killing six people with a bomb in Claudy, a town 10 miles from Derry, the same day.[40] In addition, military operations such as Operation Motorman further emphasize the imbalance of power among those who might come to a negotiating session.

Terrorizing in Great Britain. The two IRAs, especially the Provos, and the Irish National Liberation Army have taken responsibility for many letter bombs, car bombs, and explosive contraptions hidden in public areas in England, Scotland, and even at British military bases overseas since 1969. Their toll in 1972–81 came to 67 people killed and 1,100 injured. Here are some examples:

A bomb in a parked car outside the officers' mess of the 16th Parachute Brigade at Aldershot in England on 22 February 1972 killed seven people it was not supposed to have hurt: five women working in the kitchen, a gardener, and a Roman Catholic priest. The Official IRA took responsibility and claimed it to be a retaliation for the Bloody Sunday slaughter of the preceding 30 January.[41]

Two car bombs in London on 8 March 1973 killed one man and injured some 200 others. The happening coincided with a plebescite in Northern Ireland on whether or not the province should remain part of the United Kingdom. A total of 604,256 (58.6 percent) of the 1,030,084 possible voters gave 591,820 (57.4 percent of the total electorate) pro-Loyalist assents. The Social Democratic and Labour and other antiunion parties asked their constituents to boycott the poll. During that day, bombs throughout the province and especially in Derry and Belfast destroyed principally property.

No group immediately took responsibility for the London incidents of violence, but British security agents arrested seven men and three women about to enplane at London's Heathrow Airport for Dublin. Of the nine later convicted, six stated they were Provos and claimed status as political prisoners. They were denied that and also a request to be incarcerated in Northern Ireland. From Dublin, the PIRA issued a statement that "in due course retribution would be exacted from the people who had inflicted such callous punishment on Belfast youth."[42]

In an interview over Independent Television on 17 November 1974, Daithi O Conaill, chief of staff of PIRA, declared that their violence in England against "economic, military, political and judicial targets" and places "where military personnel have established haunts" would be increased. Apparently this included the disastrous pub bombing in Birmingham on 21 November 1974. At about 8:20 p.m., bombs in two public houses there killed 19 and injured 182. Two more died later. A warning telephone call minutes earlier to the Birmingham *Post and Mail* did not function to clear the pubs in time. Many victims were under the age of twenty. Official Sinn Féin blamed the event on the PIRA, and the latter stated on 23 November that "it has never been and is not the policy of the IRA to bomb non-military targets without giving adequate warnings to ensure the safety of civilians."

Six men were sentenced on 15 August 1975 to life imprisonment for the happening, and two received shorter terms. Their convictions were based chiefly on "confessions" that the Manchester *Guardian* and Dublin *Irish Times* revealed had been beaten out of them. All eight were long-time residents of Birmingham, a city with 100,000 Irish inhabitants. Whether or not they had functioned for the PIRA did not become clear. A telephoner to the Press Association at the time of the bombings asserted that the two explosions were the work of "Red Flag 74," a Manchester student body. The bombings were also coincident with the Aer Lingus transportation of the body of one James McDaid to Dublin, and that may be significant.

McDaid, a local PIRA leader, had accidentally killed himself on 14 November, one week before the pub bombings, while trying to place a bomb in a Coventry telephone exchange. The Birmingham Roman Catholic archbishop increased the tension surrounding McDaid's death by refusing to permit a requiem mass for him in the local cathedral. The fascist National Front added to the excitement by demonstrating against those carrying the coffin from the morgue. When Belfast's Aldergrove airport would not handle the coffin, it had to be routed via Dublin and then by road to Belfast. Priests there did pray over the grave.[43]

Meanwhile, a variety of letter bombs, incendiaries concealed in cigarette packets, car bombs, and bombs that could be thrown were also being used against such stores as Selfridge's and Harrod's in London, government offices, and military posts and clubs from time to time.

The Irish National Liberation Army (INLA) is said to have carried out a number of operations against the UDR, RUC, and army, many ascribed to the PIRA, but after assassinating Airey Neave, it started to take responsibility. Neave, the Conservative spokesperson on Northern Ireland in the Westminster Parliament, was "executed" at 3:00 p.m. 30 March 1979 with a mercury-triggered bomb in his car as he drove away from the House of Commons.[44] An official statement by the INLA Army Council the next day, published in their periodical *Starry Plough* (Dublin) 1 April, bragged that they "successfully breached intense security at the House of Commons to plant the device." They had "especially selected" Neave for assassination because of "his rabid militarist calls for more repression against the Irish people and for strengthening of the SAS [Special Air Service] murder gang."

A pair of PIRA's more spectacular events in England occurred on 20 July 1982 in London. To bring the conflict "home" to the English, without warning at 10:45 a.m. they skillfully nail-bombed 16 men of the Queen's Household Cavalry, two policemen, and their horses on parade in Hyde Park. They thus killed 4 cavalrymen and wounded 3 others, the 2 policemen, and 17 bystanders. Seven horses died. Two hours later in Regent's Park, they detonated a bomb under a bandstand on which 30 Royal Green Jackets were playing. This killed 6 of the soldiers and injured 24 more and 4 civilians. As an observer stated: "Fear rippled through London today as the police searched for more explosive devices. Streets were cordoned off and there were major traffic jams. A garden party planned by Queen Elizabeth was delayed after a car was found parked near Buckingham Palace with gasoline cans in the trunk." The PIRA acknowledgment of the catastrophe contained this sentence: "Now it is our turn to properly invoke Article 51 of the United Nations statute and properly quote all Thatcher's fine phrases on the right to self-determination of a people." PIRA thus wished to equate Ireland's cause with that put forward by Prime Minister Margaret Thatcher for the English colony in the Falkland Islands against Argentine claims.[45]

Terrorizing in the Twenty-Six Counties. Six spectacular terrorist acts in the Irish Republic helped to dramatize the relationships between the two parts of the island:

A crowd attacked the British Embassy in Merrion Square, Dublin, on 31 January 1972, the day after Derry's Bloody Sunday. The police (Gardai) arrested 15 who threw petrol bombs and stones at the building. Then, on 2 February, some 20,000 to 30,000 people, gathered for an anti-British demonstration, converged on the embassy and burned it to the ground. The building had been evacuated, but 68 civilians and 3 Gardai were injured.[46]

On 1 December 1972, the Irish Parliament (Dáil Éireann) was considering a bill to strengthen that government's powers in coping with membership in illegal organizations. It had the form of an amendment to the Offences Against the State Act. It was to help the Irish police and military limit the cooperation of Irish groups with the Northern Ireland paramilitaries. During that discussion, two bombs in Dublin killed 2 and injured 73. One bomb wrecked Liberty Hall, a center for trade unionist activities.

Not only the Provisional and the Official IRAs but also the Ulster Defence Association denied all responsibility for the explosions. A Provo statement contended that the bombs were probably placed by "cowardly agents provocateurs" who wanted to speed the enactment of the pending bill which the Executive Council of the Irish Congress of Trade Unions called "repressive and retrograde."[47] Their implication was that pro-British agents were responsible. That is what led the Loyalist UDA to register its denial.

At 5:30 p.m. on 17 May 1974, with no previous warning, bombs in the crowded center of Dublin killed 25 (17 women, 6 men, 2 baby girls) and in the town of Monaghan at 7:00 p.m., 5; in all, 151 others were injured. The Irish Prime Minister (Taoiseach), Liam Cosgrave, asserted that these "unforgiveable acts" helped to "bring home to us here what the people of Northern Ireland have been suffering for five long years." The Ulster Defence Association and the Ulster Volunteer Force, the chief loyalist paramilitaries, denied responsibility for what the Provisional IRA called "vile murder."[48] Despite the UDA denial of responsibility, its press officer, Samuel Smyth, asserted: "I am very happy about the bombings in Dublin. There is a war with the Free State [of Ireland] and now we are laughing at them." The outrage was later attributed to the extremist Protestant vigilantes, the Red Hand Commandos, a body with some relations with the Ulster Volunteer Force.[49]

Three other events in the Republic are mentioned just to indicate PIRA's continuity of effort there. In October 1975, the Dutch industrialist Tiede Herrema was kidnapped near Limerick in order to try to get three PIRA prisoners released. Herrema was released on 7 November, and his kidnappers were captured. Christopher Ewart-Biggs, British ambassador to the Republic, and his secretary were killed by a landmine in Dublin on 21 July 1976. The assassination of Earl Mountbatten on 27 August 1979 is discussed below.

Was the Dublin-Monaghan "Bloody Friday" calculated to distract attention of twenty-six county leaders from possible resistance to the

Protestant-led strike then in progress in the north? At any rate, here are some relevant facts:

Loyalist Strikes Against Power Sharing. During this controversial period, both Protestant and Roman Catholic workers have engaged more in Nationalist and ethnocentric than in class struggles. In 1973–74, Loyalist groups in the north were actively working to destroy the power-sharing executive for Northern Ireland that took office 1 January 1974. They wanted to return the province to the form of Orange dictatorship they had enjoyed for a half century. The three main Loyalist parties, as the United Ulster Unionist Coalition or Council, demanded the resignation of the devolved government and the discarding of the idea of a Council of Ireland advanced in the 1973 "Sunningdale Agreement" among British, Northern Irish, and Irish leaders.

To force a showdown, the militant Protestant Ulster Workers' Council (UWC) called a general strike. Even though the official trade union movement and many political leaders opposed this effort, the refusal of the Secretary of State, Merlyn Rees, "to negotiate with the strike leaders, played into the strikers' hands." In addition, the UDA entered the picture to block streets in Belfast and elsewhere in the province. The UWC thus "demonstrated its ability to control directly the supply and distribution of electricity, gas, public transport, petrol, foodstuffs and animal foodstuffs, and indirectly, many retail outlets, places of entertainment, private motoring and other sectors of economic life."[50]

In consequence, on 28 May, Brian Faulkner as chief executive and his colleagues all resigned, and the United Kingdom again resumed direct control. It is thus likely that the Dublin-Monaghan Bloody Friday did keep the twenty-six county Irish from involving themselves in the coincident UWC strike.

A further effort at political striking by the UWC in 1977, stimulated by Paisley, failed to gain much support. It lacked the backing of the Official Unionist and the Vanguard political parties.

The Miami Showband Slaughter, 31 July 1975. The killing of three of the five members of the Miami Showband near Newry highlighted an aspect of the festering situation. The musicians were returning to the Republic from an engagement at Banbridge in Northern Ireland. After the murders, two of the Ulster Volunteer Force members involved in it blew themselves up trying to destroy the Showband's van. One was an ex-Ulster Defence Regiment member, and the weapons used had been taken from a UDR depot.

That there were close relations and duplicating membership between the UDA and UVF and the UDR had often been alleged. As the previous chapter mentioned, the UDR came into existence in 1970 as a partly part-time and partly full-time replacement for the Ulster Special Constabulary, or "B" Specials. The latter had achieved a notorious reputation as an instrument of Orange oppression of the Roman Catholic minority. Where the USC had been a provincially controlled body, the UDR was presumably to be under the more objective domination of the British army, "excluding anyone found to have extremist political views," with regular army personnel to be present in all UDR patrols. Such was demonstrably not the case. In January 1973, for example, the Conservative U.K. Under-Secretary for the Army, Peter Blaker, asserted that "there is no obligation on a U.D.R. member to tell us if he belongs to the U.D.A. or not, since this is not an illegal organisation." This suggests why the Roman Catholics in the UDR declined from about 18 percent in 1971 to 3 percent in 1975 and 2 percent more recently.[51] An investigative reporter concluded that an "important factor in the decline of Catholic support for the UDR has been, over the years, the use of the regiment by loyalist paramilitary groups as a base for training and operations." He said that the "attempt to divorce the UDR from sectarian influence has been a notable failure."[52]

Mountbatten and Warrenpoint, 27 August 1979. A 50-pound remote-controlled bomb on his fishing boat off Mullaghmore in County Sligo on the eastern coast of Ireland killed Admiral of the Fleet Earl Mountbatten of Burma and two companions and wounded four others, one fatally. The same day, 27 August 1979, two remote-controlled bombs resulted in the ambush death of six paratroopers and twelve of the Queen's Own Highlanders in southeastern Northern Ireland at Warrenpoint (Narrow Water). Radio devices such as are used to guide toy airplanes set off these bombs.

PIRA in Belfast took responsibility for the murders. They called the Mountbatten affair a "discriminate operation to bring to the attention of the English people the continued occupation of our country." The embarrassed twenty-six county government quickly arrested two Provos for the Mountbatten crime, but convicted only one of them.

What did Provo leaders hope to accomplish by the Warrenpoint slaughter? A spokesman asserted that it "completely demoralised" British soldiers. He added: "The war has now gone on for ten years, and then there is this massive blow and there is no sign of victory."[53]

British and American media dramatized especially Mountbatten's death. As a cousin of the queen, his royal connections rated him a spectacular funeral in Westminster Abbey. A television series on his life (produced under his personal direction just before his death) quickly made its appearance and prolonged the impact of his assassination.

Particularly notable in the Warrenpoint scenario was its second "act." The six paratroopers had been killed by a bomb hidden in a truckload of hay. It destroyed their lorry, one of a three-vehicle convoy. A "quick reaction force" helicopter flew the wounded Highlanders to a nearby spot in order to provide first aid and support. That spot contained the second bomb![54]

All sides tried to exploit these events. Probably most significantly, they stimulated meetings among British, Northern Ireland, and Irish officials. On 5 October 1979, a joint ministerial statement "agreed that every effort should be made to make fuller use of the 1976 extra-territorial legislation which allows terrorist suspects to be brought to trial in one jurisdiction for offences committed in the other."[55] This was scarcely a consequence sought by the PIRA.

Assassinations of particular foes and symbolic figures continues in Northern Ireland. For example, on 15 October 1980, Loyalists killed two Irish Republican Socialist Party leaders in West Belfast. On 14 November 1981, the PIRA shot the Reverend Robert Bradford, Westminster MP for South Belfast. Bradford had been urging even more extreme measures against the PIRA.

Hunger Strikes. Perhaps the most effective tactics that PIRA and INLA have had available for dramatizing to the world their struggle have been the hunger strikes of 1980-81.

The impact of the publicity about the deaths of ten strikers in 1981 recalls that about the spaced-out executions by the British of fifteen leaders of the 1916 Easter Rising that 3-12 May in Dublin and subsequent trials leading to suspended death sentences and to one further execution on 3 August.[56] It also recalls the propaganda impact of the hunger strikes to death against the British in 1920 as part of the Irish independence war, especially that of the Lord Mayor of Cork Terence MacSwiney after 70 days well covered by the news media.[57] MacSwiney wrote to his fellow hunger-strikers three weeks before his death: "Comrades, if we twelve go in glorious succession to the grave, the name of Ireland will flash in a tongue of flame through the world, and be a sign of hope for all time to every people struggling to be free."[58]

The hunger strike was used a number of times during the 1970s. Here are some examples:

A hunger strike in the Crumlin Road prison, Belfast, in June 1972 plus overcrowded conditions led to the introduction of the controversial "special category status" for any prisoner sentenced to more than nine months "who claims political motivation and who is acceptable to a compound leader at the Maze or Magilligan Prisons."[59]

Such PIRA leaders as Joe Cahill, Ruairi and Sean Ó Brádaigh, and Sean MacStiofain made hunger protests that year in Eire against what they regarded as unjust imprisonment.

More attractive to the media were the strike and endured forced feeding of Dolores and Marian Price, who sought to be transferred from an English to the Armagh jail. Their protest lasted more than 200 days until 7 June 1974; they were finally moved 18 March 1975.

Two strikers for political status died in their attempts. They were Michael Gaughan, a member of OIRA who succumbed in the Parkhurst prison on the Isle of Wight 3 June 1976. Frank Stagg of the PIRA died 12 February 1976 in Wakefield prison in England. The police, the Provos, and family members all quarrelled over control of Stagg's body when it arrived in Ireland. The police buried it under a heavy concrete slab and watched over it for six months. Then, with the police watch ended, on 6 November 1976, the body was recovered and buried in a Republican plot. He is honored with three tombstones, one over each of his two graves and another over an empty plot his brother had purchased.

Daithi O Conaill led a mass hunger strike by the PIRA in the Irish Portlaoighise prison against being imprisoned that lasted 47 days until 22 April 1977. General pressure from priests and colleagues stopped that strike because the "prospects of mass death appalled everyone."[60]

The most spectacular and publicized hunger strike arose out of the continued protest by prisoners and their friends against mistreatment and especially since 1976 against further "criminalisation" through the phasing out of special category status. The reports of such bodies as Amnesty International, the admissions by British investigative commissions, and the complaints to the European Commission and Court of Human Rights and their decisions on prison brutalities throughout this struggle are discussed in chapter 6.

The on-the-blanket initiative began with Ciaran Nugent on 14 September 1976. When he was sentenced for hijacking a van, he "vowed 'that they would have to nail the clothes to my back' if an attempt was made to criminalise him" through making him wear prison clothing.[61] This pattern of protest spread not only in the Maze Prison but also among the women in the Armagh jail. It also came to include loyalists as well as nationalists.

An appeal to the European Commission of Human Rights to force the U.K. government to grant political status to the "blanket protesters" was rejected in June 1980. The Commission scored the U.K.'s inflexibility, but it decided that the debasing conditions of the protest were "self-inflicted" and "designed to create maximum sympathy and to enlist public support for their political aims."

On 27 October 1980, seven Republican prisoners began a hunger strike in the H Blocks of the Maze Prison; 342 others were then on-the-blanket, or in what is called the "dirty protest." This strike ended 18 December on its 53rd day and with no deaths. For parts of that period, three Republican women in the Armagh jail and 23 other Republican men in the Maze joined in the strike. On 12–17 December, six Protestant Ulster Defence Association members incarcerated for murder and arms offences also started a hunger strike for "political status" and segregation from Republicans. At that time, 143 of the 300 Loyalist prisoners in the Maze were refusing to do prison work, and 18 would not wear prison clothing.

The strike was stopped by family and priestly pressures and also by an apparent "agreement" or "private assurances" or a misunderstood reinterpretation of the prison behavior code. At any rate, not long after the end of the strike, it became obvious to the inmates that the Northern Ireland Office was not going to improve prison conditions very much, especially because of extreme Protestant pressure generated by rumors of what was interpreted as a Nationalist victory. Thus, to the Nationalists, the British appeared to be reneging.

By the beginning of the new year, Nationalist paramilitaries had killed 18 prison staff members in two and one-half years. Terror dramas continued. On 16 January, former U.K. M.P. Bernadette Devlin McAliskey and her husband, Michael, were seriously wounded by Loyalist paramilitaries in their home near Coalisland, County Tyrone. On 21 January, PIRA members killed two former members of the Northern Ireland House of Commons, Sir Norman Stronge and his son, James, in their home at Tynan Abbey, County Armagh. The PIRA called this a "deliberate attack on the symbols of hated Unionism" and a "reprisal for a whole series of loyalist assassinations and murder attacks on nationalist people and nationalist activities."[62]

Plans to renew the hunger strike were developing. Bobby Sands, a leader of PIRA prisoners, began the new strike on 1 March 1981, the fifth anniversary of the withdrawal of special category status for offences committed after that date. Sands was serving a 14-year term for possession of a gun. Provisional Sinn Féin announced the next day that 411 prisoners in the

Maze and 28 in Armagh on the "dirty protest" had quit their effort so that attention might be focused on the hunger strike.

The death of the U.K. M.P. for Fermanagh-South-Tyrone, a strongly Nationalist area, provided an opportunity for Sands to be run—even though in prison—to succeed him. Sands won the contested by-election 9 April, and then died 5 May. His election and that of his campaign manager, Owen Carron, on 20 August to succeed him on his death demonstrated vividly a degree of popular support that governmental spokespeople had long denied. Two other Long Kesh (Maze) prisoners (one on hunger strike) were elected to the Irish parliament at about the same time.[63]

The media impact of Sands' protest, election, and death, and of related incidents and deaths, at least equaled or exceeded that of any other terrorist theatrical described. Part of it were massive parades in Belfast, Dublin, and English cities; debates in parliament and many official statements; and riotous activities, shootings, and bombings. For the TV coverage of Sands' funeral, 164 crews—including 4 each for the American NBC and CBS networks—were made available. But, as a reporter put it, Sands "died as much from lack of truth as from food" for his "hunger-strike was presented in stark isolation to the events and political decisions that caused it."[64]

This 1981 hunger strike continued until 3 October and cost ten strikers' lives. In April–September, 61 other people (32 civilians, 14 soldiers, 15 police) were killed.

PIRA claimed that they had "discouraged the prisoners on numerous occasions when they felt that a hunger-strike was the only logical means of bringing public attention to their plight and public pressure to bear on the British."[65] Like PIRA, INLA—three of whose members died in the strike—asserted that the hunger-strike decision was made by the prisoners themselves, but that the effort is "the price to be paid for the winning of National Liberation."[66]

Other Nationalist organizations, such as the Social Democratic and Labour Party, reacted negatively to the hunger strikes as well as to the "blanket" protest. In contrast, a political editor of the London *Guardian* newspaper, Ian Aitken, stated on 13 August: "Many [British] Ministers have been distressed by the Provisional IRA's propaganda victory in Europe and America over the H-Block hunger-strikes. ... A few of them ... believe that the government should at least take steps to see that the procession of dying hunger-strikers is halted."

Predictably, the Ulster Volunteer Force journal, *Combat*, called the hunger effort "this life-wasting tactic" and cited how "indirectly they have caused the deaths of others ... not to mention the countless cost of injuries and damage to property."⁶⁷

On the religious side, it presented a difficult ideological issue: Were the dead hunger strikers murdered, as PIRA and INLA contended, or were they ;ides? Suicide is an ultimate and thus to Roman Catholics an unforgiven sin. The coroner's inquest into the ten hunger deaths refused to examine motives and ruled that deaths were due to starvation.⁶⁸ Cardinal Tomás O'Fiaich stated on 21 May 1981, after several of the deaths, that the British government should think about "the wrath of the whole Nationalist population" if it insists on maintaining its "rigid stance" on the strikers' welfare. Roman Catholic Bishop Edward Daly of Londonderry went further; he asserted that Sands' death was "not suicide."⁶⁹ On 3 October, in calling off their protest, the hunger strikers stated: "We have been robbed of the hunger strike as an effective protest weapon because of the successful campaign waged against our distressed relatives by the Catholic hierarchy, aided and abetted by the SDLP [Northern Ireland Social Democratic and Labour Party]."

As prisoners had lapsed into unconsciousness toward the end of their fast, their families had taken control and sanctioned forced feeding. A leading PIRA officer, Gerry Adams, asserted: "While we must adopt a compassionate and fraternal attitude to those families who intervened, one cannot underestimate the enormity of their action or the manner in which the defeatist and demoralising campaign by some clergymen influenced their decision."

Three days after the end of the strike, the Northern Ireland Secretary of State James Prior conceded one of the strikers' demands, the right to wear their own clothes. In response to their objection to doing prison work, he raised "the possibility of widening the scope of work in prisons" and said he hoped "to encourage a system where the very advanced training and educational facilities available ... may be freely used by all prisoners."⁷⁰

The five-year-old blanket protest had thus stopped, but such problems as prison work remained, and some 300 prisoners still possessed the special category status—with its political implications—for which their colleagues had been striking.

Terror Theater's Audiences. These dramatic terrors are brought intimately into the lives of everyone in Northern Ireland and even in the twenty-six counties and Great Britain either directly or indirectly. Television in particular has vividly injected the terrors into their lives. As social scientist Crane Brinton has it, "the Terror touches great and small with the obsessive power of a fashion." It dissipates somewhat for the time political indifference, "that mainstay of the modern state."⁷¹ Nevertheless, as an editorial in the Dublin weekly newspaper *Hibernia* of 30 August 1979 notes, "The people most directly concerned with the violence on this island—namely those living in NI—are incapable, politically, of doing anything about it." The U.K. officials in control of the province are "removed from the worst effects of the conflict." Their government "rates the problem very low in its political priorities," and that of the republic, "having no power in that jurisdiction, can and does manage to avoid any constructive political participation."

To determine the pervasiveness of experiences with violence, British Opinion Research Centre pollsters asked people in Northern Ireland in 1978: "Have you personally seen an act of terrorism in Northern Ireland?" Almost half (49 percent) the Catholics had been witnesses: 34 to street rioting, 29 to "building blown up," 16 to a vehicle hijacked, and 13 to murders. More than one-third (36 percent) of the Protestants had had such experiences: 26 to building destruction, 20 to street rioting, 9 to vehicle hijacking, and 7 to murders.⁷² With that wide a witnessing of violence, further extended and deepened by gossip and the mass media, the obsessiveness and broad diffusion of this "fashion"—as Brinton calls it—is apparent.

Do the Protestant and Roman Catholic—"Loyalist" and "Nationalist"—extremists credibly represent popular causes in a manner satisfactory to substantial constituencies? Do the British soldiers? What about the army's Ulster Defence Regiment of largely Protestant part-and-full-time soldiers? How do members of the Royal Ulster Constabulary stand?

Are the Prods and Provos really small, unrepresentative, criminal groups of gangsters who use a cause as a pretense for exploiting people, settling personal grudges, robbing banks and postoffices, operating rackets, and having illegal "fun"? Are the soldiers uninformed, prejudiced, and otherwise unemployed youths who approach the Orange and Green "paddies" as dehumanized problems? Are the UDR and RUC representative only of the Orange community? Evidence on all these questions has been presented in the foregoing, but let us look at their implications more from an audience point of view.

These questions suggest the great significance that participants in the conflict place upon their being recognized and labeled as "political" and thus representative rather than "criminal." This issue was crucial in many of the events described. As one social scientist put it, "There exists ... a consciousness in volunteers which provides an immunity to the imputation that their activities are criminal, mad or merely 'Irish.' " They see themselves as "soldier-politicians." They are not criminalized by "doing time for the movement" in prison; it is "an occupational hazard" of a revolutionary.[73] The Brit "soldiers of the Queen" and the police have a similar social garment thrown traditionally around them that provides them with "immunity to the imputation that their activities are criminal." They are told they are being properly "British." As we have seen, the political establishment cooperates with the military and the police in preserving that immunity as intact as possible.

Surveys conducted in Northern Ireland, the twenty-six counties, and England bear out these presumptions by the paramilitaries, police, and soldiers that they have substantial and wide support.

A comprehensive report on attitudes concerning the Northern Ireland situation conducted under the auspices of the Economic and Social Research Institute of Dublin by Earl E. Davis and Richard Sinnott, published in 1979, reported responses to controversial questions: In the twenty-six counties, instead of the overwhelming rejection of the motives and activities of the IRA so freely contended in the mass media and by major politicians, this report finds that 41.8 percent of the population is sympathetic with its *motives* (10.8 strongly, 15.8 moderately, and 15.2 slightly). Only 33.5 percent reject them (11.7 slightly, 11.3 moderately, and 10.5 strongly). With regard to IRA *activities*, 20.7 percent had supportive opinions (2.8 strongly, 5.3 moderately, and 12.6 slightly). The opposition to its *activities* came to 60.5 percent (25.0 slightly, 17.8 moderately, and 17.7 strongly).[74]

The report also makes significant comparisons of attitudes in the Republic, in Northern Ireland, and in Great Britain. For example, on whether "British withdrawal from Northern Ireland without the consent of the parties involved, would lead to a great increase in violence," 59.4 percent in the Republic agreed, as did 87.5 percent of the Protestants and 67.4 of the Roman Catholics in Northern Ireland and 48.0 of the respondents in Great Britain. On whether "British withdrawal ... without the consent of the parties involved, would lead to a negotiated settlement," there was a similar level, this time of disagreement: 48.6 in Eire, 81.1 among northern Protestants, and 60.2 among northern Roman Catholics.[75]

The Northern Ireland Attitude Survey, conducted in the summer and autumn of 1978 by E. Moxon-Browne of Queen's University of Belfast, indicated that 70.7 percent of the Protestants in the province oppose the creation of a united Ireland even "by peaceful means," and 82.8 percent of the Roman Catholics favor it, a basic contrast. Those supporting the more extreme political parties include 11.8 percent for the Democratic Unionist Party, led by the flaming propagandist, the Reverend Ian Paisley, and 2.3 percent for the Republican Clubs, OIRA's political affiliate. About two-thirds of both segments of the whole population (64.3 percent of the Protestants and 67.4 percent of the Roman Catholics) agreed that the "British Government does not really care what happens in Northern Ireland as long as there is not too much unrest." As to whether the Irish government "is doing its best to ensure that the IRA is unable to operate from the Republic's side of the border," 91.1 percent of the Protestants and 41.3 percent of the Roman Catholics said that it was not.[76]

In looking at such figures for the Republic and the north, an editorial writer for the Dublin *Irish Times* on 16 October 1979 concluded, "We are what we are. 'No Surrender' [an Orange battle cry] and 'Up the Republic' [a Green one] still seem to summarize the attitudes of the majority of people on this island."

Viewed from a different perspective, it can be said of both Orange and Green extremists in official and vigilante ranks that the revolutionary pattern is "repeatedly filled by the youth of another generation unaware of their elders' hypocrisy ... [or] alienated by the prim and dishonest compromises of their elders or disgusted with a system based on lies and habit."[77] The paramilitaries and the militaries provide dramatic roles that attract idealists, adventurers, misfits, the aimless, psychopaths, and criminals. Ensuing experiences tend to shift many about among these rough categories. Understandably, the more experienced and opportunistic of these people seize and use positions of leadership and power. Their dramas of terror reach vast audiences, but do they contribute to the solution of problems or merely become preoccupying symptoms? Too often, the outrageous dramas take the place in the mass media of the rankling and persisting causes, the oppression with which so many of the masses throughout the British Isles are living.

Notes

1. Eileen O'Brien, "Call for Conflict in the North," Dublin *Irish Times*, 21 April 1972, p. 12.
2. Malcolm X (with Alex Haley), *Autobiography* (New York: Grove, 1965), chap. 19.
3. Cathal Goulding, quoted by Renagh Holohan, "Goulding Orates at McCann Grave," Dublin *Irish Times*, 19 April 1972, pp. 1, 11.
4. Frank Kitson, *Bunch of Five* (London: Faber & Faber, 1977), p. 283.
5. Vera M. Roberts, *Nature of Theatre* (New York: Harper & Row, 1971), pp. 277-78; cf. Antonin Artaud, *The Theatre and Its Double* (New York: Grove, 1958).
6. Cf. Ovid Demaris, *Brothers in Blood* (New York: Scribner's, 1977), p. 365.
7. Robin Evelegh, *Peace-Keeping in a Democratic Society* (Montreal: McGill-Queen's University Press, 1978), pp. 38-39.

8. Northern Ireland Information Service: *Northern Ireland: Facts and Figures* (Belfast: July 1982), p. 24; British Information Services, *Northern Ireland,* rev. ed. (New York, 1981), p. 3; plus updating materials from British Information Services, New York, and U.S. data from National Center for Health Statistics, Washington, D.C.

9. Evelegh, *Peace-Keeping*; *Fortnight*, no. 185 (March–April 1982): 14.

10. J. L. Barkas, "Adapting to Violence," *New Leader* (New York), 15 March 1976, pp. 3-4, p. 4 quoted.

11. Northern Ireland Information Service, *Northern Ireland*; W. D. Flackes, *Northern Ireland* (New York: St. Martin's, 1980), p. 211; *Fortnight* (Belfast), no. 183 (October–November 1981): 13.

12. Flackes, *Northern Ireland*, p. 211; Workers' Research Unit, "The Security Industry North and South," *Belfast Bulletin,* no. 10 (Spring 1982): 5-16, at p. 9; J. M. Glover, *Northern Ireland: Future Terrorist Trends*, Ms. Reference No. D/DINI/2003 (London: Ministry of Defence, 15 December 1978), p. 5.

13. Michael McKeown, "Chronicles: A Register of Northern Ireland's Casualties: 1968-80," *The Crane Bag* (Holmsdale, Co. Wicklow) 4, no. 2 (1980): 1-5, at pp. 4-5.

14. Paddy Prendiville, "Prevention of Terrorism Act," *Rights* (London) 5, no. 2 (November–December 1980): 10-11; *Hibernia* (Dublin), 20–27 December 1979, pp. 1, 8.

15. *Fortnight*, no. 185 (March–April 1982): 16; *Magill* (Dublin) 5, no. 10 (July 1982): 60.

16. Amnesty International, *Report of an Amnesty International Mission to Northern Ireland (28 November–6 December 1977)*, AI Index: EUR 45/01/78 (London: AI International Secretariat, June 1978), p. 4.

17. H. G. Bennett, chairman, *Report of the Committee of Inquiry Into Police Interrogation Procedures in Northern Ireland* (London: HMSO, Cmnd. 7497, March 1979), part 6.

18. *Fortnight*, no. 180 (March–April 1981): 11.

19. Flackes, *Northern Ireland*, p. 7.

20. Justice Scarman, chair, Tribunal of Inquiry, *Violence and Civil Disturbances in Northern Ireland in 1969* (Belfast: HMSO, Cmd. 566, April 1972): 1: 15, 76 (footnote), 243.

21. Russell Stetler, *The Battle of the Bogside* (London: Sheed and Ward, 1970), p. 157.

22. "A Short History of the Plastic Bullet," *Fortnight*, no. 182 (July–August 1981): 4-5; "Plastic Bullets," *Fortnight*, no. 186 (May–June 1982): 4; "Plastic Bullets—But the Deaths Are Real," *Rights* (London) 6, no. 4 (March–April 1982): 3; Leonard Doyle, "Bans Plastic Bullets," New York *Guardian,* 26 May 1982, p. 13; "Euro Parliament Says 'Ban Plastic Bullets,' " *Troops Out* (London) 5, no. 8 (June 1982): 4; Information on Ireland, *They Shoot Children* (London, 1982).

23. *Fortnight*, no. 182 (July–August 1981): 12, and no. 185 (March–April 1982): 15.

24. *Fortnight*, no. 181 (May–June 1981) 13, and no. 183 (October–November 1981): 16.

25. J. D. Stewart, "Gun Happy," *Fortnight*, no. 11 (19 February 1971): 7; *Fortnight*, no. 186 (May–June 1982): 15.

26. Glover, *Northern Ireland*, pp. 4, 16, 17.

27. Campaign for Free Speech on Ireland, *British Media in Ireland* (London: Information on Ireland), p. 35.

28. Niall Kiely, "Provisional IRA: What Now After La Mon?" *Hibernia* (Dublin), 23 February 1978, p. 5.

29. Lord Widgery, *Report of the Tribunal Appointed to Inquire into the Events on Sunday, 30th January 1972 ... in Londonderry* (London: HMSO, H.L. 101, H.C. 220, 1972), p. 6.

30. Ibid., p. 8-9.
31. Ibid., p. 12.
32. Ibid., p. 26.
33. Ibid., p. 38.
34. Samuel Dash, *Justice Denied: A Challenge to Lord Widgery's Report on "Bloody Sunday"* (New York: International League for the Rights of Man, 1972), pp. 7-8.
35. Richard Deutsch and Vivien Magowan, *Northern Ireland: 1968–73*, 2 vols. (Belfast: Blackstaff Press, 1973–74), 2:152-53.
36. *Keesing's Contemporary Archives*, 22–29 July 1972, pp. 25383-84.
37. Deutsch and Magowan, *Northern Ireland*, 2:199.
38. John McGuffin, *Internment!* (Tralee, Ireland: Anvil Books, 1973), p. 161.
39. *Keesing's Contemporary Archives*, 16–23 September 1972, pp. 25381, 25480-82.
40. Ibid., pp. 25481-82.
41. British Information Services, *Northern Ireland*, p. 3; *Keesing's Contemporary Archives*, 8–15 April 1972, p. 25188.
42. Deutsch and Magowan, *Northern Ireland*, 2: 278–79; *Keesing's Contemporary Archives*, 16–22 April 1973, p. 25829; 23–29 April, p. 25852; 24–31 December, pp. 26254-55.
43. Jacqueline Kaye, "Behind the Birmingham Bombs Trial," *Hibernia*, 5 September 1975, pp. 7-8; T. P. Coogan, *The I.R.A.*, rev. ed. (Douglas, Isle of Man: Fontana Paperbacks, 1980), p. 487; *Keesing's Contemporary Archives,* 22–28 September 1975, p. 27346.
44. Coogan, *The I.R.A.*, p. 569.
45. Steven Rattner, "2 I.R.A. Bomb Attacks in London," *New York Times,* 21 July 1982, pp. A1, A11; John Brecher and Ronald Henkoff, "The IRA's Return to Terror," *Newsweek*, 2 August 1982, pp. 31-32.
46. *Keesing's Contemporary Archives*, 19–26 February 1972, p. 25107.
47. Deutsch and Magowan, *Northern Ireland*, 2:246.
48. *Fortnight*, no. 84 (7 June 1974): 10.
49. Deutsch and Magowan, *Northern Ireland*, 3:59.
50. Louis Boyle, "The Ulster Workers' Council Strike, May 1974," chap. 8 in *Violence and the Social Services in Northern Ireland,* ed. John Darby and Arthur Williamson (London: Heinemann, 1978), p. 155.
51. Jack Holland, "U.D.R.: The Queen's Rebels," *Hibernia*, 5 September 1975, pp. 4, 10, at p. 4.
52. Ed Moloney, "The UDR: Nine Years of Killings and Controversies," *Hibernia*, 29 March 1979, p. 10; cf. *Fortnight*, no. 177 (July–August 1980): 9.
53. Provisional IRA Spokesman, "Interview with Provisional IRA," *Hands Off Ireland* (London), no. 9 (November 1979): 11-13, at p. 11.
54. *Keesing's Contemporary Archives*, 25 January 1980, p. 30049.
55. Ibid., p. 30050.
56. Robert Kee, *The Green Flag* (New York: Delacorte, 1972), pp. 572, 580.
57. Dorothy Macardle, *The Irish Republic*, 2nd rev. ed. (New York: Farrar, Straus and Giroux, 1951), pp. 391-92.
58. Calton Younger, *Ireland's Civil War* (London: Frederick Muller, 1968), p. 106.
59. Lord Gardiner, chairman, *Report of a Committee ... Measures to Deal with Terrorism in Northern Ireland* (London: HMSO, Cmnd. 5847, January 1975), p. 34.
60. Coogan, *The I.R.A.*, chap. 21.
61. Coogan, *On the Blanket: The H Block Story* (Dublin: Ward River Press, 1980), p. 79.

62. *Fortnight*, no. 178 (October–November 1980): 11; no. 179 (December–January 1980–81): 13-14; and no. 180 (March–April 1981): 9-10; "IRA Hunger Strikes," *Keesing's Contemporary Archives*, 22 May 1981, pp. 30875-78; Gerry Foley, "The Making of a Martyr," *Magill* (Dublin) 4. no. 8 (May 1981): 11-14, at p. 14; "8-Strong Fast," *An Phoblacht: Republican News* (Dublin), 26 September 1981, p. 2.

63. "8-Strong Fast," *An Phoblacht: Republican News*, 26 September 1981, p. 2.

64. Tom McGurk, "The War of the Worlds," Dublin *Sunday Tribune*, 17 May 1981, p. 27.

65. "IRA Attitude on H-Block," *An Phoblacht: Republican News*, 5 September 1981, p. 20.

66. "The Price of Freedom," *Starry Plough* (Dublin), June 1981, p. 1.

67. "Bobby Sands, M.P., and Francis Hughes," *Combat* (Belfast) 4, no. 41 (1981): 1.

68. *Fortnight*, no. 185 (March–April 1982): 13.

69. Ibid., no. 182 (July–August 1981): 13-14.

70. William Borders, "Belfast Prisoners End Hunger Strike," *New York Times*, 4 October 1981, pp. 1, 17; *Keesing's Contemporary Archives*, 20 November 1981, p. 31194.

71. Crane Brinton, *The Anatomy of Revolution,* rev. ed. (New York: Vintage, 1965), p. 177.

72. Richard Rose and others, *Is There a Concurring Majority About Northern Ireland?* (Glasgow: Centre for the Study of Public Policy, University of Strathclyde, 1978), p. 10.

73. Frank Burton, *The Politics of Legitimacy; Struggles of a Belfast Community* (London: Routledge & Kegan Paul, 1978), p. 125.

74. E. E. Davis and Richard Sinnott, *Attitudes in the Republic of Ireland Relevant to the Northern Ireland Problem*, paper no. 97 (Dublin: Economic and Social Research Institute, 1979), p. 99.

75. Ibid., p. 88.

76. E. Moxon-Browne, *The Northern Ireland Attitudes Survey*, Ms. report (Belfast: The Queen's University, May 1979), pp. 11-12, 21, 26.

77. J. B. Bell, *The Secret Army: A History of the IRA 1915–1970* (London: Sphere Books, 1972), pp. 444-45; cf. Bell, *The Secret Army: The IRA 1916–1979* (Dublin: Academy Press, 1979); cf. Bill Rolston and Mike Tomlinson, "Spectators at the 'Carnival of Reaction'? Analysing Political Crime in Ireland," pp. 21-43 in *Power, Conflict & Inequality*, ed. by Mary Kelly, Liam O'Dowd, and James Wickham (Dublin: Turoe Press, 1982).

CHAPTER 9

Quests for Peace

Everyone in Northern Ireland has long wished for peace to break out, for the siege mentality of hatred and violence to dissipate. But what does "everyone" mean by "peace"? Peace on whose terms? Peace under what conditions? As we have seen, it can mean anything from a sort of tolerant social stalemate to complete integration of the province into the United Kingdom, to restoration of the Orange dictatorship under British sponsorship or in an independent statelet, to integration into the Irish Republic, to a socialist reorganization of society. To achieve any such goal, all sorts of violent and nonviolent methods are being advocated and tried. This chapter outlines a variety of the nonviolent methods and plans of action now being discussed or used.

In all this, too few of those involved have done as did a lower-class Protestant leader who points out: "We have looked across the fence at the 'Taigs' [Roman Catholics] and have seen that they are living in the same conditions as we are living ... that our working-class constituency is suffering just as the 'Taigs' suffer."[1] Or as a middle-class Irishman is quoted as replying when asked whether or not the struggle is one between Protestants and Roman Catholics or one between haves and have-nots: "Neither. It's a fight between the have-nots on both sides. The haves stand above it and laugh all the way to the bank."[2]

Sincere efforts are being made on many different levels to help constitute a more livable social situation. Whether they are effectual or not remains to be seen. Some of the procedures and goals have at least helped mitigate some of the bitterness. They will be outlined here as activities of these organization: (1) agencies of religious denominations and groups of denominations; (2) voluntary social work, demonstration, and protest societies; (3) political actionist bodies; (4) political parties more generally; (5) insurgent political parties; and (6) governmental agencies. These categories are not mutually exclusive, but they appear to be workable for the purposes of comparison and contrast.

Religious Agencies

Any degree of cooperation among all principal religious denominations, including the Roman Catholic, is a very recent development, precipitated by the current "troubles." It is well to bear in mind that the "present uneasy union of interests" among "all Protestant groups to the disadvantage of the Catholics in N. Ireland is a historically recent event."[3] It is not so long since the dissenting churches—Presbyterian, Methodist, and others—were disadvantaged as rebels against the Church of Ireland (Anglican). Members of these churches are still called Dissenters rather than Protestants in Northern Ireland.

Interdenominational agencies concerned with conciliating activities include the Fellowship of Reconciliation, Friends of Corrymeela, Protestant and Catholic Encounter (PACE), and Glencree Community. In addition, in early 1969, the Irish Council of [Protestant and Dissenting] Churches and the Roman Catholic Church began to sponsor a Joint Group on Social Questions with many Working Parties. Out of its consultations grew, among other projects, the Church Leaders' Peace Campaign initiated at Christmas time 1974.

The Fellowship of Reconciliation was begun by Quakers in the United States in 1915. It had its start in Northern Ireland in 1949 in a modest way. A Roman Catholic organizer for the International FOR, Hildegard Mayr, in 1957 helped make it more interdenominational there. Its small membership sought to stimulate the concern of churches in a series of social issues related to conflict and peace and to organize a series of conferences. In 1960 it became more substantial with a "War on Want," and from 1969 it sponsored such projects as workcamp play-schemes for youth from the opposing groups. The FOR even made an effort to put together a "nonviolent third force" to help offset interethnic violence, but this did not get very far.

Friends of Corrymeela derived from an organizing meeting in September 1964 in the Presbyterian Centre at the Queen's University in Belfast. Ray Davey, a clergyman who headed that facility, provided the leadership. By the next June, the group had collected enough money to gain possession on the northeastern coast of an estate appropriately called "Corrymeela," Gaelic for "The Hill of Harmony." To repair the structure on it, the Friends assembled interdenominational groups of willing workers. These working parties not only did physical labor, but they also by doing so together got the Corrymeela program of reconciliation into some action. The object of the Centre is to build bridges of understanding among the opposing factions n Northern Ireland. The view is stated: "At a workcamp people get to know each other, they get to trust each other, and a sense of comradeship and unity develops."[4]

Through a range of programs, Corrymeela Community "has brought different groups together, it has tried to create dialogue and, more important, to keep that dialogue going when the delegates from each group have gone back home."[5] It has a center in Belfast to help maintain interests nurtured at Corrymeela. It has apparently been especially helpful with children and families who were victims of violence and intimidation.

PACE, or Protestant and Catholic Encounter, was "formed in 1968 to oppose growing bitterness of the time by showing that people from all communities could live and work harmoniously." A representative, Eddie Gurley, reports: "All kinds of activities go on in sub-groups: self-development, councils, leisure-time action. We offer support to all reconcilers."[6]

Glencree Community is housed in a former British army barracks and reformatory with a 30-acre farm attached in County Wicklow of the Republic. It came into existence in 1974, sponsored by religious and peace-promoting groups including Friends of Corrymeela, to help people from the north through providing holidays from the troubles and contact and conference facilities. It has also used working parties as a medium of reconciliation.[7]

The Church Leaders' Peace Campaign since 1974 has featured chiefly statements and actions by the top officials of the four principal churches in the province: the Church of Ireland (Anglican), the Presbyterian, the Methodist, and the Roman Catholic. These leaders "appeared together on television, placed full page advertisements in the press, met the Secretary of State [for Northern Ireland], the Prime Minister [of the United Kingdom] and the Taoiseach [Prime Minister of the Republic of Ireland], and were in conference together seventeen times in the course of a few weeks."[8]

Coincident with the launching of the joint campaign by the leaders of the four denominations came an effort by "some Protestant churchmen acting on their own initiative" to arrange a conference with representatives of the Provisional IRA. They met at Feakle, County Clare, in the Republic, on 9–11 December 1974. This conference resulted in a cease-fire agreement, at first to be for the Christmas season but later extended "indefinitely." In addition, the "Provisionals agreed to set up a number of 'Incident Centres' which would investigate and report to the Northern Ireland Office [the government] on any alleged breaches" of the cease-fire.[9]

The coincidence of the Feakle development and the launching of their own interchurch campaign at first worried church leaders. Such brash actionism unsettles middle-class thinking. A Working Party of the continuing

Joint Group on Social Questions of the churches stated in a subsequent report that at first blush they were afraid the coincidence "would confuse the public and perhaps undermine the Church Leaders' Campaign, but eventually it became clear that this practical step had reinforced in the public mind the appeal of the Church Leaders and had exemplified ways in which individual Christians could respond to the appeal put out by the official leaders."[10] But the lull did not last, and it was not used as constructively as it might have been.

Other reconciliation programs have been sponsored by individual denominations. The Religious Society of Friends (Quakers) and their Friends' Service Committee have long been active in trying to offset recourses to violence and to help in social work programs. Their contributions extend back to their arrival in Ireland in the seventeenth century. "From start to finish, the story of nonviolent action in Ireland is closely connected with the Quaker story."[11] As a commentator puts it:

> In the history of Ireland the Quakers have been a conspicuous minority ... honest, skillful capitalists ... part of the economic establishment, but of that benevolent relatively nonexploitative part. They have constituted the most acceptable face of Irish capitalism. ...
>
> [The] Quakers were able to act as a critical communications medium between the colonial class and the millions of people who suffered the consequences of colonial dispossession. The Quakers belonged to neither class and were acceptable to both sides.[12]

The combination of benevolence and a nonproselyting policy also made them acceptable to Roman Catholics, Protestants, Dissenters. This tiny sect has thus had influence out of all proportion to its size.

Pax Christi, a Roman Catholic body, started in France and Germany in 1945; it got under way in Ireland in 1967. It works for peace and in particular to try to implement the encyclical of Pope John XXIII, "Pacem in Terris." This church's Servite Order also has a priory at Benburb that offers facilities for interdenominational conferences.

Peace Point, dating from June 1973, is an offshoot from the Methodist Council of Social Welfare. Its original program called for highlighting constructive happenings in the north. It even had a public relations firm to publicize its findings, but this proved impractical. It now looks upon itself as a service group for other peace groups, especially in offering leadership training for people from such groups.

These cautious religious agencies offer chiefly a more benign possibility in intergroup relations. They operate on the level of societal moral idealizations rather than of the compulsive group mores in terms of which people work, fight, and play. Reactions to the Feakle initiative are instructive. Except for the Feakle, Quaker, Corrymeela, and Glencree projects, the focus is on intentions rather than actions.

Voluntary Agencies

In a land in which religious labels are so prominent, it is difficult to differentiate voluntary agencies from religious ones, but the relative autonomy of the voluntary agencies is their distinguishing characteristic. Noteworthy examples from among the many are the International Voluntary Service, Women Together, Witness for Peace, and the Community of the Peace People. Many others "from 1968/69 onwards ... have mushroomed all over the country, some disappearing almost as fast as they came."[13]

International Voluntary Service organized workcamps beginning in 1955. It attempts to combine reconciliation with personal development through such camps and through holidays for Protestant and Roman Catholic children.

Women Together took shape at a public meeting of some 400 in September 1970. According to one of its own printed handouts, it has been busy

> separating rival gangs in riots by using themselves as shields (in Andersontown and Ardoyne), stopping children and youths setting fire to property (Broadway), dispersing a gang of youths with knives who were attacking a boy from the "other side" (Newtownards Road), defending neighbours who were having windows broken, and going out night after night talking to tartan gangs [of Protestant youth] (East Belfast), giving sympathy and practical help when it was needed and showing concern generally.[14]

Their office was burned out by a bomb in 1976, but they have continued their work. The simplicity of their program "has proved the greatest strength of the movement, allowing it to chime in with the life style of the membership."[15] Saidie Patterson, an experienced trade union leader, became chairperson of Women Together from 1973. She attracted international funds and broadened the body's work to include "shared holidays for Protestant and Catholic children from 'peace-line' areas."[16]

Witness for Peace was created by the Reverend Joseph Parker after bombings in Belfast on Bloody Friday, 21 July 1972, killed his son and ten others, including two soldiers. Some 40,000 signed his declaration as individual Christians to work and witness for peace. He held cross-planting ceremonies in remembrance of those killed in the continuing struggle, maintained a scoreboard on the death toll in the center of Belfast, and gave recognition to individuals and groups working for peace. Parker became frustrated in 1975 and emigrated to Canada, but the mentioned activities of his Witness for Peace have continued.

The Community of the Peace People is an initiative with similarities to Women Together, but it is more charismatic in its leadership, has more aggressive public relations, and at least for a time was able to obtain more establishment backing. It dates from 10 August 1976, the day that British soldiers shot and killed the driver of a car they were chasing. Out of control, the automobile killed two small Roman Catholic children, mortally wounded a third, and seriously hurt their mother. Their aunt, Mairead Corrigan, and a friend, Betty Williams, emerged as symbols of a fresh quest for peace under the guidance of a journalist, Ciaran McKeown, as director and publicist. "These two women," states McKeown, "had instinctively, intuitively, called into the light of day the will of a probable majority of the Northern Irish people to seek a new loving, peaceful way forward after the long night of violence."[17]

On a high tide of popular revulsion against violence, with the aid of the mass media, both Protestants and Roman Catholics flocked to demonstrations, marches, and vigils led by Corrigan and Williams. For a gathering in Belfast's Ormeau Park that 21 August, media estimates placed the attendance at as many as 50,000 people. "The police and the military, who were keeping the crowds under close, but discreet, surveillance, were astonished at the huge number of people, and especially of women and children."[18]

As basic themes of the movement, Corrigan and Williams read a "declaration of peace" that came to be known as the Declaration of the Peace People. Some of its key sentences are:

> We want to live and love and build a just and peaceful society.
> We want for our children, as we want for ourselves, our lives at home, at work and at play, to be lives of joy and peace.

We recognise that to build such a life demands of all of us dedication, hard work and courage.

We recognise that every bullet fired and every exploding bomb makes that work more difficult.

We reject the use of the bomb and the bullet and all the techniques of violence.

We dedicate ourselves to working with our neighbours, near and far, day in and day out, to building that peaceful society in which the tragedies we have known are a bad memory and a continuing warning.[19]

They summed this up as an acceptance of the implications of Pope John Paul's statement: "If you want peace work for justice."[20]

Like many popular movements, this one started out chaotically. Like many other nonviolent initiatives, this one accumulated some opponents immediately and others more slowly as implications of the organization's goals and methods became more widely perceived and understood. The Provisional Sinn Féin immediately stated in its Belfast *Republican News* of 20 August 1976 that the new peace movement was actually seeking "peace at any price" and not "peace with justice." PIRA pickets and counter-demonstrators harassed participants in many of the Peace People's events.

Establishment support came readily at first. Labor unions on the whole announced their backing. Corrigan, Williams, and McKeown among them jetted to Norway, Germany, The Netherlands, France, Canada, Australia, New Zealand, and the United States to raise money for the Peace People's program. As by-products of this international promotion campaign, Corrigan and Williams received recognition from the Queen of England, the Nobel Peace Prize, the Norwegian People's Peace Prize, and honorary doctorates from Yale University. As the French journalist Richard Deutsch puts it, " ... the list of the hundreds and hundreds of public and private organizations, which have lent their support, would cover many pages. Ulster once meant bombs and murder. Thanks to the media, Betty and Mairead are presenting a new image all over the world. When they travel, they not only collect money, but they also try to persuade manufacturers to invest in Ulster and build factories there."[21]

It was not possible to keep up the succession of marches and other events in many Irish and British cities that launched the Peace People's program. As Corrigan said in 1981, "The early days of mass rallies will never return unless there is some desperately bad crisis, which I pray to God will never happen." As Steve McBride, editor of *Peace by Peace*, the organization's fortnightly periodical, puts it, "The movement has become more concentrated," and he adds, "Everyone in Northern Ireland is, or has been, a guilty accomplice in the pattern of prejudices and mistrust which has created the overt violence of the gunman; everyone has a part to play in breaking down those patterns and proving that Northern Irish people can live and work together for the good of the whole community." He contends that the "nine day wonder of 1976, written off a hundred times by the press, will be around as long as it takes to build that just and peaceful society." Even though "there aren't as many people active as there were in the early days," he claims that those active are more effective, "doing specific things as distinct from milling around, attending meetings, making a lot of fuss."[22]

With the funds available at the outset, Peace People purchased a Belfast headquarters building, Fredheim (Norwegian for "Peace Home"); continued to hold a variety of intergroup events including children's sports; organized intersectarian community groups; loaned or donated funds to self-help projects; and held spring and autumn Peace People assemblies to give direction and further publicity to the movement. They are active in working out resettlement arrangements for members of the paramilitary bodies who want to quit and emigrate, and they have distinguished themselves with the submission of human rights proposals to government agencies.

The movement developed formal recommendations to the Northern Ireland Office on such subjects as "The Case for the Replacement of the Emergency Provisions Act" (1978), "Time for a Change [in the governmental control of the province's affairs]" (1980), "The Hunger Strike in the Maze Prison" (October 1980), and "The H-Block Protest, Hunger Strikes and Emergency Law" (February 1981).[23]

If the Peace People had merely continued to have intercommunity meetings at which their declaration was solemnly recited, a Belfast columnist would not have come to this conclusion in 1978: "No doubt the movement can continue to exist and do some good work as a charitable and benevolent foundation, but as a movement it seems to have lost its way." It was the writer who had not found their way: He claimed that "an appeal to abandon force means an appeal to abandon the attempts to change the present constitution." He contended that "any peace movement means supporting the status quo."[24]

The problem was that Williams, Corrigan, and many of their constituents go beyond pacifist opposition to violence. They wish to use nonviolent methods to change the character of society, to erase sectarian barriers, oppression, and injustices. As this became evident, it brought them into confrontation with powerful vested interests opposed to change, and it also forced them to try to deal with the fears of middle-class people asked to place their life styles at risk in order to work for a more viable society. The bulk of their followers were and are lower-class people with less to lose in taking such a risk.

The Peace People oppose the use of force whether by the PIRA, UVF, UDA, police, or army. They want to offset "the vicious spiral of fear and vengeance in which Northern Ireland has been trapped." They realize that "today's victors must pay the price in resentment and revenge tomorrow," as McBride words it. Whether or not this is an acceptable position depends upon one's social preparation for understanding the consequences of brutal and murderous activities. Establishment myths concerning how to maintain public safety surely do not prepare people in Northern Ireland to want to take nonviolent risks in order to achieve a more viable society, even though, as we have pointed out, more has been accomplished that way than any other. The disabled and the dead become martyrs who haunt society as constant reminders of brutality and inequality; only concessions wrung from those in power by nonviolent procedures can make for the egalitarian relationships needed in modern society.

As the investigative reporter Jill Tweedie indicates in the Manchester *Guardian* of 19 February 1980, violent "protectors" turn benign and helpful faces toward "their own people" even though they—whether vigilantes, police, or soldiers—turn "monstrous faces" toward others. As she says, "unless we recognise the human beings beneath the masks we shall never understand how they gain and keep support and so never resolve the war." As McBride points out in *Peace by Peace* of 20 August 1982, this is what the Peace People are attempting in their effort "to build a peaceful society in which Protestant and Catholic moderate and ex-terrorist could all share a future." Little wonder that, after all the high publicity of 1976 and 1977, when Corrigan spoke before a London conference of the National Council for Civil Liberties on 9 November 1978, the media failed to report her remarks. She criticized the army and the Royal Ulster Constabulary and complained about the suppression of freedom of speech and of the press.

The Peace People continue their courageous quest, but, like the Quakers and other devoted advocates of social action to achieve justice through nonviolent procedures, they only occasionally ride an emotional mass wave, even though they do have influence out of all proportion to their numbers. As McBride sees it:

Peace is not the absence of terrorism. Peace is a situation in which the dignity and the rights of the individual are respected....

For a long period there was very acrimonious debate within the movement in which people like myself were accused of being IRA-lovers because we suggested it was not enough to criticise the IRA, it was necessary to deal with the things that caused the IRA.

Those people eventually left the movement, and things have become a lot clearer since.[25]

Political Actionist Agencies

The organizations to be mentioned in this connection are the Northern Ireland Civil Rights Association (NICRA), People's Democracy (PD), the Association for Legal Justice (ALJ), and Amnesty International (AI). This is a "mixed bag," but they have in common programs seeking to cope with the conflict situation in Northern Ireland constructively and nonviolently. Much of this work is described elsewhere in this book. It is merely brought into relationship with other quests for peace at this point.

From 1964, the Campaign for Social Justice, and then from 1967, its successor, NICRA, devoted themselves to fact-gathering and educational work concerning religious discrimination and social injustice more generally. As chapters 3 and 7 point out, NICRA at the outset was patterned on the British National Council for Civil Liberties, a politically eclectic lobbying, litigating, and educating organization. As we have seen, it also in 1968–72 involved itself in organizing or cosponsoring nonviolent civil rights marches, the one in Derry on 30 January 1972 with tragic but effective consequences.

When in 1969–70, the Sinn Féin Officials and Provisionals and then the OIRA and PIRA split their organizations, the Officials in their radical and more secular ideology favored a current emphasis on agitation, demonstration, and organization rather than on the violent procedures on which the Provisionals concentrated. The OIRA thus became interested in NICRA. This helped move NICRA from a middle-class libertarian viewpoint toward a more radical actionist type of nonviolent operation.

This does not mean at all that the Officials oppose the use of violence at all times and in all places, and with their influence in NICRA, it may also reflect on that body. Cathal Goulding, OIRA chief of staff, put it this way shortly after the split: "I don't see any establishment ... handing the wealth over to the ordinary people unless the people have the necessary physical force to support their political ideas."[26] In other words, the current policy of the Officials calls for consciousness-raising and organization preparatory to an eventual seizure of power. Their commitment to nonviolence is strategic, not categorical. Goulding contended in 1978 that the current use of violence by the PIRA and others on the Nationalist side has been "a total failure and ended only in a tricolor [the Irish flag] on a coffin," that in the current situation "anything in the nature of a military campaign would be reactionary, counter-revolutionary and would play into the hands of the British imperialists."[27]

Since 1972, NICRA has again concentrated on fact-gathering for the purposes of litigation and agitation and to the support of compatible agencies. The National Association for Irish Freedom, its U.S. support body, reflects NICRA's current strategy in a 1978 *NAIF Fact Sheet* by asserting: "Only through nonviolent mass action can democracy be won in Northern Ireland."

Helpful in providing enthusiastic nonviolent "muscle" for civil rights demonstrations was People's Democracy, formed 9 October 1968 by students of the Queen's University of Belfast. This body was said by a governmental commission to have "reckless bravery" and to engage in "calculated martyrdom."[28] Chapter 4 describes PD's most celebrated event, the four-day, 75-mile march from Belfast to Derry on 1–4 January 1969. In spite of ambushes by Protestant mobs supported by police, the remnants of the march finally "arrived to a rapturous welcome from a huge crowd" in Guildhall Square, Derry.[29] In the February 1969 Stormont general election, PD fielded eight candidates, but none was elected. A 1972 policy statement advocated a secular, all-Ireland republic and opposed any merging of Northern Ireland with the existing Republic. Its original leadership, such as Bernadette Devlin, Kevin Boyle, and Michael Farrell, have moved into other organizational media.

Extensive internment and interrogation operations in August and September 1971 "had the effect of uniting the Roman Catholic community in opposition to current security policies." With this support, a group of Belfast lawyers undertook to provide advocates and legal briefs for active litigation. As the Association for Legal Justice, they "set out to encourage the use of legal processes to deal with allegations against the security forces and thus to help lessen the risk of direct retaliatory action against them."[30]

As the ALJ continued its work, Amnesty International brought into the picture its broader prestige and facilities for organizing legal and other social pressures. AI's official statement of purposes, carried on many of its publications and on its letterhead, states that it is "a worldwide human rights movement which works impartially for the release of prisoners of conscience; men and women detained anywhere for their beliefs, colour, ethnic origin, religion or language, provided they have neither used nor advocated violence." The body's opposition to torture and capital punishment "in all cases and without reservation" and its advocacy of "fair and prompt trials for all political prisoners" made it a source of hope for the Northern Irish minority and an encouragement to such nonviolent efforts as NICRA, the Peace People, and ALJ.

As we have seen, AI has investigated the mistreatment of prisoners and their detention without trial both in Northern Ireland and in the Republic. The findings of its commissioners have done much to strengthen faith in nonviolent procedures and to bring pressures in behalf of more humane practices.

The professionals who do the work of the ALJ and AI only involve lower-class individuals and groups as clients, but this helps give direction and credibility to organizations with direct lower-class representation such as NICRA and the Peace People. The latter channel data and cases to the former.

Religious, Voluntary, and Political Actionist Agencies

The first two sorts of nonviolent "peace" body discussed, the religious and the voluntary, are on the whole typical middle-class-controlled efforts to make the existing structure of the province at least appear more benign, hopefully to be more benign. They provide conscience-soothing exercises in reconciliation and to some extent the means to help create a more just social order.

In the foregoing, there is a contrast apparent between the concern for "justice" and that for "reconciliation." Concern for "justice" more directly suggests a desire for some degree of social change. It also implies a willingness to struggle for modifications in the control of social power. Change to obtain more justice has the drawback, so far as the in-group of the structure is concerned, of requiring concessions upon the part of those who are entrenched. "Reconciliation" could mean something similar to "justice," but too often it is used to suggest striving for a kind of truce, peace with no change in the social structure, no gain to the out-group's members, to the deprived.

In so-called nonviolent and pacifist circles, this noteworthy contrast is often to be observed between organizations catering to the "haves" and organizations more directly serving the "have-nots," as in the present situation. The Feakle incident of realistic interclass collaboration "turned off" the middle-class groups and had no effective follow-through at the time other than that provided by PIRA. Few middle-class people even in Northern Ireland can face realistically the implications of Russell Stetler's statements: "Britain's 'civilisation' has rested on centuries of violent racism, colonial conquest and social injustice. The Northern Ireland problem is rooted in these traditions."[31]

From their standpoints, just how can the security forces and community welfare specialists differentiate between nonviolent and violent efforts? The dividing line—especially in the case of massive confrontations or blockades but also in certain less spectacular situations—is not an easy one to draw. Nonviolence clearly includes traditional pacifism, refusal to fight, willingness to "turn the other cheek." It also comprises many kinds of nonviolent action "used to control, combat and destroy the opponent's power by nonviolent means of wielding power."[32] These techniques can include the linking of arms to block streets, sit-ins, and other devices that employ physical strength just short of violence. In contrast with many violent kinds of action, nonviolent procedures often require the participation of large numbers of people with a high degree of dedication, training, and discipline for them to be effective. At the same time, as such instances as Bloody Sunday well indicate: "There are times when the civil-rights movement has no greater friend than its enemy. It is the enemy of civil rights who again and again produces the evidence to convince this nation [speaking of the United States] that we cannot afford to stand still."[33] This statement by the U.S. political leader Emanuel Celler was prompted by the opposition to Martin Luther King, Jr., and his associates. Similarly, even by sacrificially precipitating injuries to themselves, NICRA members forced their enemies to produce convincing evidence of the need for more egalitarian conditions.

Few lower-class people develop a political capability at all comparable to that of the lower-class Irish labor leader James Connolly (1868–1916). Even Connolly got turned aside from a nonviolent approach by his comrades, and in 1916 participated in the aborted Easter Rising. This cost him his life before a British firing squad. Similarly, Bernadette Devlin McAliskey became a promising potential heroine of nonviolence during early stages of the current civil war, but she got distracted to violence and to other moves that destroyed that image. Mairead Corrigan, as we have seen, has more consistently followed a nonviolent course.

Lower-class people usually depend, as in this situation, on leaders drawn from the upper classes. Too often they are offered only the opportunity of following middle-class "front people" whose policies fall far short of lower-class needs and expectations.

Political Parties in Northern Ireland

The English social science weekly *New Society* reminded its readers in 1970 that the "present constitution of Northern Ireland was not smoothly adopted as the consensus of some national assembly. It was imposed by the Westminster parliament and then redrafted to conform to the consequences of civil war a half century ago." Civil conflict continues. The Northern Irish still seek to change that basic law by "extra-constitutional agitation," the "means they know."[34] In view of English inflexibility and preoccupation with vested interests, other means do not appear to be available. Unfortunately, the Northern Irish hold such sharply contrasting views about the form that a representative and acceptable constitution might take it is difficult to perceive how they might wisely use the power to draft one if they should acquire such power.

Since the beginning of the conflict in 1968, there have been "a series of ostentatious attempts to encourage a local compromise among selected representatives—each failure demonstrating the irreconcilability of the 'natives' and the extent of British commitment to pursuing a just settlement."[35] This has been most helpful to the English in their national and international propagandas but of little aid in developing a more livable situation in the province.

The numerous Northern Ireland political parties, if they are to make any contribution to a more viable statelet, have to do so through influencing the major British parties. Both Labour and Conservative politicians in Great Britain have done much to preserve what is well called a bitter stalemate in the province.

The six counties appear to be well furnished—so far as numbers and variety of viewpoint are concerned—with political parties. During the current conflict, the principal ones have been the Ulster or Official Unionist Party (OUP), in 1921–72 in control of the province; Paisley's rising Democratic Unionist Party (DUP); the Alliance Party of Northern Ireland (APNI), an effort at intersectarian bridge-building; and the largely Roman Catholic Social Democratic and Labour Party (SDLP). The relative success of each of these and of other Unionist parties at the polls is indicated by the tabulation of vote percentages shown in table 3.

Table 3

Voting Percentages by Party

	1969	1973	1975	1977	1981	1982[16]
DUP	4	4	15	13	27	23
OUP	53	17	25	30	26	30
Other Unionist	13	35	22	10	6	5
APNI	4	14	10	14	9	9
SDLP	7	13	24	21	18	19
Other	19	17	4	12	14	13

The "other" category in the table includes Labour, Liberal, Socialist, Nationalist, and Republican parties. Such a class-labeled party as the Northern Ireland Labour Party declined in this period from about 8 percent of the vote to a mere shadow, less than 1 percent in 1977–82. OIRA's Republican Clubs or Workers Party hovered between 3 and 2 percent, but Provisional Sinn Féin got 7 percent in 1981 and 10 percent in 1982.

The most dramatic changes in these percentages have been the rise of the DUP at the expense of the OUP and other Unionist parties, the rise and then weakening of the APNI and SDLP, and the recent votes for the Provos. The London *Economist* of 30 May 1981 called the 1981 results "a defeat for moderation." The Belfast *Fortnight* of July/August 1981 had this significant generalization to offer: "Given that Alliance draws most of its support from the middle class, it is beginning to look as if class politics may be emerging within the Unionist ranks, with the DUP taking the working class vote, and the Official Unionists sharing the middle class vote with Alliance." In the 1982 Assembly election, most of the Roman Catholic 37 percent of the electorate voted for candidates pledged to abstention from that Assembly. Thus 14 SDLP and 5 Sinn Féin of the 78 members would not take part in that advisory body dominated by Unionists.

Let us look briefly at what the more prominent of these parties would like to accomplish in the quest for a more viable society.

Paisley's DUP's emphasis on terrorists as scapegoats rather than on the causes of terrorism sounds much like right-wing agitators in the United States. As Paisley stated in 1980: "[The] majority of the Unionist population is not really convinced that HM Government has the will to win the battle against terrorism. ... I, for one, am dedicated to bringing to an end the system of undemocratic colonial rule which has prevailed here for too long. We are looking for the highest possible degree of devolution within the UK."[37] Neither does he wish any further experimentation with any power sharing in government with the SDLP, such as was tried briefly in 1974 and which his opposition helped to destroy. What he and his followers appear to desire is a nearly independent statelet dominated by his fundamentalist Protestant party, something at least as discriminatory as the old Orange province. They also seek to eliminate proportional representation, to strengthen bars against Sunday commercial and recreational activities, and to restore capital punishment.

The more general proposals of the OUP appear similar to those of the DUP, but in specifics they make conciliatory gestures to the ethnic minority. For example, the OUP Manifesto calls for "such a system of devolved government as will neither endanger the Union [with the U.K.] nor confer contrived privileges on any section of the community." That formula is probably supposed to suggest a protection for the minority against the majority, but, depending upon administrative control, it might also mean the opposite.

Like the churches, this party is quite concerned about the schools as ideological instruments. As their Manifesto puts it: "We shall continue to oppose the destruction of our own varied system of school education simply to replace it by a universal comprehensive organisation. Ulster people have the right to choose their way of life without doctrinaire and alien patterns being imposed on them."[38] The demand for the perpetuation of separatism or ghettoization is even clearer in a 1972 OUP statement, "Safeguards for Minorities: A Bill of Rights." In this request for "a precise and comprehensive Bill of Rights," the party asks for guarantees of freedom of speech, the press, political association, practice of religion, the person, right to trial, and from discrimination on religious grounds. They admit that there is something of a bill of rights in the 1920 Government of Ireland Act, and they therefore feel impelled to answer the question: "Will it be used?" After all, the existing sureties had "often been overlooked." Here is their explanation:

> The fact is that these have existed for over 50 years without being resorted to (for instance, alleged acts of housing discrimination could easily have been tested in court as could the validity of endowing Church schools or RI [religious instruction] in State Schools). The answer may be that those who complained were not anxious to have their claims legally examined or that they found it difficult to do so by reason of lack of means or evidence.

> In either case, we would argue that the precise nature of a Bill of Rights—its comprehensive coverage of issues—combined with the availability of judicial remedies or legal aid should ensure that public pressure is put on those complaining to seek recourse to the law. The dramatic nature of a Bill of Rights would give this incentive.[39]

They do not mention that law and precedent do not oppose de facto inequality of treatment. Under existing law and precedent, a discriminatory *intention* must be proven to gain recourse, a most difficult task, as chapter 6 discusses and illustrates.

In drafting proposals in 1980 to influence the most recent effort to evolve a Northern Ireland government, the OUP made these gestures at living with the ethnic minority:

> Safeguards and remedies against discrimination on religious or political grounds should be maintained as elsewhere in the U.K. and should also be applied effectively to the actions of United Kingdom ministers and their departments. ...
>
> No entrenched powers, responsibilities or privileges would be assigned to majority or minority parties or groupings as such.

In place of such "entrenched" power-sharing briefly tried in 1974, the Governor as the U.K. monarch's personal representative "would appoint the parliamentary member who appeared to him" to be appropriate to designate as "the salaried Leader of the Opposition and to be a Privy Councillor for Northern Ireland." Membership in departmental select committees would also "be so chosen as to ensure that the composition of each committee (and the total membership of all select committees) reflected the composition of the House as a whole."

What about proportional representation in a Stormont parliament? The OUP recalls that it was actually used in the province in the general Stormont elections of 1921 and 1925 and that it was at OUP insistence that in 1929 legislation changed voting over to a simple majority system, the same as for the Westminster Parliament. That assured the predominant party of more overwhelming control. But that experience is not rehearsed in the 1980 proposals. In them, the OUP called for a single chamber parliament and again wanted "the representatives of single member constituencies elected by a simple majority."[40] No proportional representation!

This is all more subtly stated than would Paisley, but the OUP proposals differ from his principally in rhetoric, in inconsequential details, and wishfully in probable control. The OUP's apparently more compromising stance is actually an effort to reinstate the Orange statelet that the OUP dominated so completely in 1921-72. In analyzing the DUP-OUP relationship, a Belfast editor concludes:

> The battle for the leadership of Unionism lies between the Official Unionists who are attempting to reach socially downwards, and the Democratic Unionists who are reaching upwards. Paisley helped to split Unionism on a class basis. ... If there is one crucial factor which will deny him [control of Unionism and of the province] ... it will be his raucous, strident, impolite style—his lack of respectability.[41]

The Alliance Party (APNI) was formed in April 1970 to serve as a political association representative of the three ethno-religious-economic groups,—Orange, Green, and West British. From the outset, it had substantial middle-class support, especially from new commercial and industrial interests, professional people and employees of multinational corporations. As a minority party, its leadership apparently seeks to make some progress in substituting current politico-economic issues for tribal appeals in political campaigns. As long as the provincial majority wishes to retain the U.K. link, APNI "is fully committed to the establishment of a regional parliament or assembly" within the union, and it adds: "We are convinced that the basic problems of sectarianism and division can only be solved by the people of Northern Ireland within a Northern Ireland context. The fact that these problems were not solved during 50 years of Stormont or during the previous 120 years of 'direct rule' does not mean that the problems are insoluble."

The devices APNI wishes to use are proportional representation (with a single transferable vote, i.e., of a recorded second choice) in elections, joint planning with the Irish Republic "for economic, social and agricultural problems facing the whole island," and the enactment of a Bill of Rights "guaranteeing to all citizens their fundamental Human Rights based on the Universal Declaration of Human Rights." Because of the party's undoubted awareness of the notorious reputation of the Ulster Defence Regiment and the Royal Ulster Constabulary for sectarian bias, the APNI "is totally committed to all security powers being retained by Westminster."[42]

Thus APNI is in part "unionist" and in part pro-SDLP, part of what now appears to be a shrinking center in the province's political life. In the 1981–82 elections, it lost particularly in the suburbs, its previous source of modest strength.

The fourth party whose quest for peace is to be characterized is the Social Democratic and Labour Party (SDLP), formed 21 August 1970. Its constituency is overwhelmingly Roman Catholic. It gained many supporters from the older Nationalist, National Democratic, and Republican Labour parties, and it did much to weaken the Northern Ireland Labour Party, a body somewhat related to the British Labour Party.

John Hume, an SDLP leader, has often said that the British guarantee of Northern Ireland's provincial status—barring a popular vote to the contrary—is an important obstacle to any realistic negotiations to resolve intergroup conflict. He contends that the British "should join the ranks of those who would persuade the Unionists that their future lies in a stable and firm political association with the rest of Ireland, and that she should use all her power and influence in that persuasion." He asserts that the proper "objective is a pluralist Ireland and that the Protestant people of the north would have a positive and guaranteed role to play."[43] As he sees it, the Unionists otherwise have only the alternatives of waiting "until they are outvoted" or until "the British pull the rug from beneath them."

Is such a forceful approach by the British to the Unionists a practical possibility? Hume likes to use a possible United States parallel: "Would it have been reasonable to suppose ... that you can't have civil rights in Mississippi because the whites might oppose it?"[44] But then the United States has a Bill of Rights and a more adequate—albeit slow and halting—implementation process for human rights guarantees and a more representative judiciary. SDLP leaders feel that sooner or later they are going to get the British to help them deal with "loyalist intransigence."

SDLP's program statement, "Towards a New Ireland," adopted in 1972, has served as its chief theme with minor modifications since then. This document claims that "the area which has come to be known as 'Northern Ireland' is inherently unstable." It continues:

> The last attempt to find a settlement to the problems of this country was THE GOVERNMENT OF IRELAND ACT, 1920. It was an imposed settlement which was at the time, unacceptable to all sectors of the people of this Island. It has failed. One of its essential elements, The Stormont Parliament, has recently disappeared and it is necessary to realise that its failure does not

simply represent the failure of the Northern System of Government but the failure of the 1920 Irish Settlement of which it was a part.

It claims that the 1920 partition of the island "institutionalised the differences between the two main traditions creating a Protestant ascendancy in the North and a Catholic one in the South, thereby preventing the positive interaction of one tradition on the other, which a unified state would have provided." With "no hint of coercion," it wants a British declaration "that it would be in the best interests of all sections of the Communities in both Islands, if Ireland were to become united on terms which would be acceptable to all the people of Ireland." It asks that the British "positively encourage the prosecution of this viewpoint." How the British would accomplish this and avoid a "hint of coercion" is not outlined.

The SDLP would work out its solution through a treaty between Britain and the Irish Republic setting up an interim system of joint sovereignty for Northern Ireland. The statelet's citizens would be recognized as citizens of either the U.K. or the Republic, but they would not be entitled to representation in either the Westminster or the Dublin parliament! They would have their own assembly and administration. The single-house assembly would be elected on the basis of proportional representation (the single transferable vote type). "Flags of both Sovereign States would have equal status," and the area might also have its own flag as well. The sovereign powers would each be represented by a commissioner. The two would both have to "sign all legislation passed by the Northern Ireland Assembly unless either or both ... are of the opinion that [it] ... is an infringement of the treaty."

The SDLP realizes that "Irish Unity" arouses deep-set Protestant fears of "Rome rule," but it contends that a gradually evolving and mutually agreeable integration is not only possible but essential. It therefore modestly put forward the recommendation of "a National Senate of Ireland" with the realization expressed that it is "the most difficult and delicate of all our proposals to implement." This Senate "would have equal representation (elected by PR) from both the Dublin Parliament and the New Northern Assembly." It would be established by treaty between the U.K. and the Republic and would be asked "to plan the integration of the whole island and the harmonisation of structures, laws and services in both parts of the island."[45]

A similar integrative line of thought has recurred in minority and British policy proposals concerning Ireland ever since the establishment of the northeastern province.

Insurgent Political Parties. An investigative reporter, Anne McHardy, writing from Belfast for the Manchester *Guardian* 23 February 1980, calls the four mentioned the "trivial legitimate political parties." At any rate, that is the status both the U.K. government and the media people ordinarily grant them. The publicity-conscious UDA and PIRA directly and through their political party affiliates attract much more attention. These affiliates are the Ulster Loyalist Democratic Party (ULDP), formerly the New Ulster Political Research Group (NUPRG), and the Provisional Sinn Féin (PSF). These groups contribute heavily to McHardy's generalization: "All British and Irish media contain people who are partial on Northern Ireland. Some of the fiercest arguments arise not because of external pressure but because of internal differences of strongly held opinion." After all, media people try to search out the colorful and controversial. This has even been attributed to the media people's "vulture mentality"!

Andy Tyrie, chairman of the UDA, and Glen Barr in January 1978 founded the New Ulster Political Research Group as an instrument to put forward a proposal for an independent Northern Ireland. Barr had been a member of the Northern Ireland Assembly in 1973–74 and Convention in 1975. He had also served as former deputy leader of the Vanguard Unionist Party and as senior political spokesperson for the UDA. He chairs the new organization. Their case for "negotiated independence" is briefly as follows:

> It is the only proposal which does not have a victor and a loser. It will encourage the development of a common identity between the two communities, regardless of religion. It offers first class Ulster-citizenship to all of our people, because, like it or not, the Protestant of Northern Ireland is looked upon as a second class British citizen in Britain and the Roman Catholic of Northern Ireland as a second class Irish citizen in Southern Ireland.

The organization calls its detailed constitution, prescription for political structures, and bill of rights something other than an effort to create "a Protestant dominated State, nor is it the stepping stone to a United Ireland." It is said to be "an opportunity for peace and stability" and for "the Ulster people to get back their dignity."[46] As UDA leader Tyrie stated in 1980: "Ulster would have a rosier future if both Britain and Eire were to move their influence and 'guard dog' image from the tortured minds of Ulster's people. ... The sooner we remove the 'orange' and 'green' from Ulster politics, singing Ulster's praises instead of Ulster's battles, the sooner we will be on that long-awaited path to peace."[47]

Ruairí Ó Brádaigh, president of Provisional Sinn Féin and in sympathy with the Provisional IRA, is opposed to six-county independence. He states "that a political solution to the present state of war in our country cannot be found other than in a 32-county context." He wants to dismantle the existing governments of Northern Ireland and the Republic "to make way for the New Ireland which the Irish people North and South, Protestant and Catholic will themselves build—a Democratic Socialist Republic." He pleas neither for "the Western capitalism of the U.S.A. with its 30,000,000 poor and hungry amid plenty nor the Eastern Soviet state capitalism (or any of its variations) with its denial of freedom and human rights." He wants to base the ownership of Ireland by the Irish people on the ancient Irish Brehon laws that provided "communal—but not State—ownership of the means of production."[48]

Each of the four traditional provinces would have a separate government under this PSF scheme; it would also be a federation of local governments. This calls for Ulster again having nine rather than six counties (an expansion threatening Protestant domination). The national government would federate the regional ones. A 1979 PSF statement about "Éire Nua" (New Ireland) develops the localism point:

> We stand for the right of each Irish community within an independent 32 County state to mould its own destiny, to develop its own talents, to be itself, having neither to compromise the values it holds dear, nor to apologise to any other group, foreign or domestic, for being what they are. ... We oppose ... the hidden persuaders who are attempting to assimilate our diverse communities into one mass-cultural grouping which can be more easily manipulated.[49]

Thus, predictably, UDA's ULDP asks for a state in which Protestants would have a majority, and PIRA's PSF wants a state in which Roman Catholics would have a majority. Both of course promise fair treatment to the "other side." Tyrie does not play with the idea of separating church and state; his Orange ties are too binding for that. On the other hand, Ó Brádaigh is even willing to go so far as to demand "the complete separation of church and state with a civil constitution and the building of a pluralist society."[50] Whether this rhetoric from extremists about cooperation and the protection of minority rights would have influence is not likely to be tested in terms of their own proposals.

Governmental Agencies

Under direct rule from Westminster, more than ever, decisions about the future of Northern Ireland are made by administrative functionaries of the British government and by the British Parliament, with little time given to learning about the nature of the Irish situation. Provincial leaders *attractive to the British* are consulted, but such leaders are not broadly enough representative. They also do not have the responsibility or power to work out basic policies and to decide how to implement them.

The off-handed and formula-ridden treatment of the Northern Ireland situation is all the more curious in view of the numerous Irish settlers and people of Irish background throughout Great Britain, especially in its principal cities. The noted English writer J. H. Plumb contends that these Irish "still feel their deprivation, hence the intensity of their feelings of kinship" with those remaining in Ireland. He even predicts: "What England faces is very probably years of urban guerrilla warfare."[51] If he were predicting class warfare, he would likely be accurate. Evidences of the assimilation of the Irish there into British conflict patterns tend to outweigh those pointing to tribal loyalties, as the PIRA and INLA have at times learned.

What are British leaders attempting to do to cope with Northern Ireland's intercommunity violence, its disastrously mounting unemployment rate, its increasing ghettoization in housing and education, its de facto inequality and discrimination in so many aspects of life, and the general sense prevalent of chaos, a lack of direction, irresponsibility, a bitter stalemate? Are they continuing to encourage their selected local leaders to engage in initiatives to resolve the deadlock that will fail in order again to prove the incompetence of the "natives" and the validity of British police state strategy?

As a response to such questions, a Northern Irish leader wrote to me in 1973 concerning the effort then to restore a devolved provincial government: "Despite the cheerful press notices, the outlook is I think gloomy. There are too many strong interest groups who are not tied into the settlement and who have the capacity to wreck it."

Wreck it they did. U.S. Senator Daniel P. Moynihan, after detailed discussions with prominent London officials in 1978, similarly stated that in "the two leading British political parties" he had found "no political will to settle" the Northern Ireland conflict—"no intention of doing anything ... except keeping the British there."[52]

Even though they lack control of their own governmental structures, the Northern Irish have done what has been accomplished to force the British to

Quests for Peace 223

make movements toward reconciliation if not toward a more viable society. Possibly now the British are finally going to yield enough influence to the Northern Irish to permit them to goad the British into some further movement.

The preceding chapters looked at many aspects of these problems. Here let us sum up briefly major governmental initiatives and developments since 1968:

The Reforms of November 1968. In response to the dramatic demonstrations concerning unfairness in housing allocations beginning in June 1968, as chapter 4 detailed, the Northern Ireland government promised (1) housing allotment on the basis of need, (2) effective machinery to investigate citizens' grievances, (3) an economic development plan for Derry, (4) elimination of the special votes for business organizations in local elections, and (5) the withdrawal of some "special powers" for the security forces.

Downing Street Declaration, 20 August 1969. The use of British soldiers in Derry's "Battle of the Bogside" and in Belfast precipitated the publication of a joint U.K.-Northern Ireland resolution "to take all possible steps to restore normality to the Northern Ireland community so that economic development can proceed at the faster rate which is vital for social stability." In joint communiqués dated 29 August and 10 October, they spelled out their plans for reforms that would provide "equality of treatment and freedom from discrimination." This program included the 1968 points and went beyond them.[53]

In announcing to the media on 18 December 1969, the legislative implementation of these Downing Street commitments, the Prime Minister of Northern Ireland, J. D. Chichester-Clark, admitted that Christmas would still have "soldiers and barbed wire in the streets of Belfast," but he asked the media "to help us in putting across the true significance of these reforms."[54] That was not an easy job. In August 1971, faced with "unsubstantiated allegations that it has failed to honour its obligations under the Downing Street Declaration," the government of Northern Ireland issued *A Record of Constructive Change* that pointed to these principal reforms:

It claimed that the Royal Ulster Constabulary had been "civilianised and unarmed" and placed under province-wide control. Prosecutions have become the responsibility of independent public prosecutors rather than of the RUC. The Ulster Special Constabulary, or "B" Specials (notoriously biased), have been disbanded and replaced by a part-time RUC Reserve and by the Ulster Defence Regiment of the British army (shortly regarded as similarly biased). With "extreme reluctance," the Special Powers Act—brushing aside many civil rights—was still being used in order to cope with "terrorists."

It also asserted that housing was being provided according to need to the extent it was available; a complaints setup "wholly independent of government" was functioning; a Ministry of Community Relations was working "to bring people together" and to monitor possible unfairnesses; an economic Development Commission had gotten under way with house building in Derry; universal suffrage in all elections was instituted for all citizens aged eighteen and more, with no special company or business votes any longer permitted in local elections; equal opportunities are offered in public employment; and greater efficiency and opportunities for popular involvement are being provided in local services.[55]

In previous chapters, the defects of such of these initiatives as the complaints procedures are documented. At best, the reforms suggested to the deprived that pressures might yield some benefits. The pressures continued.

Direct Rule Introduced, 1972. The fragmentation of the Unionist political organization, Derry's Bloody Sunday of 30 January 1972, and other continuances of dissent and violence made the Stormont Parliament's claims to political legitimacy increasingly questionable. In March 1972, therefore, the U.K. Parliament suspended ("prorogued") the Northern Ireland (NI) one, provided for NI legislation to be made by order in council, and designated a secretary of state for NI to assume the responsibilities of the provincial government and to hold a seat in the U.K. cabinet. It was said that this was not intended to be a permanent or more than a temporary arrangement.[56] Immediately, it ushered in a continuous series of discussions as to the form that a future devolved government might take and as to interim measures.

On 8 March 1973, as a propaganda ploy helpful in support of direct rule, all citizens of Northern Ireland aged eighteen and over were asked to vote by mail whether NI should remain part of the U.K. or be joined with the Irish Republic. The antiborder parties (pro-Republican) boycotted the vote. The loyalists to the U.K. registered about three-fifths of the possible vote. Few actually cast votes for an Eire link.[57]

Under direct rule in 1973, the 73 local governmental authorities were replaced by 26 district councils, and the first full local governmental elections were held that used proportional representation. As part of this reorganization, education, planning, and health and social services were centralized in control under ministries of the provincial government. Both these moves were said to be to provide better representation for minority interests.

These reforms were presented as being adequate to satisfy those who had been crusading for civil rights. That their actual implementation did not do so in any adequate manner led two U.S. Congress members investigating the situation in 1978 to conclude "that individual human rights are being violated every day in Northern Ireland." They added:

> While strongly deploring the violence of the Provisional IRA, the delegation believes the continued suppression of individual legal, human and civil rights—itself, a form of violence—can only force disregard for authority. ...
> The British experience in Northern Ireland tends to demonstrate that the application of severe measures has made little impact on deterring violence.[58]

These conclusions were also apparently held by a great many of Northern Ireland's deprived. The bitter stalemate continued in spite of the reforms.

Constitution Act of 1973. On 20 March 1973, the U.K. government offered the results of various discussions in the form of a White Paper making constitutional proposals for Northern Ireland. It suggested a single legislature elected by proportional representation. It urged that both legislative committees and administrators should be broadly representative. This became known as "power sharing." It also asked for a recognition of "the Irish dimension," the existence of common interests between the Republic and Northern Ireland.[59]

The Constitution Act adopted that year embodied these proposals. It also eliminated the regal office of governor. The election of the new assembly took place in July 1973.

In the assembly election, no party gained a majority of the 78 seats. The results were as follows: Official (pro-White Paper) Unionist Party, 24; SDLP, 19; "anti-White Paper" and other loyalist parties, 26; Alliance Party, 8; and Northern Ireland Labour Party, 1. In consequence, the OUP, SDLP, and APNI leadership got together to discuss the setting up of a power-sharing executive for the new government. They also agreed to a three-sided conference of their executive group with representatives of the U.K. and Eire. This conference, held at Sunningdale, led to the proposal to set up a Council of Ireland of seven Irish and seven North Irish ministers, a consultative assembly, and a secretariat.

End of Direct Rule. On 1 January 1974, the new Northern Ireland executive was sworn in, with a chief executive, his deputy, and nine ministers, seven of them department heads. These were shortly supplemented by two more department heads and two others, a total of 15 that included 7 Unionists, 6 SDLP, and 2 APNI. But anticonstitution Unionists were already destroying the basis for the new government. Brian Faulkner as chief executive lost the support of his OUP. Even though he continued as executive, insurgent Unionists led by Paisley disrupted the 22 January assembly meeting; 18 of them, including Paisley, were ejected by police. The position of the insurgent loyalists was further strengthened in the province, however, by the results of the U.K. general election of February 1974. In that election, the anticonstitution loyalists got 51 percent of the vote and elected 11 of the 12 NI members of the U.K. House of Commons.

The final and crushing blow to both the Sunningdale agreement concerning the Council of Ireland and to the current Northern Ireland power-sharing executive was the May general strike of the Ulster Workers' Council, a Protestant body with some 300,000 members. On 14 May, the power-sharing executive had won a vote in the Assembly 44 to 28 on the Sunningdale agreement. The general strike was a consequence of that vote. It continued until Faulkner and his Unionist colleagues in the executive resigned. The next day, 29 May, the UWC called off the strike, and the U.K. government suspended the Assembly.[60]

Direct Rule Again, 1974. After a period of renewed discussions, the suspended Assembly was finally dissolved at the end of March 1975 to clear the way for voting on membership for a constitutional convention in May. It was to be a "consultative" convention. It was to try to find provisions that "would be likely to command the most widespread acceptance throughout the community." Its product, possibly subject to a popular referendum, was finally to be submitted to the U.K. Parliament.

The results of the convention election rather assured the outcome of its deliberations. The pro-Orange-statelet United Ulster Unionist Council (or Coalition) won 46 (OUP, 20, Vanguard Unionist, 14, Paisley's DUP, 12) of the 78 seats. The distribution of the other seats was Independent Unionist, 1; Unionist Party of NI (Faulkner's split from the OUP), 5; SDLP, 17; APNI, 8; and NI Labour Party, 1. Torn by basic conflicts of interest, the convention adopted a report and dissolved itself on 7 November 1975.

Merlyn Rees, as Secretary of State for Northern Ireland, submitted the proposals of that report to Parliament on 20 November, but their echoes of Orange statelet provisions made them unacceptable. He therefore gave convention members a detailed reaction and asked them to reconvene in February 1976 for a further four weeks of discussion. Significant points of his disagreement included his unwillingness to transfer control of security arrangements in more than a slow and gradual manner to the new Northern Ireland government. "So long as the Secretary of State remains responsible for security policy, responsibility for emergency legislation would remain with the United Kingdom Parliament." Only with a "peace-time level" of violence would control of the police be given to the new legislature and executive. Rees also pointed to the need for more convincing provisions to assure power sharing among the political parties and for a recognition of the necessary "Irish dimension" for consultation and cooperation with the other twenty-six counties even if a Council of Ireland is not acceptable. When "it became clear that there was no prospect of agreement between the parties," the convention was finally dissolved in March 1976.[61]

The majority report of the 1975–76 constitutional convention was not yet dead in May 1977. Secretary of State for Northern Ireland Roy Mason on 2 May told the U.K. House of Commons:

> A body calling itself the United Ulster Action Council seeks to bring Northern Ireland to a standstill by calling for a stoppage of work from midnight tonight. Most of the militant Loyalist paramilitary organizations are associated with the Council, whose membership includes the Ulster Workers' Council, the newly-formed United Ulster Unionist Party led by Mr. [E. A.] Baird, and the Democratic Unionist Party led by the Hon. Member for Antrim North [the Rev. Ian Paisley]. The Action Council are asking for the implementation of the majority Report of the Constitutional Convention, which was rejected by this House a year ago.[62]

The strike continued until 13 May. It failed because it lacked the support drawn by the 1974 strike.

Discussions have continued since, but the three-sided deadlock persists and hinges on these basic issues: The ethnic Protestant majority wants to rule in its own way. The ethnic Roman Catholic minority pushes for a degree of power sharing to permit it to have some representation in all aspects of government. The British do not care to have to deal again with the rigidities of an Orange statelet. They need "reasonable and appropriate arrangements to take account of the interests of the minority." They also desire to be secure in the character of the control of their province, its relative stability and freedom from disruptive influences.

Humphrey Atkins as Secretary of State for Northern Ireland made an effort in 1979 to break this deadlock through trying to arrange a four-party conference. Lack of agreement to participate delayed the meeting until 7 January 1980. Even then, the OUP declined to attend. It, together with its current affiliates in the Ulster Unionist Council, the United Ulster Unionist Party, and the Unionist Party of NI, had polled 53 percent of the vote in the May 1979 election. SDLP, APNI, and DUP, with 42 percent of that vote, agreed to participate in the Atkins conference. James H. Molyneaux, OUP leader, submitted a memorandum in behalf of the Ulster Unionist Council that made a few concessions to the minority, but, rhetoric aside, reiterated much of the position—so far as potential control was concerned—of the 1921–72 Orange government and more closely of the 1975–76 convention's majority report.[63] Details of the proposal are given above in the discussion of political party "peace" initiatives.

The conference continued until 24 March 1980. It did not result in detailed agreement. Atkins claimed that it "clarified the parties' view, and it has increased my understanding, and theirs, of what our aims must be and the problems that must be solved." When a member of the opposition in the House of Commons asserted to Atkins that the conference had failed, he stated, "It was extremely valuable to the Government and, I believe, to those parties which attended." He attached significance to the agreement of all those present to seven principles that he had laid down in an advance working paper for the conference. The vagueness of these principles can be judged by the third and fifth ones:

> Under any new arrangements, existing safeguards and remedies against discrimination on religious or political grounds should be at least maintained, and, if possible, improved. ...
>
> In the foreseeable future, given the Government's overriding commitment to combat terrorism, responsibility for law and order will ... remain with Westminster.[64]

Apparently Atkins was working on the assumption that he should grasp at whatever even vague agreements might exist and then try to build what he could upon them. He told the House of Commons on 2 July 1981, that his "exhaustive discussions over the past two years with Northern

Ireland political leaders have driven me to the conclusion that it isn't yet possible to confer executive or legislative powers upon a representative Northern Ireland body." He therefore told the House that he was going to establish a representative Northern Ireland Council, made up of elected members of the Westminster Parliament, European Parliament, and Northern Ireland local councils. This was to be a purely consultative body.[65] Before Atkins had time to go ahead with this idea, James Prior took over as Secretary of State for Northern Ireland and dropped the council idea.[66]

As a result of these and other procedures, such as Anglo-Irish talks about cooperation, and also prodded by the 1980 and 1981 hunger strikes' worldwide publicity, Prior announced in April 1982 that another effort would be made to set up a Northern Ireland Assembly. This body, "from its inception, will have scrutinising, deliberative, and consultative functions." It would be asked to recommend "arrangements under which the whole or part of the range of legislative and executive responsibilities previously transferred under the Northern Ireland Constitution Act 1973 could be exercised by the Assembly and by a devolved administration answerable to it." If "certain criteria are satisfied," the U. K. government will implement the recommendations of the Assembly.[67] The "certain criteria" include the principal commitments specified for the 1974 Assembly that helped to destroy it.

In the 30 October 1982 election, 49 of the 78 Assembly seats went to the Unionist parties (26 to OUP, 21 to DUP, and 2 to others), and 10 were controlled by Alliance. SDLP got 14 memberships, and Provisional Sinn Féin got 5. These latter 19 seats, as mentioned above, were all committed in advance to nonparticipation in the Assembly. These 19 appeared to be aware that, with the forthcoming expansion of the Northern Ireland delegation to the U.K. House of Commons from 12 to 17 members, the Unionists in the Assembly would be even less likely than those in 1974 to compromise. They could then move their power among the larger British parties.

In a post-election plea to SDLP to participate in the Assembly, Prior asked its members to "have a real voice and put pressures on the Unionists, and the public generally, to show what it is that they were aiming to achieve." He stressed how economic problems "have probably given the Provisional Sinn Fein the size of their vote." These problems include "the unemployment amongst young people, the destitution, the poverty of a lot of Catholic families."[68] He did not deal with minority disillusionment with the repetition of the same old British gestures toward the lower class and toward ethnic minorities both in Northern Ireland and Great Britain. He also did not face popular awareness of the gross lack of implementation of civil liberties safeguards.

The investigative journalist Gerald A. Fitzgerald concludes: "Within the province no London government has yet found an alternative to direct rule, and none is likely to emerge until Ulster's two main confessional groups—Protestants and Catholics—can achieve an acceptable minimum of material and ideological satisfaction."[69] More than a century ago, Karl Marx's daughter, Jenny M. Longuet, put the matter thus:

> Theoretical fiction has it that constitutional liberty is the rule and its suspension an exception, but the whole history of English rule in Ireland shows that a state of emergency is the rule and that the application of the constitution is the exception.[70]

Is there no end to it all?

Notes

1. James Gilhooley, "On the Road to Drogheda," *Commonweal* (New York), 18 March 1977, pp. 178–80, at p. 178.
2. Quoted by Rona M. Fields, personal communication.
3. Desmond Wilson, "The Churches and Violence in Ireland," *The Month* (London), February 1977, pp. 41–42, 44, at p. 41; J. C. Becket, *The Anglo-Irish Tradition* (London: Faber & Faber, 1976), p. 90.
4. Alf McCreary, *Corrymeela: Hill of Harmony in Northern Ireland* (New York: Hawthorne, 1976), p. 31.   5. Ibid., p. 107.
6. Eddie Gurley, quoted by D. J. Bowman, ed., *Information Bulletin* no. 20 (Ireland Program, National Council of the Churches of Christ in the U.S.A., September 1978), p. 3.
7. Howell Evans, *From Revolution to Reconciliation—the Story of Glencree* (Bray, Co. Wicklow: Glencree Community, 1977).
8. C. B. Daly and R. D. E. Gallagher, joint chairpersons, *Violence in Ireland: A Report to the Churches*, rev. ed. (Dublin: Veritas, 1977), p. 68.
9. Ibid., pp. 39-40.
10. Ibid., pp. 68-69; cf. W. D. Flackes, "Feakle Talks," pp. 57-59 in his *Northern Ireland* (New York: St. Martin's Press, 1980).
11. Rob Mitchell, "Peace Groups Since the 'Thirties,' " *Dawn* (Dublin), nos. 38-39 (no date): 18-24, at p. 18.
12. Garreth Byrne, "Quaker Non-Violence in Irish History," *Dawn*, ibid., pp. 7-10, at p. 9.
13. Mitchell, "Peace Groups," p. 22.
14. Ibid.
15. David Bleakley, *Peace in Ulster* (London: Mowbrays, 1972), p. 84.
16. Bleakley, *Saidie Patterson: Irish Peacemaker* (Belfast: Blackstaff, 1980), p. 77.
17. Ciaran McKeown, *The Price of Peace* (Belfast: McKeown, 1976), p. 12.
18. Richard Deutsch, *Mairead Corrigan, Betty Williams*, trans. Jack Bernard (Woodbury, N.Y.: Barron's, 1977), p. 87.
19. Ibid., p. 86.

20. Community of the Peace People, "Breaking the Cycle of Violence," pp. 18-20 in *The Administration of Justice in Northern Ireland: The Proceedings of a Conference* (Belfast, 13 June 1981), p. 18.
21. Deutsch, *Mairead Corrigan*, p. 172.
22. Mairead Corrigan and Steve McBride, quoted by John Conroy, "A Noble Crusade Five Years Later," *Baltimore Sun*, 21 August 1981; and McBride, "Six Years on," *Peace by Peace*, 7, no. 13 (20 August 1982): 2.
23. Community of the Peace People, "Cycle of Violence," p. 19.
24. Calvin Macnee, "Peace in Pieces," *Fortnight*, no. 166 (28 April–12 May 1978): 2.
25. Steve McBride, quoted by Conroy, "A Noble Crusade"; and McBride, "Life at Ground Zero," *Peace by Peace*, 7, no. 12 (July 1982): 4-5, at p. 5. See also D. P. Barritt, *Northern Ireland* (London: Quaker Peace & Service, 1982), chap. 6, and Eric Gallagher and Stanley Worrall, *Christians in Ulster: 1968–1980* (New York: Oxford University Press, 1982), chap. 11.
26. Cathal Goulding, quoted by Gerry Foley, *Ireland in Rebellion* (New York: Pathfinder, 1971), p. 25.
27. Goulding, "Right Wing Defeated," *United Irishman* (Dublin) 36, no. 6 (June 1978): 5.
28. Lord Cameron, chairman, Commission Appointed by the Governor of Northern Ireland, *Disturbances in Northern Ireland* (Belfast: HMSO, Cmd. 532, September 1969), p. 47.
29. Michael Farrell, *Northern Ireland* (London: Pluto Press, 1976), p. 251.
30. Tom Hadden and Paddy Hillyard, *Justice in Northern Ireland* (London: Cobden Trust, 1973), p. 30; Kevin Boyle, Hadden, and Hillyard, *Law and State: The Case of Northern Ireland* (Amherst: University of Massachusetts Press, 1975), p. 130.
31. Russell Stetler, *The Battle of the Bogside* (London: Sheed and Ward, 1970), p. xi.
32. Gene Sharp, *The Politics of Nonviolent Action* (Boston: Sargent, 1973), p. 4.
33. Emanuel Celler, chairperson, Judiciary Committee, U.S. House of Representatives, quoted in *New York Times*, 8 July 1966, p. 26.
34. Editorial, "No Place for Sentiment," *New Society* (London), 2 July 1970, p. 3.
35. Liam O'Dowd, "Shaping and Reshaping the Orange State," Chap. 1 in O'Dowd, Bill Rolston, and Mike Tomlinson, *Northern Ireland* (London: CSE Books, 1980), p. 1.
36. The percentages given are from these elections: 1969 Stormont Parliament, 1973 local government, 1975 Northern Ireland Constitutional Convention, 1977 local government, 1981 local government, and 1982 Assembly. Where there was a choice, the percentages are based on first-preference votes only.
37. Ian Paisley, "End Undemocratic Colonial Rule," Manchester *Guardian*, 18 February 1980, p. 7.
38. "Official Ulster Unionist Manifesto," 1 sheet, n.d.
39. Ulster Unionist Party, "Towards the Future," pp. 45-57 in Northern Ireland Office, *The Future of Northern Ireland* (London: HMSO, 1972), p. 55.
40. Ulster Unionist Council, *The Government of Northern Ireland* (Belfast, January 1980), pp. 2-3. A submission by James Molyneaux as leader of the OUP to Prime Minister Margaret Thatcher.
41. David McKittrick, "The Class Structure of Unionism," *The Crane Bag* (Holmsdale, Co. Wicklow, Ireland) 4, no. 2 (1980): 28-33, at p. 33.
42. Alliance Party, "Proposals for a Political Settlement in Northern Ireland," pp. 55–61 in Northern Ireland Office, *Future of Northern Ireland*.

43. John Hume, "Unity Should Be UK Policy," Manchester *Guardian*, 18 February 1980, p. 7.

44. Hume, "Interview," by Seamus Deane and Barré Fitzpatrick, *The Crane Bag*, 4, no. 2 (1980): 39-43, at p. 40.

45. Social Democratic and Labour Party, "Towards a New Ireland," pp. 72-82, at pp. 72-75, in Northern Ireland Office, *Future of Northern Ireland*.

46. New Ulster Political Research Group, *Beyond the Religious Divide* (Belfast, March 1979), p. 3.

47. Andy Tyrie, "Independence Is the Only Alternative," Manchester *Guardian*, 18 February 1980, p. 7.

48. Ruairi Ó Brádaigh, *Our People Our Future: What Éire Nua Means* (Dublin: Sinn Féin, 1973), pp. 13, 8; for a discussion of ancient Breton land laws, see P. W. Joyce, *A Societal History of Ancient Ireland,* 2nd ed. (Dublin: Gill & Son, 1913), vol. 1, chap. 7.

49. Sinn Féin (Provisional), *Éire Nua Is Local Democracy* (Dublin, 1979), p. 2.

50. Ruairi Ó Brádaigh, "How to Restore Power to the People," Manchester *Guardian*, 18 February 1980, p. 7.

51. J. H. Plumb, "Letter From London," *New York Times Magazine*, 16 December 1973, pp. 50-51, 55, 58, 60, 65, at p. 51.

52. D. P. Moynihan, quoted by Jackson Holland, "The Big Four Turn Around," *Hibernia* (Dublin), 26 April 1979, p. 7.

53. Government of Northern Ireland, *Text of a Communique Issued Following Discussions Between the Secretary of State for the Home Department and the Northern Ireland Government in Belfast on 9 and 10 October 1969* (Belfast: HMSO, Cmnd. 4178, 1969).

54. J. D. Chichester-Clark, "Significance of Reforms," *Policy Statements* (New York: British Information Services, 18 December 1969), pp. 1-3, at p. 1.

55. Government of Northern Ireland, *A Record of Constructive Change* (Belfast: HMSO, Cmd. 558, August 1971), esp. pp. 2-8.

56. Northern Ireland (Temporary Provisions) Act 1972.

57. R. J. Lawrence and S. Elliott, *The Northern Ireland Border Poll 1973* (London: HMSO, Cmnd. 5875, January 1975).

58. Joshua Eilberg and Hamilton Fish, Jr., *Northern Ireland ... Report by Two Members of the Committee of the Judiciary, Ninety-Fifth Congress* (Washington, D.C.: Government Printing Office, 1979), p. 220.

59. Secretary of State for Northern Ireland, *Northern Ireland Constitutional Proposals* (London: HMSO, Cmnd. 5259, March 1973).

60. Northern Ireland Act 1974; Secretary of State for Northern Ireland, *The Northern Ireland Constitution* (London: HMSO, Cmnd. 5675, July 1974), pp. 1-11.

61. Secretary of State for Northern Ireland, *The Northern Ireland Constitutional Convention* (London: HMSO, Cmnd. 6387, January 1976), esp. pp. 3-6; British Information Services, *Northern Ireland* (New York, 1978), pp. 18-19.

62. Roy Mason, "Northern Ireland: Strike Threat," *Policy Statements* (New York: British Information Services, 2 May 1977), p. 1.

63. Ulster Unionist Council, *Government of Northern Ireland*; Secretary of State for Northern Ireland, *The Government of Northern Ireland* (London: HMSO, Cmnd. 7763, November 1979).

64. Secretary of State for Northern Ireland, ibid., pp. 2-3; Humphrey Atkins, "Northern Ireland: The Way Ahead," *Policy Statements* (New York: British Information Services, 7 April 1980), pp. 1-2.

65. Humphrey Atkins, "Northern Ireland: Advisory Council Proposals," *Policy Statements* (New York: British Information Services, 7 July 1981), p. 2.

66. James Prior, "Northern Ireland: The Way Forward," *Policy Statements* (New York: British Information Services, 13 October 1981), p. 5.

67. Secretary of State for Northern Ireland, *Northern Ireland: A Framework for Devolution* (London: HMSO, Cmnd. 8541, April 1982), p. 8.

68. British Information Services, "Northern Ireland: The Election Results," *Policy Background* (New York: 26 October 1982), p. 2.

69. G. A. Fitzgerald, "Public Opinion and the Slippery Road to Peace in Northern Ireland," chap. 4 in W. P. Davison and Leon Gordenker, eds., *Resolving Nationality Conflicts* (New York: Praeger, 1980), p. 62.

70. J. M. Longuet, "Letter to *Marseillaise*, 18 March, 1870," quoted in *Power, Conflict & Inequality*, ed. Mary Kelly, Liam O'Dowd, and James Wickham (Dublin: Turoe Press, 1982), p. 41.

CHAPTER 10

Is There No End To It All?

Technological change, the shrinking world with its integrating market economy, and the disastrously increasing threats of military destruction have vastly complicated human conditions of life and living. As part of all this, the mass media tell millions of people of opportunities others enjoy but of which they may be deprived. The glittering prints, sounds, and screens do this in effect without succeeding to impart as well the justifications for inequality traditional in so many utterances from pulpits and other establishment podiums. Thus the impression has been getting around that lack of necessities or even of privileges is not inevitable and "natural." Many are learning that they can and might as well try to achieve some sort of improvement in their way of life.

Formulas and organizations through which to find relief appear together with enticements to work for change, but the patterns offered are confusingly varied. Often one scenario is most attractive. It is the one with which people have "grown up." It is the one that many times offers the least in the way of change!

Since the "Irish" are oppressed by the Brits, what about Irish "nationalism"? Since the "Scotch-Irish" are apparently threatened by a "Papist takeover," what about loyalism to the United Kingdom, to the Orange Order, to Ulster? Since the Northern Irish—regardless of class, religion, or party—tend to be second-class citizens in either England or the twenty-six counties, what about Ulster nationalism, an independent state? Since the middle- and upper-class English appear to fare very well in British society, shouldn't middle- and upper-class Ulsterites seek that identification with its proper manner of speaking and school ties? Since lower-class Brits appear to have done fairly well with their trade unions and Labour Party, shouldn't lower-class North Irish forget about sectarian squabbles and join together to make gains from the class that dominates them? All these questions get positive answers, but the class-oriented ones may now be gaining.

These questions depend for answers upon one's conception of Northern Ireland society, one's ideological bent. Analysts characterize such conceptions in great variety, in terms of at least eleven different models. A popular one is the "double-minority" model offered by the journalist Harold Jackson. He sees the dominant Protestant establishment in the province, a minority on the island, as "acting under the stresses of a besieged minority." The Roman Catholics, the minority in the six counties, have "a burning sense of grievance" at not possessing a say in the government.[1] The political scientist Arend Lijphart found these other ten conceptions of the province's situation in the current literature: the binational state, the religiously divided society, the plural society, the biracial society, the colony, the fragment society, the arena of guerrilla warfare, the arena of class struggle, the majority dictatorship, and the besieged democracy.[2]

All these conceptions, even the fictional one of a biracial society, have some descriptive utility, refer to actual aspects of the situation, but the adoption of any one of them as *the* model distorts what is happening. Blaming the conflict, for example, on the "virus" of nationalism or religious bigotry overlooks the fundamental politico-economic inequalities, irritants, and processes that nurture such symptoms of social disorder. One's choice of one or more of the models would have much to do with how one might answer the question: Is there no end to the current conflict in the six counties?

Rather than choose any one or several of these models, it is to be suggested here that the answer to that question—to the extent that there might be an answer—can best be found by looking at sociohistorical processes rather than at anything so static as a model. In that light, all the conceptions labeled have some relevance, especially in the propagandas of the contestants.

As a result of bitterly contested political steps, twenty-six counties of one of Britain's oldest colonies became what appears to be an independent country. The other six counties may remain in the direct control of Westminster, become a more or less devolved statelet, or even try to set themselves up as a separate realm. In the world of the neoimperialists, however, such political results are more apparent than actual gains in autonomy. While people were using their talents and even giving their lives to achieve these modifications in the Irish map, the growth of plutocratic neoimperialism in the Western world has been threatening to make such matters as relative autonomy for Northern Ireland and the Republic less and less relevant to the lives of the Irish people.

Both the United Kingdom and Ireland have entered the European Economic Community with its potentialities for supranational exploitation by industrial and financial corporations. Just how to project the growth of that

Community and its manipulators is a tricky matter. Few are equipped to penetrate all the disguises, protective colorations, and other subterfuges of those who play on the vast gaming tables of the neoimperialists.

Just ponder, as part of all this, the many inducements offered by the Westminster-controlled government of Northern Ireland for the investment of foreign capital. Following the announcement by General Motors that it planned to open new plants in Northern Ireland, the secretary of state, Roy Mason, asserted: "A company of vast resources has checked out Northern Ireland and found it can provide the kind of facilities it needed—skilled, trainable labour, an excellent history in the crucial field of labour performance and a well developed communications network."[3]

With no export duties, the opportunities for corporate tax-dodging through artificial transfer prices between Northern Ireland and other units of a multinational corporation are extensive; locally admitted and thus taxed profits within the United Kingdom can thus be quite arbitrary. In addition, there are cash grants toward plant building and low rentals for government-constructed facilities, depreciation allowances of up to 100 percent, 75 percent reductions in local taxes on manufacturing installations, and free instruction in state schools for employees and also cash grants for labor training. "There is no bar on the remittance of profits and dividends or the repatriation of capital." This all combines with low wage rates, high unemployment (more than 21 percent of the economically active in 1982), low absenteeism, and few strikes. As a Department of Commerce prospectus puts it: "Most plants have trade union representatives on the shop floor; these unions are cooperative."[4]

If the European, American, and Japanese enterprisers controlling the principal business interests of the Western world succeed in achieving a reasonably efficient exploitation of the human and material resources of Northern Ireland, are there likely to continue to be underprivileged and underemployed minorities and classes? Without effective social organization to the contrary, it is more than likely. After all, such enterprisers engage in social planning only for their own corporate goals and often do what they can to sabotage social planning of a broader and more humane sort. Capital flows in the direction of the greatest anticipated profits if it is not controlled for more broadly human concerns. As part of this, competition among class and ethnic segments becomes more remote and abstract and thus more easily obscured from public discussion and redress.

This sweeping integration of power does not mean that there is no recourse for the deprived and unrepresented. It merely provides the evolving setting in which efforts at change necessarily have to take place.

More than intolerable life conditions are needed to stimulate open rebellion. Without the hope aroused by some apparent possibility of modifying one's lot or that of one's group for the better, people try to "live with the devil they know." They persist under distressing deprivation rather than experiment with fearful consequences from openly defying the vested interests of those who control them. In many parts of the world, including Northern Ireland, nevertheless, media "good news" imparts that hope—a disturbing consequence of media diffusion rarely intended to be such by their entrepreneurial owners.

Lacking an incentive to rebel openly, the deprived often turn to secret conspiracies to develop protection and other advantages and to inflict reprisals. The oppressed Irish—both Green and Orange—turned not only to religious "holier-than-thou" and secular nationalist ways of rationalizing their lots and of finding dignity; they also, and at the same time, elaborated ways to deal with their oppressors, especially the ways called "stage Irishness." As the writer J. H. Plumb notes, "In many ways it [Ireland] was England's South—the Irish, our blacks," and the Irish reacted similarly to the blacks by being "given to foolish stories and more foolish behavior, yet hospitable and courteous." He points out that these are "all protective devices, dodges to get away with what they could, to hide the bitterness and the sorrow, to mask the hate."[5]

On the one hand, the Irish—Orange and Green—have thus gotten the reputation for producing what Italians call *preti presbiteriani* ("Presbyterian," or puritanical, Roman Catholic and Protestant clerics) in contrast with their own more comforting functionaries. On the other, they are said to offer the dehumanizing stereotype of the "feckless, childish, whimsical, and violent Irishman, who ... served as a convenient scapegoat ... of countless Englishmen."[6] The caricatures are significant in propaganda, but how different are the real people, as the anthropologist Henry Glassie discovered in making his detailed study of a community of Protestants and Roman Catholics in County Fermanagh during the current troubles. He brushes aside journalists' characterization of the situation "as an anachronistic religious squabble." From becoming friends with both Protestants and Roman Catholics, he realizes that it is a "variety of economic-cultural conflict." He believes it "will continue to erupt in small countries, once colonies, for the rest of our days."[7]

These deepset characteristics and movements provide the base upon which openly rebellious nonviolent and violent initiatives have been developed in Northern Ireland by civil rights actionists, pacifists, politicians, social workers, teachers, legal specialists, clergy people, and paramilitary leaders.

Many students of revolt contend that preventive therapy would have kept efforts at change from reaching a terrorist stage so many times in Irish history and elsewhere. The political scientist C. J. Friedrich asserts, in line with many other liberal theorists, that, to avoid or minimize threats of revolutionary activity, "effective change has to be organized to make possible recurrent adaptations of the institutions and processes of political order to evolving values, interests, and beliefs by gradual transformation of such an order."[8]

Such preventive therapy has to be something other than a cosmetic effort, however, and it must be frequent and timely. It may be useless after rioting breaks out. Another writer, Robert Moss, reminds us that "often it is not until the guerrilla threat has emerged that the ruling elite becomes conscious of the urgent need for reform."[9] Before that period of crisis, those with vested interests in the establishment brush aside pleas for adaptation as visionary. As both British and Unionist behavior demonstrate in Northern Ireland, even after a crisis arises, those with vested interests still try to hold on to them and avoid compromises. Crisis therapy of some sort thus too often prevails, and it, as we have seen, usually focuses on symptoms rather than causes, on socially destructive repression as an instrument rather than on social adaptation.

Such superficial crisis therapy, as the sociologist Walda Katz Fishman points out, gets caught up in the basic conflict between human rights and profits, politico-economic domination. Referring especially to "periods of economic crisis and political upheaval when profits and human rights cannot both be supported," she notes that "the most reactionary sector of the capitalist class offers the right-wing solution, that is, the violent repression of the working people."[10] In writing about the intellectual orientation common to members of the dominant class, the sociologist Franco Ferrarotti tells how "human relations tend to be replaced by the market relationship. Life is progressively being 'dried up' from the emotive point of view."[11]

We have recited what various participants in the provincial troubles appear to expect from what they are using as crisis therapy—especially from terrorism in some form and from contrasting proposals for institutional change. This probably all looks chaotic and discouraging, but fortunately there are some reasons for optimism in the whole situation, as difficult as such reasons may be to perceive.

The psychologist Ken Heskin, for example, has challenged journalistic and political commentators who insist that in the Northern Ireland situation "a point may have been reached, or may be about to be reached, beyond which Northern Ireland society will teeter into chaos." The

Taoiseach (prime minister) of Ireland put it that the "fabric of society" of the six counties is threatened. After studying all the criteria he could find, as well as from his own extensive field experiences in Northern Ireland, Heskin concludes that "there is no evidence that crime in Northern Ireland is on the brink of epidemic proportions at this time [1980], as a result of the civil conflict." He discovered that crime trends were similar to those in Great Britain and in the twenty-six counties for the same period. He therefore warned that the visibility of violence "becomes an excuse for glossing over other possible aspects of the problem, such as unemployment, low wages, high prices, poor housing and so forth." He goes even further by asserting that "it also serves to distract public attention from similar problems" elsewhere in the British Isles.[12]

Even under great stress, the "fabric of society"—especially the informal "fabric" in terms of which people do their living—has a surprising amount of strength and resilience. To an extent even because of stress, people tend to rise to challenges and do what they can to make life more livable again. The civil rights movement, the nonsectarian Alliance Party, the Belfast students' People's Democracy, the Friends of Corrymeela, Women Together, the Community of the Peace People, the Feakle negotiations, All Children Together, and the ministrations of involved attorneys and clergy people, social workers and teachers all tell how people care and try nonviolently to maintain humane values, to create a more egalitarian and viable society.

A factor in the changing social situation that is also encouraging is the expansion of both the Orange and Green supply of educated people, including professionals. This is in part a function of rising expectations as a result of broader participation in the world community through the mass media and through the emigration and return of thousands of individuals. It was also given an important impetus by the Education Act (NI) 1947. That legislation obliged local education authorities to make available not only more adequate primary and secondary schooling but also to provide that qualified students might go on for further education, in part at least at state expense. This included an increase in the funding for Roman Catholic schools. Those educated in the public colleges and universities experienced mixed ethnic associations, often for the first time. They may also have lived or later moved into mixed middle-class neighborhoods. These are the people who have given substance and many times leadership to the nonviolent organizations that are creating a groundswell toward a more equable society.

Changes achieved through nonviolent confrontations and pressures do not leave the scars of civil war that may distort social life through many subsequent generations. In any meaningful sense, the "end to it all" in Northern

Ireland is not likely to be a spectacular event. It would be better otherwise. After all, a victory always leaves the vanquished, and there are enough victims and martyrs in Northern Ireland already. The outcome is much more likely to result from the growing social consciousness and more adequate organization of those dedicated to a humane reorganization of society. A consistently nonviolent movement of an effective sort many times can cope with monopolized state power more effectively than can violent procedures. Even, and perhaps especially, when they are met with violence, nonviolent confrontations gain attention and popular support even behind a police state's complicated politico-economic defences.

Notes

1. Harold Jackson, *The Two Irelands—A Dual Study of Inter-Group Tensions* (London: Minority Rights Group, Report No. 2, 1971), p. 4.
2. Arend Lijphart, "Review Article: The Northern Ireland Problem: Cases, Theories, and Solutions," *British Journal of Political Science* 5 (1975): 83-106.
3. Roy Mason, quoted in *Bulletin of Industrial & Commercial News from Northern Ireland* (Belfast: Department of Commerce Press Office, June 1978), p. 2.
4. Industrial Development Organization for Northern Ireland, *Industrial Investment in Northern Ireland* (Belfast: Department of Commerce, 1978), esp. pp. 4-6, 17.
5. J. H. Plumb, "Letter from London," *New York Times Magazine,* 16 December 1973, pp. 50-51, 55, 58, 60, 65, p. 51 quoted.
6. L. P. Curtis, Jr., *Anglo-Saxons and Celts* (Bridgeport, Conn.: University of Bridgeport, 1968), p. 65.
7. Henry Glassie, *Passing the Time in Ballymenone: Culture and History of an Ulster Community* (Philadelphia: University of Pennsylvania Press, 1982), p. 15.
8. C. J. Friedrich, "An Introductory Note on Revolution," in Friedrich et al., *Revolution* (New York: Atherton Press, 1966), pp. 8-9.
9. Robert Moss, *The War for the Cities* (New York: Coward, McCann & Geoghegan, 1972), p. 240.
10. Walda Katz Fishman, "Right-Wing Reaction and Violence: A Response to Capitalism's Crises," *Social Research* 48 (1981): 157-82, at p. 182.
11. Franco Ferrarotti, "Social Marginality and Violence in Neourban Societies," *Social Research* 48 (1981): 183-222, at p. 185.
12. Ken Heskin, "Social Disintegration in Northern Ireland: Fact or Fiction," *Economic and Social Review* (Dublin) 12 (1980-81): 97-113, at pp. 97, 110-11; *cf.* D. P. Barritt, "Peaks and Troughs of Hope," chap. 1 in his *Northern Ireland* (London: Quaker Peace & Service, 1982).

Index

Abbott, Simon, 41
Adams, Gerry, 193
Aitken, Ian, 192
Advisory Council for Education, 114, 124
Alderman, Geoffrey, 40
Aldershot, 183
Alexander, Yonah, 97
ALJ: Association for Legal Justice
All Children Together, 115, 239
Alliance Party, 153, 213, 217–18, 225–26, 228–29, 239
Allport, G. W., 41
American Psychological Association, 28
Amnesty, 90, 155; International, 128–29, 131, 140–41, 173, 190, 197, 209–11
Ancient Order of Hibernians, 150
Andrews, F. M., 16
Anglican Catholic: Church of England
Anglicans: Episcopalians
Anglo-Saxonism, 2, 22–23, 28–29, 31, 33, 38–39, 49
Antrim, 87
AOH: Ancient Order of Hibernians
APNI: Alliance Party of Northern Ireland
Apprentice Boys of Derry, 46, 82, 90, 174, 177
Aristotle, 20, 21, 39
Armagh, 47, 78, 86–87, 91, 93, 134, 143 163, 190–92
Army, 11–13, 16, 33, 44–46, 50–52, 60, 77, 96, 99, 102–03, 112–13, 118, 120–22, 126, 128, 132, 144–48, 154–55, 158, 163, 168–69, 172, 175–77, 179–83, 185, 188–89, 196, 202, 205, 208
Arnold, Matthew, 40
Artaud, Antonin, 196
Asquith, H. H., 50
Association for Legal Justice, 153, 209–11
Atkins, Humphrey, 228, 232–33

Baader-Meinhof gang, 6
Bailyn, Bernard, 16

Baird, E. A., 227
Ballykelly, 179
Ballymena, 181
Banbridge, 187
Bancroft, Edward, 8
Bangor, 181
Barkas, Janet L., 171, 197
Barnes, H. E., 39
Barr, Glen, 220
Barritt, D. P., vii, 123, 233, 240
Barzilay, David, 165
Barzun, Jacques, 40
Bates, Dawson, 75
Beard, C. A., 4, Mary R., 4
Beattie, Emily, 78–79
Beckett, J. C., 47, 57, 230
Belfast, 77, 83, 87, 89–94, 99, 107–13, 116, 148, 150, 153, 155, 160–61, 164, 169–71, 175–78, 182–84, 188, 190, 192, 201–02, 205, 207, 210, 217, 223; Andersontown, 174, 182, 204; Ardoyne, 90, 92, 117, 121, 204; Divis, 174; East, 159, 181, 204; Falls, 92, 158, 174, 176; Peace Line, 176, 205; Shankill, 113, 120–21, 176–77; South, 189; Unity Flats, 90; West, 109, 159, 189; Aldergrove Airport, 184; Centre for Teacher Education, 116, College of Technology, 36; Europa Hotel, 169, 174; *Fortnight*, 214; *Irish News*, 178; *Newsletter*, 36, 178; Queen's University, 83, 153, 195, 201, 210; *Republican News*, 206; Royal Victoria Hospital, 170
Bell, Geoffrey, 166
Bell, J. B., 16, 199
Benburb, 203
Benewick, R., 76
Bennett Committee, 129, 130–31, 143, 145, 174; H. G., 41, 129–31, 140, 164–65, 197
Berkeley, George, 33, 41
Berry, Peter, 166

Bill of Rights, 34, 215–18
Bindman, Geoffrey, 39, 42
Birmingham, 184; *Post and Mail,* 184
Black and Tans, 54
Blaker, Peter, 188
Blanket protest, 134–35, 190–91, 193
Bleakley, David, 167, 230
Bloody Friday, 178, 180–82, 186–87, 205
Bloody Sunday, 37, 178–80, 182–83, 212, 224
Blue-shirts, 70
Blumenthal, M. D., 16
Boehringer, Kathleen, 123
Bolt, Christine, 40
Bombings, 172–74, 177–78, 182–86, 194, 204–05
Booth, Arthur, 123
Borders, William, 199
Boulton, David, 57, 166
Bowman, D. J., vii, 230
Boylan, Henry, 76
Boyle, Kevin, vii, 58, 75, 130, 137, 140–41, 210, 231; Louis, 198
Boyne, battle of the, 46, 68, 90
Bradford, Robert, 189
Bradshaw, Kenneth, 41
Brady, Brian, 166
Braverman, Harry, 142
Brecher, John, 198
Brehon laws, 221
Breslin, Jimmy, 59, 75, 94, 98
Brinton, Crane, 17, 193–94, 199
British government, 26–27, 29, 33–37, 49–50, 52, 55, 84, 93, 95, 107, 127, 131, 136, 143–44, 147, 151, 155, 157–58, 162, 182–83, 185, 191–92, 196, 200, 213, 216–19, 222–30, 234, 238–39
British Broadcasting System, 56; Defense Intelligence, 144; Information Services, 133, 141, 197–98; Official Secrets Acts, 147; Labour Party, 214, 218, 234; Opinion Research Centre, 194; Union of Fascists, 70
Brooke, Basil, 68
Brown, John, 76, 166
Browne, Vincent, 160, 166–67
Brutality, defined, 127–28

Brynmor-Jones, David, 40
"B" Specials: Ulster Special Constabulary
Buchanan, R. H., vii
Buckland, Patrick, 60, 75
Buckley, W. F., Jr., 5, 16
Bugler, Jeremy, 76
Bunting, Ronald, 86–88, 90, 151
Burgess, E. W., 40
Burke, Maurice, vii, 165, 167
Burntollet Bridge, 87–89, 177
Burt, Cyril, 28
Burton, Frank, 162, 167, 199
Butt, Isaac, 49
Byrne, Garrett, 230

Cahill, Joe, 190
Caledon, 78–79, 177
Calvert, Harry, 58
Cameron Commission, 62–64, 72–76, 78–79, 82–84, 89, 97, 146, 157; Lord, 75, 97, 165, 231
Campaign for Democracy in Ulster, 71
Campaign for Free Speech on Ireland, 197
Campaign for Social Justice, 71, 79–80, 209
Campion, D. R., 94, 98
Capitalism, 13, 38, 50, 101, 138–39, 203, 221, 236, 238; see Colonialism; Corporations, multinational; Imperialism
Carlton, David, 97
Carrington, E. T., vii
Carron, Owen, 192
Carson, J. T., 98
Carter, C. F., 123
Castlereagh, 143, 178
Case, C. M., 17
Casey, W. Van E., 95, 98
Casualties, 52, 91, 93, 117–18, 125, 127, 132–33, 144, 160–61, 168, 170–73, 175–76, 178–79, 181–83, 186–88, 191–92, 194, 205
Causation, 5, 7, 92–97, 126, 169, 238–39
Celler, Emanuel, 212, 231
Celticism, 2, 29, 31, 39; Celts, 22–23, 26, 30, 38, 49
Central Intelligence Agency, 16, 162, 167

Index

Chall, L. P., vii
Chamberlain, H. S., 21, 39
Channon, Paul, 183
Chibnall, Steve, 18, 41, 165
Chichester-Clark, James, 90, 92, 223, 232
Chilver Review Body, 116
Christianity, 95–96, 100, 114–15, 117, 203, 205
Chubb, Basil, 76
Church of England, 20, 27, 44
Church of Ireland, 44, 94, 115, 201, 202
Church Leaders Peace Campaign, 201–03
Civil Liberties, 27, 33, 215, 229; Movement, 77, 79, 81–82, 87–88, 146, 149, 151–52, 157, 212; rights, 37, 126, 135, 153, 177, 224–25, 237; see Human rights, Bill of Rights
Clan na Gael, 48
Clark, K. B., 75
Class, social, 2–3, 10, 13, 15, 19–25, 28–32, 34, 38, 51, 55–56, 78, 99–100, 103, 107, 110, 117, 138, 163–64, 173, 187, 203, 214; upper, 10, 12–14, 19–20, 24–25, 29, 34–35, 47, 60, 69, 100–01, 125–40, 149, 164, 177, 218, 234, 238; middle, 22, 31–32, 34, 46–47, 69, 72, 79, 100, 102–03, 111–13, 117, 119, 131, 143–44, 149–52, 154, 164, 200, 207, 211, 213–14, 222, 234, 239; lower, 22, 32–34, 44, 47, 60, 69, 100, 102–103, 111–13, 120, 122, 125, 131, 144, 146–48, 150, 154, 162–64, 200, 212–13, 234; underclass, 100, 102–03, 109
Claudy, 183
Clergy, 112–14, 116, 237–39
Clogher, 92
Coagh, 181
Coalisland, 81, 191
Coles, Robert, 123
Collins, Chris, 42
Colonialism, 1–3, 8, 25–27, 32, 37, 44–45, 128, 140, 203, 212, 215
Combat, 155–56, 192
Commissioner of Complaints, 136, 141
Complaints procedure, 145, 224
Compromise, 14–15, 104, 149, 155, 213, 229

Compton Committee, 127; Edward, 127, 140; P. A., 124; report, 128
Conlon, Lil, 123
Connell, K. H., vii, 57
Connolly, James, 13, 17, 38, 42, 48, 50, 52, 55–58, 110, 123, 212
Connor, 92
Conrad, Joseph, 7, 16
Conray, John, 113, 124, 231
Conway, William, 98
Coogan, T. P., 71, 76, 159, 163–64, 167, 198
Cookstown, 109
Cooley, C. H., 107, 123
Cooper, I. A., 84
Coote, Anna, 41–42
Corporations, multinational, 24, 31, 33, 38, 100–01, 138, 140, 236
Corrigan, Mairead, 205–08, 212, 231
Corrymeela, Friends of, 201–02, 204, 239
Cosgrave, Liam, 186
Costello, Joe, 165
Costigan, Giovanni, 47, 57
Council of Ireland, 54–55, 187, 226-27
Courts, see Judiciary
Craig, James, 60, 75; William, 82, 84–85
Craigavon, Lord, 68
Crime, criminals, 7, 101–02, 131, 134, 148, 155, 194, 239; "criminalisation program," 134, 190; "criminal status," 134
Cromwell, Oliver, 46
Crowd control, 83, 89, 127, 144, 175; see CS gas, Plastic and Rubber bullets
Crowley–Farrell, Marybeth, vii
Crumlin Road prison, 190
CS gas, 147, 174–75, 179
Culture, 21–22, 30, 34, 43, 48–49, 99, 118, 122; defined, 103–05
Currie, Austin, 78–81
Curtis, Edmund, 40, 57–58; L. P., Jr., 40–41, 57, 165, 240

Dáil Éireann, 53–55; see Irish government
Daly, C. B., 57–58, 98, 230; Edward, 176, 193
Darby, John, 150, 166, 198
Darlington, Roger, 41–42

Darwin, Charles, 9
Dash, Samuel, 198
Davey, Ray, 201
Davis, E. E., vii, 195, 199
Davison, Joseph, 68; W. P., 233
Dawson, Helen, 57
Deane, Seamus, 232
de Burca, Mairin, 165
Debray, Regis, 17
Declaration of Independence, 53
Defenders, 47
de Gobineau, J. A., 21, 39
Delinquency, 102, 109, 119
Dellinger, David, 17
DeLorean, J. Z., 138–39, 141
Demaris, Ovid, 196
Democracy, 1–2, 6–7, 13, 38, 77, 87, 136, 152, 155, 158, 168, 210
Democratic Unionist Party, 138, 151, 153, 162, 195, 213, 215, 217, 226–29
Deportation, exclusion, 33, 37, 67
Derry, 73, 77, 81–92, 102, 109–10, 113, 131, 148, 156, 174–83, 210, 223–24; Bogside, 88, 90, 131, 175, 177, 181–82, 223; "Free Derry," 89; Creggan, 182; Citizens' Action Committee, Defence Association, 84, 87, 90, 157
Detentions, 67, 133, 130–31, 133, 173; see Internment, Interrogations
Deutsch, Richard, 97, 198, 206, 230–31
de Valera, Eamon, 7, 54, 58, 68–69
Devlin, Bernadette, see McAliskey, B. D.; George, 97
Dewar, M. W., 76, 166
Dillon, Martin, 166
Diplock courts, 75, 129, 133; Lord, 75, 98, 128–29, 140–41
Direct rule, 224–30
Dirty protest, see Blanket protest
Discrimination, social, 19, 35–36, 45, 55–56, 60, 67, 73, 136–38, 204, 209, 216, 222–24, 228; see Anglo-Saxonism, Celticism, Ethnocentrism
Diskin, Matt, vii
Disraeli, Benjamin, 27, 40
Dissenters, 9, 32, 43–45, 48, 95, 149, 201, 203
Dixon, R., 17

Dolci, Danilo, 75
Down, 92
Downey, James, 140
Downie, Leonard, Jr., 164
Downing Street Declaration, 223
Doyle, Leonard, 197
Drogheda, 46
Dromore, 92
Dublin, 110, 157, 160, 173, 184–86, 189, 192, 194–95; *Irish Times,* 176, 184, 196
Dummett, Ann, 42, 165
Dungannon, 73, 78–82, 87, 91, 93, 109
Dungiven, 87, 90–91
Dunleath, Charles, 124
Dunmurry, 139
Dupertuis, C. W., 57

Eames, Edwin, 41
Easter Rising, 11, 48, 51, 155, 158, 189, 212
East India Company, 35
Economic and Social Research Institute, 195
Edison, T. A., 9
Edmonds, Sean, 166
Education, -ors, 24, 28–29, 32, 34–35, 54, 60, 99, 103, 108, 112, 114–16, 118, 149, 193, 209, 222, 224, 236, 239; Acts, 115, 239; see Schools
Edwards, L. P., 17; O. D., 45, 57; R. D., 18, 40
Egan, Bowes, 97
Eilberg, Joshua, 232
Einstein, Albert, 9; Lewis, 16
Eire, 68, 70–71, 158, 171, 190, 220, 225; see Irish government
Elections, 67–68, 153, 179, 183, 192, 210, 214, 216, 219, 224–25, 228–29
Elizabeth I, 45, 185; II, 185, 206
Elliott, Denis, 143; Ruth, 124; S., 232
Ellis, P. B., 57
Elterman, Howard, vii
Emergency Powers Acts, see Special Powers
Emerson, R. W., 8, 16
Emigration, 15, 28, 32, 46–47, 100
Empire Loyalists, 178
Engels, Friedrich, 10, 17

England, -ish, 10–11, 19–20, 23–27, 29–30, 32–33, 35–36, 38, 43–45, 48, 50, 56, 60, 69, 77, 100, 131, 135, 178, 183, 185, 190, 192, 213
Episcopalians, 43, 45, 56; see Church of England, of Ireland
Equal Opportunities Commission, 137
Establishment, 12–13, 15, 38, 126, 146, 160, 203, 206, 208, 235; see Class, upper; Power, social
Ethnicity, 20–25, 43–44, 78, 99, 103, 107, 110, 113, 117, 119, 125, 138, 149–50, 164, 173, 176, 211, 227, 239
Ethnocentrism, 2–3, 19–22, 38, 100, 111, 147, 187
Eugenics, 21, 28
European Commission of Human Rights, 128, 153, 190–91; Convention of Human Rights, 86; Court of Human Rights, 128, 140, 150, 190; Economic Community, 39, 140, 235–36; Parliament, 151, 153, 175
Evans, Howell, 230; Gwynfor, 57
Evason, Eileen, 123
Evelegh, Robin, 135, 141, 164–65, 169–70, 196–97
Everton school, 117, 120
Ewart–Biggs, Christopher, 186

Fair Employment Agency, 36, 103, 137–38
Family life, 22, 102, 104, 106, 109–12, 114, 116–17, 119, 150, 191, 193
Famine, 15, 25–27, 45–46
Farley, Peter, 165
Farrell, Michael, 36, 42, 75, 97, 210, 231
Faul, Denis, 141, 153, 166
Faulkner, Brian, 132, 187, 226
Feakle negotiations, 202, 204, 239
Fellowship of Reconciliation, 201
Fenian Brotherhood, 47–48, 120
Ferguson, William, 40
Fermanagh, 237
Ferrarotti, Franco, vii, 238, 240
Feuer, L. S., 17
Fields, Rona M., vii, 111, 123, 163, 167, 230
Fish, Hamilton, Jr., 232
Fishman, Walda K., 39, 238, 240

Fitt, Gerard, 81, 83
Fitzgerald, G. A., vii, 230, 233; Julie, vii
Fitzpatrick, Barré, 124, 232
Flackes, W. D., 98, 165–67, 197, 230
Flynn, Elspeth, vii
Foley, Gerry, 199, 231; Michael, 123
Fraser, Morris, 111, 122–24, 163, 167
Free Presbyterian Church, 95, 150
Freud, Sigmund, 9
Friedrich, C. J., 123, 238, 240
Friends, Religious Society of, see Quakers

Gaine, Hugh, 8
Gallagher, Eric, 231; R.D.E., 57–58, 98, 230
Galton, Francis, 21, 28, 39–41
Games, 121–22, 164
Gangs, 112–13, 117, 119, 163
Gardiner Commission, 133–34; Lord, 128, 133, 141, 198
Garnett, David, 17
Garland, Sean, 160
Gaughan, Michael, 190
General Motors, 138, 140, 236
Geneticism, 19–22, 28–29, 49
George, D. L., 24, 52, 54
George III, 9; V, 54
Gibbon, Peter, 57
Gibbons, Patricia A., 165
Gibson, N. J., 96, 98
Gifford, Lord, 165
Gilhooley, James, 230
Gladstone, W. E., 49
Glass, D. V., 41
Glassie, Henry, 237, 240
Glencree Community, 201–02, 204
Glover, J. M., 158, 167, 197
Goldaber, Irving, vii
Gombeen, 110
Good, G. E., 98
Goodfellow family, 78–79
Gordenker, Leon, 233
Gossett, T. F., 40
Goulding, Cathal, 161, 167–68, 186, 209–10, 231
Governmental agencies, 222–30
Government of India Act, 1833, 35; of Ireland Acts, 54–55, 126, 136, 215, 218

Graham, H. D., 16
Grramsci, Antonio, 16
Grant, Lawrence, 39, 41–42
Gray, Tony, 57–58
Greaves, C. D., 57
Green: Irish nationalist
Greenberg, William, 41–42
Gregg, Richard, 17
Greig, Ian, 17
Grindal, B. T., vii
Group characteristics, 99–122
Guerrillas, 6, 70, 125, 144; theatre, 169; warfare, 222; see Vigilantes
Guevara, E. C., 17
Guida, Ann, vii
Gumplowicz, Ludwig, 21–22, 40
Gurley, Eddie, 202, 230
Gurr, T. R., 16

Hackett, John, 148, 165
Hadden, Tom, 75, 130, 140–41, 231
Haley, Alex, 196
Hanna, G. B., 62, 75
Harbinson, J. F., 166
Harbison, Jeremy, 124; Joan I., 109, 123–24
Hardman, J. B. S., 16
Harkaway, Jack, 1
Harland and Wolff, 102
Harlow, R. V., 16
Harris, Marvin, 41
Hayes, M. N., vii
H–Blocks, see Maze Prison
Head, K. B., 16
Hechter, Michael, 40
Hemyng, Bracebridge, 4
Hench, J. B., 16
Henkoff, Ronald, 198
Henriques, H. S. Q., 40
Henry II, 43; VIII, 20, 44
Herman, E. S., 106, 123
Herrema, Tiede, 186
Heskin, Ken, 111, 124, 238–40
Hibernia, 173, 194
Hillyard, Paddy, 75, 130, 140–41, 231
Himsworth Committee, 175
Hinkle, Warren, 16
Hoffman, Abbie, 17

Hoggart, Richard, 18
Holland, Jack, 123, 145, 165–66, 198, 232; Mary, 76
Holmes, Colin, 40; Erskine, 120–21, 124
Holocausts, Irish, 45–46, 48
Holohan, Renagh, 196
Home rule, 50–51, 54; League, 49
Hooton, E. A., 57
House searches, 66–67, 147
Housing, 34, 36, 45, 60, 73–74, 80, 85, 90, 93, 96, 108, 117, 181, 222–24, 239; Authority, 176
Howson, Roger, 40
Huberman, Edward, vii; Elizabeth, vii
Hughes, Francis, 166, 199
Hull, Roger, 76
Humanism, 2, 21, 116
Human rights, 33–34, 36, 59–74, 82, 85, 136, 207, 210–11, 225; see Civil rights
Hume, John, 153, 218, 232
Humphrey, N. D., 4
Hunger strikes, 9, 135, 162, 168, 178, 189–93, 229
Hunt, John, 165

ibn Khaldûn, Abd–al–Rahman, 21, 39
Immigration, 28, 32; Act, 37
Imperialism, 2, 24, 27–28, 30, 32, 35, 38–39, 60, 78, 96, 100, 140, 162, 168, 210, 236; see Corporations, multinational
Incident Centres, 202
Independent Television, 184; Unionist Party, 226
INLA: Irish National Liberation Army
Insurgents, 125, 154, 169–70, 180, 200
Intellectuals, 12–14, 32, 108, 116
Interethnic conflict, 19–42
International: Fellowship of Reconciliation, 201; League for the Rights of Man, 180; Voluntary Service, 204; Working Men's Association, 11
Internment, 109, 118, 120, 131, 177, 179, 210
Interrogation, 64, 67, 77, 127–31, 143, 145, 147, 159, 168–69, 173–74, 210
IRA: Irish Republican Army

Irish government, 51, 53–55, 60, 68–69, 128, 186, 188, 196, 200, 219–20; see Dáil Éireann
Irish Army Comrades Association, 70; Association of Democratic Lawyers, 153; Congress of Trade Unions, 186; Council of Churches, 45, 96, 201; National Liberation Army, 154, 160–62, 179, 183, 185, 189, 192–93, 222; Nationalist Party, 53; National Volunteers, 49, 51, 54, 64; Republican Army, 6, 30, 49, 53–54, 64, 70–71, 81–82, 90–91, 93–95, 103, 127, 135, 143, 152, 155, 157, 159, 184, 195–96, 209; Republican Brotherhood, 47, 49, 51, 53, 64; Republican Socialist Party, 160, 189; Revolutionary Brotherhood, 47
Irwin, Robert, 143

Jack, R. I., 40
Jackson, Harold, 235, 240; J.A., vii
Jacobs, Glenn, vii
James II, 46, 82, 90; William, 108, 123
Jefferson, Thomas, 1
Jensen, A. R., 41
Jews, 3, 20, 22, 27–29, 45, 70
Johnston, William, 155
Journalists, see Propaganda
Joyce, P. W., 232
Judiciary, 33, 35–36, 54, 61, 64–65, 67, 75, 120, 127, 129–31, 133–35, 137, 144–45, 176, 211, 215–16
Juveniles, 102, 130, 144; see Education, Family life

Kahn, R. L., 16
Kamin, L. J., 28, 41
Kaye, Jacqueline, 198
Kee, Robert, 56–58, 198
Keesinge's Contemporary Archives, 97, 141, 198
Kelly, H., 140; James, 166; Mary, 199, 233
Kennedy, R. E., Jr., vii, 40, 57
Kettle, Martin, 165
Kiely, Niall, 197
Kiernan, V. G., 41
Kilmore, 92

King, M. L., Jr., 212
Kipling, Rudyard, 28
Kitson, Frank, 16–17, 42, 164–65, 169, 196
Kluckhohn, Clyde, 123
Knightley, Philip, 164
Kohn, Hans, 20, 39
Kramer, Jane, 123
Kriesberg, Louis, vii, 17
Kroeber, A. L., 123
Ku Klux Klan, 2, 6
Kyle, Charles, vii

Lagan College, 115
La Mon Restaurant, 178
Land clearance, 25–26
Langer, W. L., 18
"Law and order," 5–7, 33, 37, 61, 77, 125–26, 163
Lawrence, R. J., 232; T. E., 14, 17
Leach, Edmund, 57, 165
Lecky, W. E. H., 44, 56–57
Lee, A. McC., 4, 16–17, 40–41, 105, 123, 124, 165; Elizabeth R. B., iv, viii, 4, 17, 124
Legal profession, 153, 239
Legislation, 35, 45, 59–74, 132, 135–36, 173
Lehane, Denis, 166
Leitch, David, 164
Lenin, V. I., 11, 13, 17
Lerner, Max, 7, 16
Lester, Anthony, 39, 42
Levenson, Samuel, 57
Lewis, J. L., 9
Leyburn, J. G., 16
Liberal Party, 214
Liebow, Elliot, 75
Liggio, L. P., 4
Lijphart, Arend, 235, 240
Lincoln, C. E., 39
Lindsay, Kennedy, 142, 165
Lisnevin School, 116
Litigation, 153, 209–10
Local government, 86, 136, 224
Lockhart, W. H., 124
LOI: Loyal Orange Institution
London, 183, 185; *Daily Telegraph,* 181;

Economist, 157, 214; Heathrow Airport, 183; *Sunday Times,* 77, 97, 141, 165; *Times,* 182
Londonderry, see Derry; Area Plan, 86
Long, S. E., 76, 150, 166
Long Kesh Prison, see Maze Prison
Longuet, Jenny M., 230, 233
Lorenz, A. L., 16
Lowry, D. R., vii, 56, 58, 137, 141
Loyal Citizens of Ulster, 84, 87; Orange Institution, see Orange Institution
Loyalist Defence Volunteers, 156
Loyalists, 36, 43, 60, 70, 72–73, 77, 82 86–88, 95, 113, 125–26, 133–34, 138, 144–46, 151–52, 154, 156–57, 162–63, 168–69, 171, 173, 176–78, 186–87, 190–91, 218, 226–27; see Vigilantes, Guerrillas
Lynch, Jack, 180
Lynd, Staughton, 17
Lyons, F. S. L., 45, 57; H. A., 164, 167

Macardle, Dorothy, 58, 75, 198
Macaulay, T. B., 27, 40
MacDiarmid, Hugh, 57
MacDonald, Ramsay, 24
MacDougall, C. D., 16
MacGiolla, Tomás, 160
MacIver, R. M., 40
MacKies, 102
Macnee, Calvin, 231
MacStiofain, Sean, 190
MacSwiney, Terence, 189
Mafia, 6
Maghera, 80, 87
Magilligan Prison, 190
Magowan, Vivien, 97, 198
Malcolm X, 168, 196
Manchester *Guardian,* 184, 208, 220
Mangione, Jerre, 75
Manning, Maurice, 76
Mao Tse Tung, 17
Maquet, J. J., 40
Martyrs' Memorial Church, 150
Marx, Karl, 10–11, 13, 17, 40
Marxist–Leninism, 71, 158, 160
Mason, Philip, 41; Roy, 227, 232, 236, 240

Mass communication, media, see Propaganda
Mayr, Hildegard, 201
Maze Prison, 113, 134–35, 190–92
McAliskey, Bernadette D., 123, 131, 157, 191, 210, 212; Michael, 191
McAteer, Eddie, 82–83, 85
McBride, Steve, 206, 208–09, 231
McCann, Eamonn, 166; Joe, 168
McCaul, S. P., 131
McCluskey, Con, 71, 79–80; Patricia, 71, 79
McConnell, Joe, 42
McCormack, Vincent, 97
McCreary, Alf, 230
McCrudden, Christopher, 137
McDaid, James, 184
McDowell, R. B., 57–58
McGuffin, John, 141, 198
McGurk public house, 178; Tom, 199
McHardy, Anne, 220
McKenna family, 78
McKeown, Ciaran, 205–06, 230; Michael, 171, 173, 197
McKittrick, David, 231
McNeilly, Norman, 166
McNeill, Ronald, 57
Mead, Margaret, 101, 123
Mehra, Ravi, viii
Menendez, A. J., 98
Methodist, 20, 43, 94, 115, 201–02; Council of Social Welfare, 203
Metress, S. P., vii
Miami Showband, 178, 187
Midgley, Harry, vii
Mill, J. S., 29, 40–41
Miller, J. C., 16
Mills, C. W., 31, 41
Mitchell, Rob, 230
Mitchison, Rosalind, 40
Moloney, Ed, 164, 198
Molyneaux, J. H., 228, 231
Monovalence, 103, 108
Montague, J. B., Jr., 41
Morals, 104–06, 112, 119, 131; see Culture
Moran, Brian, 147
Mores, 104–06, 119, 131; see Culture
Moss, Robert, 17, 238, 240

Mountbatten, Lord, 161, 178, 186, 188
Moxon–Browne, E., 167, 195, 199
Moynihan, D. P., 222, 232
Mullaghmore, 188
Multivalence, 22, 34, 103–08, 121
Murray, Gilbert, 39; Raymond, 141, 153, 166

Nairn, Tom, 40–41
Narrow Water, 161, 188
National Association for Irish Freedom, 210; Council for Civil Liberties, 36, 61–63, 65–66, 71, 75–76, 80, 138, 141, 157, 208–09; Democratic Party, 218; Front, 184; Union of Protestants, 150
Nationalism, –ists, 23–24, 30, 34, 38–39, 43–44, 48, 50–51, 53, 60, 64, 82, 94, 126, 133–34, 147, 154, 158, 177–81, 187, 190–91, 193, 210, 234, 237
Nationalist Party, 84–85, 132, 214, 218
Nationality Act, 37
NCCL: National Council for Civil Liberties
Neave, Airey, 185
Newry, 91, 109, 160, 187
New Society, 131, 213
Neewsweek, 139
New Ulster Political Research Group, 156–57, 220
New University of Ulster, 96
New York Times, 71, 179
NICRA: Northern Ireland Civil Rights Association
Nixon, R. M., 9
Nobel Peace Prize, 206
Nonviolent methods, 14–15, 26, 48, 62, 72, 81–82, 84–85, 100–01, 104, 126, 132, 135–36, 153–57, 169, 200–33, 237, 240
Nonwhites, 30, 33, 35–37, 44, 59, 77, 102, 168, 237
Nordheimer, Jon, 179
Northern Ireland government, 38, 51, 54–55, 60–62, 64–74, 79, 84–88, 92–93, 95, 126, 135–36, 138–39, 151, 157–58, 176, 191, 202, 213–19, 222–30, 235; Assembly, 229; Constitution Act, 1973, 136, 225, 229; Constitutional Convention, 1974, 226–29; Office, 141; "Irish dimension," 227
Northern Ireland Association of Socialist Lawyers, 153; Attitude Survey, 162, 195; Civil Rights Association, 71–72, 79–87, 90, 93, 97, 132, 152–53, 157, 179, 209, 211–12; Information Service, 123, 141–42, 165, 172, 197; Labour Party, 132, 214, 218, 225–26
Northern Irish society, conceptions of, 234–35
Notting Hill race riots, 35
Nugent, Ciaran, 190
NUPRG: New Ulster Political Research Group

Oak–Boys, 47
Oberschall, Anthony, 17
Ó Brádaigh, Ruairi, 190, 221, 232; Sean, 190
O'Brien, C. C., 167; Eileen, 196
O Conaill, Daithi, 184, 190
O'Connell, Daniel, 26–27, 48
O'Day, Alan, 97
O'Donaghue, Joseph, vii; Nancy, vii
O'Dowd, L. G., vii, 137–38, 141, 165, 199, 231, 233
Official Irish Republican Army, 14, 71, 152, 154, 158, 160–62, 168, 181, 183, 186, 190, 195, 209–10, 214; Sinn Féin, 161, 184, 209; Unionist Party, 120, 152, 156, 213, 215–17, 225–26, 228–29
O'Fiaich, Tomás, 135, 141, 193
O'Hanlon, T. J., 123
OIRA: Official Irish Republican Army
O'Kane, J. M., vii
Ombudsman, 85, 136
O'Neill, Conor, 99, 122; P., 167; Terence, 72–73, 84–85, 87, 90, 152, 155
"One man, one vote," 86
Operation Motorman, 178, 182–83
Opinions, 105, 194–96
Orange: Northern Irish loyalist; Society, Order, Institution, 47, 49–50, 60, 67, 69, 73, 88, 103, 118–19, 146, 149, 152; statelet, 43, 55, 59–74, 156, 162, 217, 227–28; Volunteers, 156
OUP: Official Unionist Party

PACE: Protestant and Catholic Encounter
Pacifism, 161, 207, 211–12, 237; see nonviolent methods
Page, Bruce, 164
Paine, Thomas, 1, 47
Paisley, I. R. K., 58, 86, 88, 90, 95, 98 149–51, 153, 162, 166, 175, 187, 195, 213–14, 217, 226–27, 231
Pakistanis, 36
Palestine Liberation Organization, 6
"Papists": Roman Catholics
Palmer, N. D., 57
Paramilitary organizations, 50, 70, 109–10, 113–14, 126, 134, 155, 162–63, 181, 186, 191, 195–96, 207, 227, 237; see Vigilantes, Guerrillas
Park, R. E., 40
Parker Committee, 127–28; Joseph, 208; Lord, 127, 140
Parkhurst Prison, 190
Parliamentary Commissioner for Administration, 86, 136, 141
Parnell, C. S., 48–49
Parri, Meurig, 147, 165
Patricianism, 34, 36, 38, 56
Patterson, Henry, 57; Saidie, 204
Pax Christi, 203
PD: People's Democracy
Peace by Peace, 206, 208
Peace, quests for, 200–30; People, Community of the, 204–08, 211, 239; Point, 203
Pearse, P. H., 51
Pearson, Karl, 21, 39
Peep-o'-Day Boys, 47
Peer groups, 22, 103–04, 106–08, 112, 119, 121–22
People's Democracy, 74, 84, 87–89, 93, 132, 157, 209–10, 239
Personality, 103–05, 107–08, 112, 121
Phillips, Ian, 147
PIRA: Provisional Irish Republican Army
Plaid Cymru, 30, 38
Plastic bullets, 144, 147, 174–75
Plato, 20–21, 39
Plumb, J. H., 222, 232, 237, 240
Plutocracy, 24, 38, 60, 140; see Capitalism
Police, 6–7,16, 37, 55, 60, 63–64, 66–67, 69–70, 77, 79, 81, 83–85, 88–90, 96, 99, 102, 119, 129–31, 138, 144–45, 147–48, 154, 175, 177, 180–82, 185, 190, 195, 205, 208, 210, 222, 226–27
Political actionist agencies, 200, 209–13; parties, 200, 213–21
"Political status," 133
Poole, Michael, 98
Pope John XXIII, 151; John Paul II, 206
Portadown, 182
Portlaoighise Prison, 190
Poverty, 108, 139, 229
Power, social, 10, 12–14, 101, 116, 187, 212–13, 215–16, 222, 236, 240; sharing, 225
Prendiville, Paddy, 173, 197
Presbyterians, 1, 8–9, 20, 43, 45, 56, 94–95, 98, 115, 150, 200, 202, 237
Price, Dolores, 190; Marian, 190
Priestley, J. B., 19, 39
Pring, David, 41
Prior, James, 193, 229, 233
Prisons, –ers, 77, 129–30, 133–35, 145, 162, 184, 191, 193, 211; see Detentions, Internment
Processions, 9, 80–84, 86–90, 103, 111, 113, 121, 151–52, 174, 177, 179–80, 205–06, 209
Prods: Protestants
Propaganda, –ists, 7–9, 12, 15, 24, 32, 34–35, 43–44, 46, 48–49, 52, 56, 60, 79, 94, 99, 103, 106, 113, 118–19, 146, 148, 151, 154–55, 159, 163–64, 168, 174–75, 179–80, 182, 184, 190, 192–93, 202, 205–07, 213, 215, 220, 224, 234, 237; armed, 169
Property damages, 93, 118, 126, 131, 155, 161, 171, 173–74, 183
Proportional representation, 67–68, 225; see Elections
Protestant and Catholic Encounter, 201–02; *Telegraph,* 151; Unionist Party, 153
Protestants characterized, 32, 43–46, 59–74
Prototypes, 103, 106, 112, 122

Provisional Irish Republican Army, 14, 17, 58, 71, 107, 111–12, 114, 154–55, 157–59, 161–62, 166–67, 169, 171, 177–78, 181–86, 188–94, 198, 202, 208–10, 220–22, 225; Sinn Féin, 71, 158, 206, 209, 214, 220–21, 229
Provo: Provisional Irish Republican Army member
Pryde, G. S., 40
Public Appointments Commission, 85; Broadcasting System, 56; Order Acts, 85; Protective Agency, 182; relations, see Propaganda

Quakers, 20, 149, 201, 203–04, 208
Queen's Household Cavalry, 185; Own Highlanders, 188; University, 83, 153, 195, 201, 210

Race Relations Acts, 35–36, 85
Racism, 1–2, 19–21, 27–33, 35–36, 44, 48, 77, 212; see Ethnocentrism, Anglo-Saxonism, Celticism, Eugenics, Geneticism
Rackets, 160, 194
Raftery, A., 17
Rattner, Steven, 198
Reagan, Ronald, 9
Red Brigade, 6; Flag 74, 184; Hand Commandos, 156, 186
Redmond, John, 50–51
Rees, Merlyn, 187, 227
Reformism, 12, 14–15, 238
Rejai, M., 17
Religious agencies, 200–04, 211–13
Religious Society of Friends, see Quakers
Republicans, 48, 53, 56, 62–63, 69–70, 81–82, 95, 121, 154, 157–58, 173, 190–91, 214; Clubs, 64, 160–62, 214; Labour Party, 132, 218; Movement, 161
Revolt, revolution, defined, 5–16
Rhys, Ioan, 57; John, 40
RIC: Royal Irish Constabulary
Rice, T. J., vii
Rioting, 89, 132, 144, 173–74, 177, 181, 238
Rising of 1798, 26, 47
Rivington, James, 8
Robbery, 158–59, 163, 171, 194

Robboy, Howard, 41
Roberts, Adam, 17; Vera M., 196
Robson, J. M., 40
Roles, social, 103–07, 112
Rolston, Bill, vii, 141, 165, 199, 231
Roman Catholics characterized, 31, 43–56
Roman Catholic Church, 20, 44, 92, 94–96, 115, 201
Romans, 22–23, 35
Roosevelt, F. D., 9
Rose, E. J. B., 42; Richard, 166, 199
Royal Black Institution, 73; Green Jackets, 135, 185; Irish Constabulary, 54, 145; Ulster Constabulary, 66, 82, 88–89, 93, 107, 121, 128–33, 143–45, 147–48, 164, 171–72, 174, 178, 182, 185, 194, 208, 217, 223; Ulster Constabulary Reserve, 93, 144, 147, 171–73, 223
Rubber bullets, 147, 174–75
Rubin, Jerry, 17
RUC: Royal Ulster Constabulary
RUCR: Royal Ulster Constabulary Reserve
Rudd, P. Joy, vii, 141
Rumour Service, 182
Ryan, Desmond, 58

Salaman, R. N., 18, 57
Samaritans, 172
Sampson, Anthony, 4
Sands, Bobby, 113, 135, 166, 191–92, 199
SAS: Special Air Service
Scarman, Leslie, 98, 124, 166, 197; Tribunal, 89–90, 92–93, 98, 151
Scenarios, 168–69, 174, 177, 189, 234; see Strategies
Schellenberg, J. A., 17
Schools, 121, 137, 215; controlled, 96, 113–16; integrated, 114, 116, 120; maintained, 115; segregated, 138, 176; see Education
Scotch–Irish, definition, 1–2, 49
Scots, 23–26, 29–30, 32, 34, 38–39, 43, 45, 100, 183
Scottish National Party, 30, 38
SDLP: Social Democratic and Labour Party
Segregation, 93–94, 96, 103, 114, 121, 149, 176, 215, 222

Senior, Hereward, 57
Servite Order, 203
Sex Discrimination Act, 35, 139
SF: Sinn Féin
Shakespeare, William, 28
Sharp, Gene, 18, 231
Shearman, Hugh, 57
Sheridan, Monica, 123
Shillman, Bernard, 40
Shuster, Alvin, 41
Simms, G. O., 93
Sinclair, Betty, 81
Sinn Féin, 30, 51–53, 71, 157, 160–61; see Official and Provisional Sinn Féin
Sinnott, Richard, 195, 199
Sloan, Sam, 113, 124
Smith, B. E., 16
Smylie, David, 82
Smyth, Martin, 150; Samuel, 186
Social control, 33, 38, 101, 228, 235; process, 105–06; science, 12–14, 27–28, 106, 108, 112, 149, 154; services, workers, 108, 123, 149, 200, 224, 237, 239
Social Democratic and Labour Party, 152–53, 183, 192–93, 213, 215, 218–19, 225–26, 228–29; Democratic Party, 132
Socialist, 158, 200; Party, 214
"Solemn League and Covenant," 43, 49
Somerdale School, 117, 119
Sorokin, Pitirim, 39
Soviet Union, 135, 159, 167
Special Air Service, 185
"Special Category" status, 133–35, 155, 190–91, 193
Special Powers Acts, 60–65, 67, 70, 74, 85–86, 126, 151, 155, 159, 223–24
Spencer, A. E. C. W., vii, 115, 124
Sports, 114, 119, 144
Spjut, R. J., 42
St. Comgall's School, 91
St. Gabriel's School, 117
St. Gemma's School, 117
St. Joseph's School, 116
St. Mary's School, 116
Stagg, Frank, 190
Standing Advisory Commission on Human Rights, 136

Starry Plough, 160, 185
Steelboys, 47
Sterling, Claire, 167
Stetler, Russell, 41, 197, 212, 231
Stewart, A. T. Q., 56; J. D., 197; Senator, 80
Stone, Lawrence, 17
Stonham, Lord, 76
Stormont, see Northern Ireland government
Strategies, –ists, 12, 101, 125, 144, 161, 164, 169, 180, 210, 222, 238–39; see Scenarios
Strikes, 109, 178, 187, 226–27; see Hunger strikes
Stronge, James, 191; Norman, 191
Subcultures, 34, 99, 103–05, 112
Subversion, 6, 12–13, 125, 143, 173
Sugden, Edward, 40
Sumner, W. G., 21–22, 39, 123
Sunningdale Agreement, 187, 226
Sutherland, Duchess of, 25–26
Symptoms, social, 5, 126, 169, 238
Syngenism, 21

Taigs: Roman Catholics
Tartan gangs, 120–21
Tawney, R. H., 40–41
Taylor, John, 80, 153
Terrorism, defined, 125–26, 168–70; Prevention of, Acts, 37
Thatcher, Margaret, 185, 231
Theatre of Terror, 125, 168–99
Thornton, A. M., 117, 121, 124
Tierman, Andrew, vii
Tomlinson, Mike, 141, 165, 199, 231
Tone, Wolfe, 47
Toome, 87
Traditionalism, 43–56
Trevor Hill, 160
Turk, A. T., 17
Twelfth of July, 113
Tynan Abbey, 191
Tyrie, Andy, 156, 220, 232
Twain, Mark, 1
Tweedie, Jill, 208

UAC: Ulster Army Council
UDA: Ulster Defence Association

UDR: Ulster Defence Regiment
UFF: Ulster Freedom Fighters
ULDP: Ulster Loyalist Democratic Party
Ulster Army Council, 156; Constitution Defence Committee, 74, 151; Defence Association, 154, 156–57, 159, 162, 181–82, 186, 188, 191, 208, 220; Defence Regiment, 93, 132–33, 145–47, 170–73, 176, 182, 185, 187–88, 194, 217, 224; Freedom Fighters, 154, 156; Loyalist Coordinating Committee, 155; Loyalist Democratic Party, 157, 220–21; Pregnancy Advisory Association, 116; Protestant Volunteers, 74, 81–82, 151; Special Constabulary, 54, 67, 74, 88–89, 91–92, 117, 145–46, 150, 176, 188, 223; Special Constabulary Association, 156; Unionist Council, 54, 228; Unionist Party, 152; Vanguard Party, 182; Volunteer Force, 49, 51, 54, 64, 145, 154, 156, 162, 186–88, 192, 208; Workers' Council, 156, 187, 226–27
Ulsterisation, 147
Unemployed, –ment, 32, 34, 55–56, 59, 70, 82, 102, 109, 113, 139, 147, 163, 222, 229, 236–39
Unionist, 43, 51, 58, 71–72, 78, 80, 84, 89, 132, 154–55, 175, 191, 213, 218, 224, 226; Party, 54, 67, 69, 73–74, 88, 138; parties, 229; Party of Northern Ireland, 226, 228
U. N. Declaration of Human Rights, 84, 185, 217
United Ulster Unionist Party, 228; Unionist Action Council, 156, 227; Ulster Unionist Coalition or Council, 187, 226, Party, 227
Untereiner, Wayne, 123
Urdang, Laurence, 16
USC: Ulster Special Constabulary
UVF: Ulster Volunteer Force
UWC: Ulster Workers Council

Valliéres, Pierre, 75
Values, 104–08, 116, 239
van der Vat, Dan, 167
Vanguard Unionist Party, 156, 220, 226
Vigilantes, 72, 84, 94, 99, 101, 110, 111–12, 114, 134, 146, 155–57, 163, 173, 176–77; see Guerrillas, Paramilitary organizations
Violence, 9–10, 15, 62, 67, 69, 77–78, 80, 82, 84, 86, 91, 94, 99–124, 126, 132, 151, 155, 184, 201, 205, 209, 211, 225
Voluntary agencies, 200, 204–09, 211–13

Wade, Nicholas, 41
Wainer, Irving, 39
Wakefield Prison, 190
Walker, Ian, 167
Waller, Willard, 123
Warrenpoint, 178, 188–89
Washington, George, 7
Weinraub, Bernard, 3–4, 122
Welsh, 23–25, 29–30, 32, 34, 38–39, 100
"We Shall Overcome," 44, 81, 84, 166
West Britons, British, English, 32, 45, 100, 217; Indians, 36
Westminster, see British government
Wexford, 46
Whiteboys, 47
Whitelaw, William, 182
Whitney, W. D., 16
Wickham, Ann, 142; James, 199, 233
Wicklow, 202
Widgery, Lord, 42, 180, 197–98
Wilkinson, Paul, 16, 97
William of Orange, 46, 90
Williams, Betty, 205–07; T. D., 18, 40
Williamson, Arthur, 198
Wilson, Desmond, 113, 124, 230; Harold, 84
Witness for Peace, 204
Winchester, Simon, 97
Women, status of, 101, 110; Together, 204–05, 239
Woodham–Smith, Cecil, 18, 40, 57
Workers Life, 161
Workers' Party, 160–61, 214; Research Unit, 165–66, 197
World War I, 50–52, 170; II, 59, 69, 70
Worrall, Stanley, 231
WP: Workers' Party

Young Socialists Alliance, 83
Younger, Calton, 198

Zimmerman, P. D., 123

WITHDRAWN
UST
Libraries

UNIVERSITY OF ST. THOMAS LIBRARIES

HV 6433 .G7 L44 1983
Lee, Alfred McClung, 1906-
Terrorism in Northern
Ireland